A
HISTORY
OF THE
UNITED STATES
IN
FIVE CRASHES

A
HISTORY
OF THE
UNITED STATES
IN
FIVE CRASHES

Stock Market Meltdowns
That Defined a Nation

SCOTT NATIONS

wm

WILLIAM MORROW
An Imprint of HarperCollinsPublishers

HarperCollins books may be purchased for educational, business, or sales promotional use. For information, please email the Special Markets Department at SPsales@harper collins.com.

A hardcover edition of this book was published in 2017 by William Morrow, an imprint of HarperCollins Publishers.

FIRST WILLIAM MORROW PAPERBACK EDITION PUBLISHED 2018.

Designed by Joy O'Meara

Library of Congress Cataloging-in-Publication Data has been applied for.

ISBN 978-0-06-246728-7

18 19 20 21 22   DIX/LSC   10 9 8 7 6 5 4 3 2 1

For Wendi

CONTENTS

CONTENTS

PREFACE

Crash. It's a kinetic and evocative word and dramatic and frightening. It means there's a story to be told, because when two cars collide or a plane plummets from the sky there's rarely a single cause. When the stock market crashes, vast sums are lost and people's lives are changed, often drastically. But equally dramatic are the stories leading up to the crashes in the stock market, because amid the wreckage there are heroes, people who recognized the causes and catalysts and warned us of the immense drop looming or who did their best to stop it once it was in motion.

We invest in the stock market for many reasons, each of them good, including funding retirements and educations. The irony is that in funding our retirement we create new jobs. In financing educations we create more technology to learn about. The impact isn't felt just here; as those investments are deployed around the world, problems are solved, new industries are created, and international economies grow—the American investor has probably done more good in this world than anyone else, with the exception of the American soldier.

The stories of markets, including of the modern stock market crashes, are ultimately fascinating personal stories. Some people saw the crashes coming, some unwittingly sped up the drop, some were more malicious, and some were just stupid or reckless.

What's engrossing, and a bit scary, is that most of the people responsible for the modern stock market crashes thought they were operating in the public good. From a president who wanted more power for himself and less for "malefactors of great wealth"; to another public official who in an effort to help a friend fed a bubble that ultimately crashed; to academics who created an ingenious methodology that was supposed to wring most of the risk out of investing but instead manufactured an enormous new risk; to those who worked to make certain that every American could enjoy the satisfaction of owning his or her own home; and finally, to the ones who thought that automation would make trading less expensive and more efficient—those at the heart of these crashes were, without exception, warned that the courses they'd set were dangerous. We'll read about the people and the warnings with the hope of learning to heed those warnings in the future.

But the subject isn't just one of personal intrigue. The impact on investors has been profound. If one had invested $1 in the Dow Jones Industrial Average on December 31, 1899, it would have grown to $156.88 at the close of trading on the day of the last modern stock market crash. If that investor had avoided just one day, October 19, 1987, the balance would instead be $202.71. If that investor had avoided the five worst days, that balance would be $319.24, more than doubling his or her return.

Unfortunately, stock market crashes cost more than just money. They breed fear that causes people to refuse to invest, making it nearly impossible to finance creation of those jobs and advancement of those economies. And they create other unforeseen but enthralling problems. For example, it was a loss of confidence and refusal to invest in the early 1970s that led to the creation of the contraption that fueled the crash of Black Monday, October 19, 1987. We'll learn the entire story.

For all the protections we put in place, stock market crashes are a function of the way markets, and the men and women who run them, operate. And that human element of the stock market is what makes crashes endlessly fascinating and also creates a unique prism through which we can view the prologue to the next crash while it is still likely years away. But as time passes, we forget the lessons learned, and as the particulars change, we lose sight of the fact that crashes don't have a single cause that is easy to recognize before the damage is done. Instead every crash is caused by a unique confluence of usually personal events. Despite understanding this and despite our best efforts, it's impossible to crash-proof our financial system, just as it's impossible to eliminate automobile accidents. No matter how well engineered the car, no matter how conscientious the driver, someone will be human, perhaps when assembling one of the thousands of critical parts, or when operating one of the thousands of critical parts, or perhaps in a combination of both. Or perhaps the weather will just be bad or the other driver will be drunk.

Confirmation that our stock market will crash again can be found in the understanding that markets continue to crash, even though the five modern stock market crashes are strikingly similar and should teach us something. They share important phenomena, and some of them should be obvious to us, including steep appreciation in the stock market. Precisely how the market appreciates is common to the crashes; two-year periods of particularly aggressive buying inside a robust decade are common just before most of the crashes. Less obvious commonalities also appear, including new financial contraptions that we are (overly) confident we understand, only to learn that they inject uncertainty and leverage into the stock market at its weakest moment. The government also makes its appearance, often in an effort to eliminate a real inequity

like competition-killing industrial monopolies or abusive leveraged buyouts. But the government often chooses the worst possible moment to intervene, having waited until the financial stresses
are finally too much for their constituencies. When an external
catalyst—often natural or geopolitical—pushes the system past the
tipping point the market crashes, and the warnings that are also
common to each of the crashes seem remarkably prescient. Why
didn't we listen?

Given the commonalities, how do we keep getting ourselves
into situations in which we convince ourselves that this time it's
different? Often it's the nature of the contraption that convinces us
that much of the risk has been wrung out of the stock market.

In the 1920s the investment trust promised professional financial management and diversification, both of which were thought
to reduce or eliminate risk, but instead the investment trusts
increased risk. In the 1980s a wonder of complex mathematics
known as portfolio insurance promised to provide a floor below
which the value of a portfolio simply could not fall. Instead it
increased the depth and velocity of the drop. Thirty years later,
investment bankers and institutional investors were seduced by
even more complex mathematics into believing that the value of
mortgage-backed securities could not fall below a certain level.

While we watch these dangers build, the unknowable or unfore-
seeable element is the catalyst that will set it off. In 1907 it was as
random as an earthquake, while in 2010 it was a riot in a place far
away. Each of the catalysts initially seemed to have little, if anything,
to do with finance. But our modern economies are intimately connected by finance—insurance in the case of an earthquake on our
west coast or the price of crude oil and geopolitical turmoil in the
Middle East, or the common European currency when it seems a
country is dissolving into violence. These unpredictable catalysts
take on critical financial importance.

The observable elements are necessary for a crash to occur but they aren't sufficient. We should be able to recognize when a crash is possible even if we can't be certain one will occur. If a catalyst is never introduced, the result will likely be years of poor stock market returns rather than the lightning bolt that creates chaos that destroys the fortunes of people who don't know how they can recover.

It's easy to believe the differences between our current financial world and that of even a few years ago—some call them advances—render another crash impossible. Unfortunately, it's often those very changes that breed the next crash. In 1907 the simple act of paying an insurance claim could take weeks. To compensate for the losses incurred in the 1906 San Francisco earthquake, gold had to be loaded onto ships in London (the insurers were overwhelmingly British); they then sailed west. In the era before the 1914 opening of the Panama Canal, the trip would take weeks, and the only way to shorten it was to make port in Boston or New York and transfer the gold to a train that would set out on the multiday trip to San Francisco.

By 2010, the time required to consummate even the most complicated financial transaction had been reduced to a fraction of a second. Traders in Chicago or New York knew that they could effect a trade in about 20 milliseconds (one-fiftieth of a second). But 20 milliseconds was an eternity compared to what could happen when communications firms erected expensive microwave towers, which could shave 5 milliseconds off execution time. This often made all the difference in a market when the focus had shifted from what something was worth to how quickly it could be bought or sold.

This very advance in speed generated its own problem. As the system that relied on the speed of nearly instantaneous electronic trading was degraded, often without humans recognizing the delay, entirely new problems were created that led to a new kind of crash.

Einstein said that imagination is more important than knowledge because knowledge is limited to all we know and understand. He could have been referring to the causes of the past stock market crashes. On the other hand, imagination allows us to understand that even though the players have changed, the game is the same and we can imagine how the market will crash again.

This book tells the stories of what led up to the crashes of 1907, 1929, 1987, 2008, and 2010, the crashes themselves, and the elements shared by each past crash. Americans in the 1930s wondered if the stock market would ever regain the level reached on September 3, 1929. Even though the Great Depression, World War II, and a quarter century intervened, the stock market eventually reclaimed that level. The American stock market has always reclaimed its pre-crash level, but the danger isn't that money is lost, it's that time is lost as Americans turn from the market, reluctant to invest and participate in the recovery if lifestyles, retirements, and educations are at stake.

The stories are fascinating, but this book is also intended to give the American investor—one who, over time, has done so much good in this world—insight into the circumstances that can foster a crash. Forewarned is forearmed. If we're paying attention.

A
HISTORY
OF THE
UNITED STATES
IN
FIVE CRASHES

PANIC
1907

After decades of gray men in gray suits, Americans woke on the morning of September 15, 1901, to find that possibly the single most energetic and vivacious of their 78 million strong—Theodore Roosevelt—was their new president after the assassination of William McKinley.

McKinley was elected twice and had been well liked. At fifty-eight, he was still a young man, even by the standard of the day. Only five foot seven, he was short but marked by a barrel chest, broad shoulders, and ample gut, in those days a sign of health and prosperity. He had three years left in his presidency, but on September 6, 1901, he was shot while standing in a receiving line at the Pan-American Exposition in Buffalo, New York. Just three days before, Leon Czolgosz, a twenty-eight-year-old anarchist, had paid $4.50 for a chromed .32-caliber Iver Johnson revolver. As he approached McKinley, Czolgosz fired twice, hitting the president in the chest and the gut. McKinley survived the initial attack and gracefully instructed his attendants to be careful when giving the news to his wife. Dr. Matthew Mann was the surgeon available at the fairgrounds, and despite the crude facilities and Mann being a professor of obstetrics and gynecology, the decision was made for Dr. Mann to operate immediately rather than transport the president to a local hospital. Even so, McKinley died eight days later, on September 14.

At the time of the shooting, Roosevelt was on a hunting trip in the remotest stretch of the Adirondacks, thirty-five miles from the town of North Creek, New York. Rather than return to Washington, Roosevelt continued hunting and McKinley died while Roosevelt was still working his way over dark roads from the Tahawus Club hunting lodge to North Creek. Roosevelt was still forty-three days from his forty-third birthday when he was sworn in as president on September 14, 1901. When McKinley selected him to replace his first vice president, who died in 1899 from a string of heart ailments, Roosevelt was serving as governor of New York. Among the reasons he got the post was that the powers-that-be in New York State wanted Roosevelt out of the governorship and making his mischief elsewhere.

Roosevelt had been the ideal candidate for governor of New York when he returned from the Spanish-American War as a hero. Never mind that some of the hero-making had been more Roosevelt's premeditated doing than sheer gallantry on the battlefield, although there was much of that. Roosevelt was a master of self-promotion. There was so little room on the ship taking his regiment to Cuba that only Roosevelt and the senior officers of the "Rough Riders" were able to bring their mounts—many of the Rough Riders had to walk into battle. But Roosevelt made sure there was room on board for reporters, photographers, and even a couple of early, crude movie cameras, despite the objections of the United States Army.

The war lasted less than four months, but the experience seemed to teach Roosevelt that every subsequent professional and political conflict should be charged with the drama and righteousness of this armed combat. Even relatively minor disagreements with potentially helpful businessmen evoked in him the furor of battle. For Roosevelt, losing the battle or being killed was preferable to missing the action entirely. When asked about the possibility that the war would conclude before he got there, he said that would be "awful." He professed the hope that all his officers would be "killed, wounded, or promoted"; coming upon a dying Rough Rider on the battlefield, Roosevelt stopped, shook his comrade's hand, and said, "Well, old man, isn't this splendid?"

Roosevelt wasn't new to politics when he entered the 1898 race for governor of New York. He'd been elected to the New York Assembly in 1882 as a twenty-three-year-old, despite being warned off by friends that those of Roosevelt's ilk, education, and wealth didn't go into politics. Roosevelt simply replied, "That merely means that the people I know do not belong to the governing class, and I intend to be one of the governing class."

As an assemblyman, Roosevelt was branded a troublemaker and reformer, a title that was anathema to the governing class. When he demanded to be heard on every issue, newspapers started calling him "the cyclone assemblyman," and while still a freshman, Roosevelt managed to anger businessmen by exposing a financial relationship between financier Jay Gould and New York Supreme Court justice Theodoric Westbrook. As he would show in Cuba, Roosevelt made every issue a fight between right and wrong, good and evil; there was no middle ground or "go along to get along" in Roosevelt. And occasionally his indignation made him appear unnecessarily and dangerously belligerent.

Even with his war record, Roosevelt needed help getting elected governor of New York. One month after Roosevelt returned from Cuba, he was summoned to the Fifth Avenue Hotel by Thomas Collier Platt, known as the "Easy Boss" of New York. Platt had served as a congressman for two terms and was in the middle of his second term as senator, but when he called for Roosevelt he had distinguished himself only as the political boss of Republicans in New York State. The *New York Times* would eulogize Platt in 1910 by saying that "no man ever exercised less influence in the Senate or the House of Representatives than he." However, the *Times* went on to explain: "But no man ever exercised more power as a political leader."

Platt offered to put that power to work for Roosevelt; he boldly offered Roosevelt the Republican nomination for governor as long as Roosevelt promised he wouldn't get carried away with his reform agenda.

The two men struck a purely political bargain; Roosevelt agreed to consult with Platt's people when it came to patronage. The election was close. Roosevelt won with 49 percent of the vote in a five-man race. But his victory would be a resounding defeat for "Easy Boss" Platt; Roosevelt simply refused to do as Platt wished, failing to support suggested nominees and, in an important harbinger, moving to regulate business. Platt quickly had enough: "I want to get rid of the bastard. I don't want him raising hell in my state any longer. I want to bury him." Platt realized the only way to "bury" Governor Roosevelt was to slide him into the job that John Adams, the first to hold the position, had called "the most insignificant office that ever the invention of man contrived or his imagination conceived." Platt would get Teddy Roosevelt out of New York by making him vice president of the United States.

Roosevelt hated the idea of the vice presidency and threatened to decline the nomination, but Platt used Teddy's fame against him and Roosevelt won every vote the 1900 Republican convention had to offer, with the lone exception of his own. Roosevelt was crushed: "I would rather be anything, say, a professor of history." Others were unhappy, too. Mark Twain, who had met Roosevelt more than once, said after he'd been inaugurated, "I think the president is clearly insane." Mark Hanna, senator from Ohio and a power in the Republican Party, asked simply of the men responsible, "Don't any of you realize there's only one life between that madman and the presidency?"

On September 14, 1901, that one life winked out, and Hanna's "madman" was in charge.

On Saturday, September 7, 1901, the first day the stock market could fully respond to McKinley's shooting (until 1952, the New York Stock Exchange was open on Saturdays for an abbreviated trading session), the Dow Jones Industrial Average lost 4.4 percent, to close at 69.03, but as hopeful news of McKinley's recovery was reported, it regained most of that loss. Only when it appeared that McKinley would not survive did stock prices break again, losing nearly 6 percent in the three days before McKinley's death, at the prospect of an antibusiness progressive "reformer" in the White House. But just when Americans were desperate to be reassured, Roosevelt's first act as president was to promise that he would "continue absolutely unbroken the policy of President McKinley for the peace and prosperity and the honor of our beloved country."

Though the prosperity Roosevelt aimed to continue had surely bypassed some, it was true that much of the country was wealthier than ever. The superintendent of the U.S. Census Bureau had said in 1890 that the western part of the country was so settled that the "frontier" had ceased to exist. Those who remained in the cities were enjoying a second industrial revolution.

The American economy had expanded rapidly from the end of 1896 to the end of 1900, when annual economic growth averaged 6 percent and the optimism was being expressed in the stock market. The Dow Jones Industrial Average rallied from 40.45 to 70.71, an increase of 74.8 percent, including gains of 22.2 percent in 1897 and 22.5 percent in 1898. Referring to 1899, when the Dow gained 9.2 percent, the *Boston Herald* reported, "If one could not have made money this past year, his case is hopeless." The American Century had just dawned when Senator Chauncey Depew remarked, "There is not a man here who does not feel 400 percent bigger in 1900 than he did in 1896, bigger intellectually, bigger hopefully, bigger patriotically."

As the frontier was disappearing and the stock market was booming, American businesses were growing in size and complexity. In 1882 John D. Rockefeller's counsel at Standard Oil had devised the "corporate trust," a novel piece of financial engineering that allowed Rockefeller and his managers to control the labyrinth of partnerships and corporations that Standard Oil had become. From that single oil trust in 1882, which controlled more than 90 percent of the nation's oil refining capacity, about eighty different trusts, covering an immense range of industries, existed in 1897. In 1898 a new corporate form was wedded to the corporate trust when New Jersey began allowing one corporation to own stock in another. Delaware followed the next year with even more liberal rules, and the holding company was born. By 1904, 318 corporate trusts were dominating the business world, from steel and copper, crude oil and kerosene, to lead and linseed oil.

On December 3, 1901, President Roosevelt delivered his first message to Congress. He began by eulogizing McKinley, then turned to the country's other business, particularly business itself, noting that the growing complexity of industrial development brought with it serious social problems, including pollution, overcrowding in the cities, and an enormous income disparity between the average workingman and the industrialists. But Roosevelt then cautioned against dealing with corporations in ways that might jeopardize the resurgence American business was enjoying. "The mechanism of modern business is so delicate that extreme care must be taken not to interfere with it in a spirit of rashness or ignorance," he said. "Many of those who have made it their vocation to denounce the great industrial combinations . . . appeal especially to hatred and fear."

As he continued, Roosevelt shifted from killing businessmen with kindness to turning on them by calling for federal regulation of the "corporate form," the legal fiction that allows a group to limit its liability and be treated as an immortal individual through the process of incorporation. Roosevelt argued that since the form, essentially all corporations, had these decided advantages that were conferred by the government, it should be regulated. He also called for the government to inspect and examine the "workings of the great corporations engaged in interstate business." He said that "artificial bodies, such as corporations and joint stock or other associations, depending upon any statutory law for their existence or privileges, should be subject to proper government supervision, and full and accurate information as to the operations should be made public regularly at reasonable intervals." And how might he regulate? Roosevelt gave a clue when he said, "Since the industrial changes which have so enormously increased the productive power of mankind, [the old laws and the old customs] are no longer sufficient."

When Roosevelt was assistant secretary of the navy, he had professed that only those "who dared greatly in war, or the work which is akin to war" were worthy. Now he seemed to have found his work akin to war and his next opponent. If businessmen were surprised by the new president's path going forward, then they simply hadn't been listening.

James J. Hill and E. H. Harriman didn't like each other, even though both had come up hard and built incredible fortunes as they established railroad empires. Hill originally wanted to be a trapper and fur trader but began his career as a clerk and freight hauler. Eventually he came to own the Great Northern Railway and much of the stock of the Northern Pacific. This meant he controlled most of the railroad business in the Northwest. Hill was largely self-educated, with only a brief period as a scholarship student at Rockwood Academy. Despite his lack of advantages, Hill's railroad empire had been built in part through his alliances in business with J. P. Morgan and the Vanderbilt family.

In 1901, Hill's roads from the Northwest extended only as far east as Minnesota, and he was anxious to expand his network to Chicago, the belching, stinking center of the industrial Midwest and the crossroads of transportation that fed it. To do so, Hill would buy the Chicago, Burlington & Quincy Railroad, known as the Burlington, for its sprawl of track from Minnesota to Chicago and back west across Iowa, Missouri, Nebraska, and Kansas. With J. P. Morgan providing the financing, the Northern Pacific, which Hill had a large stake in but did not yet fully control, reached an agreement to buy the Burlington and its eight thousand miles of track, much of which paralleled that of E. H. Harriman's Union Pacific.

Edward Henry Harriman had quit school at the age of fourteen—Hill's age when he was forced to leave Rockwood Academy—to take a job as a messenger on Wall Street. Eight years later, Harriman was a member of the New York Stock Exchange. Harriman entered the railroad business when he was forty-nine. Initially he'd been a mere investor, but by the turn of the century he controlled the Southern Pacific and Union Pacific railroads, and as such, much of the railroad business in the West and Southwest. Harriman did so by aligning himself with the Rockefeller and Gould families.

On hearing of Hill's plans, Harriman requested that they buy the Burlington together. After all, Harriman already owned a sizable chunk of Burlington stock, and the Burlington routes served as feeders to much of Harriman's Union Pacific. But Hill rejected Harriman's proposal, leaving Harriman's railroads in a supremely precarious situation. Not only might Hill use the Burlington routes to freeze Harriman out of Chicago, but the Burlington routes west of Chicago could compete directly with Harriman's Union Pacific routes once they were strengthened via the combination Hill imagined.

This prompted Harriman to make an audacious decision: If he couldn't acquire enough of the Burlington to guarantee access to Chicago and prevent competition elsewhere, then he would acquire the acquirer of the Burlington. After confirming that Hill and Morgan controlled the board of the Northern Pacific, but owned less than a controlling percentage of the outstanding stock, Harriman began buying Northern Pacific shares quietly. On April 22, 1901, with the Dow at 74.56, Northern Pacific was trading at $101 a share. By April 30, it was $117. On Monday, May 6, it was at $133. At this point Harriman quit being quiet, as he realized Morgan had figured out what he was up to. Both camps began buying madly; the next day Northern Pacific, a company that had just emerged from bankruptcy, reached $149, while the Dow, at 75.02, was little changed since the buying in Northern Pacific commenced. By Thursday, May 9, Northern Pacific briefly reached $1,000 a share as the Hill-Morgan team finally secured a controlling interest.

May 9, 1901, the day Northern Pacific reached its peak, became known as "Blue Thursday" because this action in Northern Pacific sucked all the air out of every other stock and caused the rest of the market to plunge; on May 8 and 9, as Northern Pacific was cresting, the broad stock market lost 10.2 percent of its value, with the Dow closing at 67.38. The headline of the May 10 edition of the *New York Times* described it as "Disaster and Ruin in Falling Market." A handful of robber barons, icons of the Gilded Age, in fighting for a relatively small railroad, the Burlington, had nearly crashed the stock market.

Eventually the protagonists realized they could go on fighting each other or they could join forces in the sort of industrial trust that Standard Oil had perfected and that was becoming so popular with Wall Street. The players came together, the chaos they had caused propelling even normally impatient businessmen to reach an agreement quickly, just twenty-two days after the panic. On June 1, 1901, an agreement was announced and "harmony" was declared; the principals would merge all their holdings into a single entity. The vessel of this harmony was the Northern Securities Company, with Morgan in charge and Hill leading the board of directors, which Harriman and several fellow raiders joined. Having regained all the ground lost in the "Blue Thursday" panic, the Dow closed that day at its highest level of 1901 to date, 76.59, up 8.3 percent for the year.

The federal government, during one of its first attempts to enforce 1890's Sherman Antitrust Act, had been beaten decisively. The Sherman Antitrust Act had been authored by Ohio senator John Sherman, a three-time candidate for president, former secretary of the Treasury, younger brother of General William Tecumseh Sherman, and a man so lacking in personal warmth that he was called "the Ohio Icicle." Breathtaking in its scope, the Sherman Act was a response to the emerging power of the industrial trusts, particularly Standard Oil. It outlawed every effort to restrain trade "among the several States."

The E. C. Knight Company controlled 98 percent of sugar refining in the United States, and in 1892 President Grover Cleveland instructed the government to sue the Knight Company under the Sherman Act as a combination acting in restraint of trade. When the case ultimately reached the Supreme Court in 1895 the ruling was a disaster for the government. Ruling 8 to 1 for Knight and against the U.S. government, Chief Justice Melville Fuller, reading his own opinion for the majority, said that manufacturing was a local activity and therefore not subject to the Sherman Act, since it was not an interstate enterprise occurring "among the several States." Fuller's decision said such combinations "could not be suppressed under the provisions of the act" but that rather, individual states would be forced to bring suit to defeat combinations in restraint of trade, a near impossibility in the case of monopolies headquartered out of state. The Knight ruling effectively put control of monopolies beyond the reach of the Sherman Antitrust Act.

The Knight ruling also provided Morgan, Hill, and Harriman a road map for deflecting any government meddling into what they called Northern Securities, which was incorporated in New Jersey on November 12, 1901, just two months after Roosevelt had become president and promised to continue McKinley's policies—presumably including not prosecuting violations of the Sherman Antitrust Act in the post–E. C. Knight world.

It's no accident that J. P. Morgan was the money and the brains behind Northern Securities. Morgan had been born into a privileged position in finance. His father, Junius Spencer Morgan, was an influential banker in London, where he made a fortune during the American Civil War selling war bonds on behalf of the U.S. government. Pierpont's education was peripatetic; he attended schools in Connecticut, Boston, Switzerland, and Germany, learning to speak both French and German while earning a degree in art history, an odd course of study for one who went on to expand his father's small banking firm into a financial colossus.

In 1901 J. P. Morgan was sixty-four and by consensus the most powerful banker in the world. Consistent with that power was an utterly intimidating manner made more disconcerting by a nose grotesquely malformed due to rhinophyma, a severe form of rosacea.

Though he had played a role in the stock market turmoil during the fight for Northern Pacific, Morgan hated chaos. His son-in-law, Herbert Satterlee, would later say Morgan loved order and, whenever possible, tried to substitute a pattern for disorder. Satterlee said this explained why Morgan played solitaire while thinking through business problems—bringing the deck of cards into an orderly sequence out of a random deal.

Morgan believed the Knight Sugar precedent had brought the Northern Securities problem to a close, but his fame was about to cause its own problems. On May 11, 1901, just two days after the stock market break he'd help set in motion, Morgan was asked about the small investors, the general public, who'd been caught in the market selloff. Didn't he owe them some consideration during his maneuverings? The *New York World* was happy to relay Morgan's pique: "I owe the public nothing." Morgan was becoming one of the most hated men in America, but he had a bigger problem: Theodore Roosevelt.

Roosevelt believed in power, having said, "I believe in a strong executive. I believe in power." And though Roosevelt hated the concentration of control of business, he said about politics, "I don't think any harm comes from the concentration of power in one man's hands." It was clear that Roosevelt meant his own hands.

As news of J. P. Morgan's injudicious quote spread, mail flooded the White House—Roosevelt had changed the name from "Executive Mansion" to "White House" shortly after moving in—urging the president to act against Morgan and the trusts. Newspapers ran editorial cartoons showing Roosevelt as a whip-wielding lion tamer with the trusts at his feet or dressed in a singlet, wrestling the railroad trusts into submission.

Even though Roosevelt had occasionally suggested that his attorney general, Philander Knox, pursue possible targets for antitrust action, none of them had been satisfactory. But after being prodded again by Roosevelt, and following a week's research that toured British philosophy, American common law, and the Knight Sugar trust case, Knox had found a target: Northern Securities. Knox determined that the Knight case had been lost because it had been badly argued, but a suit against Northern Securities could be won, and Knox would argue it himself. Roosevelt had been in office less than five months but he'd found an endeavor that was akin to war, and his enemy would be the monopolies.

On February 19, 1902, Knox issued a statement: "Some time ago the President requested an opinion as to the legality of this merger [Northern Securities], and I have recently given him one to the effect that, in my judgment, it violates the provisions of the Sherman Act of 1890, whereupon he directed that suitable action should be taken to have the question judicially determined." The next day the stock market lost 1.3 percent, but the loss was quickly recovered. Roosevelt didn't seem to worry investors.

Morgan was aghast. He thought trusts like Northern Securities were good for the country because they fostered calm, as opposed to the pandemonium of "Blue Thursday." He also thought the Knight Sugar case provided judicial cover. On February 22, Morgan went to the White House to meet with Roosevelt and Knox. He said he thought Northern Securities should be given the opportunity to make changes in its makeup before charges were brought:

Roosevelt: That is just what we did not want you to do.
Morgan: If we have done anything wrong send your
man [Attorney General Knox] to my man,
and they can fix it up.
Roosevelt: That can't be done.
Knox: We don't want to fix it. We want to stop it.

On March 10, 1902, Knox filed the official complaint against Northern Securities in federal court in Minnesota, a state with deep antipathy toward the railroad trusts, and commenced preparing for trial, which began in February 1903. When the verdict was announced on April 9, 1903, it was as resounding a victory for the government as the E. C. Knight decision had been a defeat.

The judges were unanimous and unambiguous; acquisition of the Northern Pacific and Great Northern railroads by Northern Securities was a conspiracy in restraint of trade.

Despite the legal thrashing of corporate trusts, the stock market held up well on Thursday afternoon and closed for the week—the next day was Good Friday—as the decision was being digested. Two days after the Northern Securities decision, Roosevelt, who was camping on Slough Creek near Yellowstone Park, tracked and shot a mountain lion. But Roosevelt must have believed he had felled bigger prey in Morgan and Northern Securities.

The next trading day, Monday, April 13, 1903, the Dow, which had been down 3 percent for the year, lost another 2.5 percent, falling to 60.79. The *New York Times* blamed the Northern Securities decision and described the action as a "sharp decline, but no panic."

As the Northern Securities case wended its way to the U.S. Supreme Court, general business conditions weakened and the drumbeat against trusts grew louder. When the former lieutenant governor of Missouri admitted to a grand jury that he had been paid, while in office, $1,000 by the sugar trust for "literary services" and another $750 by the tobacco trust, and had been offered a similar amount by the baking powder trust, the drumbeat got more insistent. With each revelation the outlook for all the trusts darkened, taking the stock market lower, since the trusts signified cooperation and size, both of which led to higher profits. As the Supreme Court sat for arguments on December 14, 1903, the Dow was at 46.70, down 27.4 percent for the year and 25.0 percent since the verdict against Northern Securities.

The case was decided by the Supreme Court on March 14, 1904. In preparation, Roosevelt had molded the Court to his ends. Two of his new justices voted for the government, along with John Harlan, the government's only vote in the Knight Sugar case, and two of the justices who had voted against the government in the Knight case. The government won by the slimmest of margins, 5–4, with Harlan's opinion stating plainly that the Sherman Antitrust Act meant that "liberty of contract did not involve a right to deprive the public of the advantages of free competition in trade and commerce."

Knox tried to calm the business world and the stock market by assuring them that there would be no "running amuck" on controlling corporations. The next day, March 15, 1904, the stock market opened at 47.73, having fallen 29.3 percent the previous twelve months as Roosevelt seemed to ready for war. It was down 5.3 percent for 1904 to date but rallied through the day to cut 1904's loss nearly in half with a gain of 2.5 percent. The stock market had taken comfort in Knox's assurance.

Roosevelt focused on raising the funds for his 1904 presidential campaign. One likely reason Knox didn't "run amuck" and file additional suits after the Northern Securities decision was that Wall Street and the business world were expected to be a significant source of Roosevelt's campaign funding. With Roosevelt and Knox otherwise occupied, the stock market was again enjoying a golden age. The Dow ultimately gained 41.7 percent in 1904 to close at 69.61, more than recovering the previous year's losses. While many had assumed that Knox's promise not to run "amuck" in March 1904 was pure political pragmatism, coming eight months before a presidential election, Roosevelt needn't have worried—he beat the Democrat, Judge Alton Parker, convincingly, winning 56.4 percent of the vote and every state outside of the solidly Democratic South. In his inaugural address Roosevelt barely mentioned business. It seemed to Wall Street that Roosevelt and Knox had moved to other battlefields.

The Dow rose another 38.2 percent in 1905 to close at 96.20. That two-year gain of 95.9 percent is still the greatest two-year return the American stock market has ever enjoyed, and the start of 1906 seemed like a continuation of the 1904–5 run. On January 12, 1906, the Dow closed above 100.00 for the first time ever, and by January 19, 1906, it was up 7.1 percent for the year, which was just sixteen trading days old. One observer early in that year described a "mammoth bull movement" running its course on the New York Stock Exchange. Jack Morgan, son of J. P., and running his father's eponymous firm while J. P. was traveling, noted in January 1906, the month that started the year so well, that it wasn't just professionals who were buying stocks: "For the first time in three years the public—with stocks at their present high prices—have begun to come in and buy heavily." This may have been the first real instance of individual investors taking a big stake in the stock market. It would end badly less than two years later.

The bad news began at 5:12 A.M. on Wednesday, April 18, 1906, when the northernmost 296 miles of the San Andreas Fault, from the California town of Hollister to Cape Mendocino, where the fault disappears into the Pacific Ocean, ruptured. The shaking lasted fifty-five seconds in what was ultimately an 8.3-magnitude earthquake. The eastern side of the fault had moved to the southeast by twenty-four feet.

In San Francisco, the earthquake was bad but the fires that resulted from broken gas lines were worse, because the quake had also broken the water mains. After firefighters pumped the sewers dry in an attempt to stop the flames, they sent word to the Presidio, the military fort overlooking the entrance to San Francisco Bay, requesting an army artillery battalion. With no water to fight the fires, the soldiers used dynamite to collapse buildings into heaps of rubble that they hoped would serve as firebreaks. More often, the explosions started new fires.

Though almost none of San Francisco was insured against earthquake, the vast majority of it was insured against fire. Having your house burn was the only way to get an insurance payment. So, in the days immediately following the quake, citizens with houses that had been heavily damaged by the quake, but spared the fires, set their own homes ablaze.

More than 27,500 buildings covering 500 square blocks, one-half of the largest city west of the Rocky Mountains and the financial center of the American West, was gone. At least 225,000 residents, more than half of all San Franciscans, were homeless. Investors understandably sold stocks off sharply on news of the quake and as they learned of the depth of destruction.

The Dow had given back most of its gains from the first three weeks of the year, but when the quake struck it was at 96.84, still slightly higher on the year. It quickly turned lower, losing more than 10 percent in the two weeks following the earthquake and closing at just 86.45 on May 3.

The San Francisco insurance market was an oddity. For decades most of the city's fire insurance had been written by British companies because the city had a great many London-based banks poised there to finance grain shipments from the west coast to Britain, as well as British trade with Asia. In 1852, the first fire insurance firm, foreign or domestic, was opened in the city when the Liverpool & London & Globe Insurance Company placed a sales agent in San Francisco. Two years later there were four British firms and just a single American firm writing policies. By 1900 approximately half of all fire insurance policies in San Francisco were still issued by British companies and the quake hit the British hard. After the fires, the *Financial Times* called San Francisco a $200 million "ash heap," as London-based insurers began loading gold on ships and watched those ships sail west even as the claims continued to pile up. Thirty million dollars in gold was sent in April, with more sent during the summer and $35 million sent in September alone. The amount of gold sent to San Francisco to settle earthquake claims was equal to 14 percent of Britain's total stockpile.

Eventually every available dollar and pound in London, New York, or Boston ended up on the American west coast. Even more money than was otherwise needed had to be sent—cash and gold in bank vaults throughout San Francisco weren't available until weeks later because bankers had to wait for the vaults to cool; they were convinced that if the vaults were opened too soon the residual heat combined with fresh oxygen would cause the stock certificates, bonds, and cash inside to burst into flame.

Gold was liquidity for a central bank like the Bank of England, and without liquidity a central bank, despite the name, wasn't much of a bank. Operating under the gold standard, this sudden outflow of gold from London was such a massive shock to the British financial system that the governors of the Bank of England did the only thing they knew to do: they raised the interest rate they were willing to pay those who left their gold on deposit—but they did so only slightly, from 3.5 percent to 4.0 percent. Ominously for the American stock market, interest rates increased worldwide as those few who had ready cash started charging higher rates for it.

Every modern stock market crash has an external catalyst at its heart. These external catalysts—some are acts of nature, such as 1906's earthquake; some are geopolitical, as in 1987 and 2010; some are political, as in 2008; and some are criminal, as in 1929—are not sufficient themselves to start a crash, though they are necessary.

Not only was the San Francisco earthquake of 1906 the catalyst for what became known as the Panic of 1907, but the analogy between earthquake and stock market crash is particularly apt. Some geologists point out that the beginning of a major earthquake, the nucleation, is identical to that of a minor tremor, but the sliding of one tectonic plate against another stops quickly in a minor tremor as friction overcomes tension. In a major earthquake, the sliding doesn't stop until all the coiled tension has been released; an earthquake is a tremor that doesn't stop. Similarly, as stocks decline in value during a correction, investors begin to recognize value and step in to buy at a discount; greed overcomes fear. During a crash, unique forces align. The decline doesn't stop as these forces overwhelm the ability to know what value is.

After the election of 1904, Roosevelt was set to resume his trust-busting after a three-year pause, during which the American stock market had enjoyed unequaled growth. While his government had filed antitrust action against some smaller concerns—including the Terminal Railroad Association, Otis Elevator, and Virginia-Carolina Chemical—since his Supreme Court victory against Northern Securities, he had conspicuously avoided the biggest trust, Standard Oil.

On May 4, 1906, sixteen days after the San Francisco earthquake and before the first shipment of British gold reached America's west coast, Roosevelt stood in the House of Representatives and delivered a message in which he resumed his battle against the trusts, focusing on the first of them, and still the most egregious offender, Standard Oil. Accusing Standard Oil of benefiting from secret rate deals with railroads, he said many of these secret rates were "clearly unlawful." Roosevelt seemed determined to remove the trusts' ability to rely on the Knight Sugar case. He would do so by pointing out that companies were evading the law by treating as intrastate commerce—and therefore protected by *Knight*—what was really a part of interstate commerce and therefore fair game thanks to the Northern Securities decision.

But then Roosevelt added that mere lawsuits weren't enough, and he called for Congress to confer on the Interstate Commerce Commission the power to impose its decisions "at once," without review. While Roosevelt conceded that the ICC should be subject to the Constitution and might "at times be guilty of injustice" under his proposal, the injustice wrought by Standard Oil was "far grosser and far more frequent." In other words, the Constitution should bend to Roosevelt's will because he believed his actions were less wrong than those of the men running Standard Oil. It was this sort of overreaching that led Joe Cannon, Republican Speaker of the House, to complain that the president had "no more use for the Constitution than a tomcat has for a marriage license."

Roosevelt began his attack on Standard Oil on June 22, 1906, when he announced that the company was officially under investigation. Roosevelt attacked on two fronts. On August 27, 1906, the U.S. government charged Standard Oil with 6,428 different violations of the Elkins anti-rebate law for accepting secret rebates on oil shipments that reduced the fare paid to about one-third of the published, minimum rate. Each violation was punishable by a fine of "not less than $1,000 nor more than $20,000." One headline announcing the charges trumpeted the potential fine of $128,560,000.

The case was assigned to a judge who had just ascended to the federal bench. Kenesaw Mountain Landis was named after the Georgia battlefield Kennesaw Mountain, where his father had been wounded during the Civil War, although no one was ever able to explain away the difference in spelling between the names of the boy and the battlefield. As a young man, "Kennie" Landis detested formal education and left school at the age of fourteen—the age at which both James Hill and E. H. Harriman left school—without consulting his parents. Two years later, Landis learned shorthand and accepted a job in a stenographer's office, where he received his first exposure to the legal system. In 1887, the year he turned twenty-one, Landis registered as an attorney despite having no formal legal education—he'd had no formal education of any kind in seven years—as was the custom of the day. Still, Landis enrolled in the Cincinnati YMCA Law School in 1889, and the next year transferred to the Union College of Law, now the Northwestern University School of Law.

Next for Roosevelt was to file suit in St. Louis on November 15, 1906, essentially demanding the breakup of Standard Oil, just as the government's anti-rebating case was nearing trial in Chicago. This second suit named John D. Rockefeller, his brother William, Henry Rogers, four other individuals, and seventy different corporations and partnerships, and sought an injunction prohibiting Standard Oil of New Jersey, as the holding company, from controlling any of its subsidiaries or paying dividends to any of the named individuals. In Landis's courtroom Roosevelt was attacking the way Standard Oil made its money; in this second case, he was targeting the way it paid out those profits.

On October 11, 1906, in an attempt to prevent the anticipated withdrawal of another two million pounds sterling of gold, the Bank of England raised interest rates from 4.0 percent to 5.0 percent, and then just eight days later to 6.0 percent, a rate seen only three times in the previous twenty years.

The beginning of December saw the American stock market down 1.1 percent for the year, as higher interest rates started to weigh on valuations and Roosevelt tried to talk the stock market higher while shifting any blame. In his State of the Union message on December 3, 1906, his first words were, "As a nation we still continue to enjoy a literally unprecedented prosperity; and it is probable that only reckless speculation and disregard of legitimate business methods on the part of the business world can materially mar this prosperity." But the rebuilding in San Francisco was still sopping up capital, and in December Jack Morgan complained that it was interfering with the natural flow of money to New York to take advantage of high interest rates. On December 18, Morgan wired colleagues in London that "things here are very uncomfortable owing to the tightness of money . . . we are likely to have a stiff money market for some time to come." On Christmas Eve he wired again, warning of an "undefined feeling that there is something wrong in New York." The Dow ended 1906 at 94.35, down 1.9 percent for the year and more than 8 percent below its high.

*   *   *

Once the trial of *Standard Oil v. United States* began on March 4, 1907, lawyers offered a laundry list of defenses: that Standard Oil had been misled to believe that the rate it paid was the lawful rate; that the Elkins Act was unconstitutional because anyone had a natural, inherent right to make a private contract; that the route in question did not constitute interstate commerce; that instead of being indicted for each shipment, just three indictments to cover the three annual contracts should have been brought; and finally, that the offense, if any had occurred, was purely technical. Regardless of the defense, public opinion was against Standard Oil.

As the proceedings slogged on, the stock market weakened, partly because the trial was thought to be going badly for Standard Oil and the railroads. On March 14, 1907, Landis ruled against a Standard Oil motion that the minimum rate they were accused of violating had never been published. That same day, an editorial in the *New York Times* asked why stocks were weak and said there was no obvious reason for the selling, explaining instead that "conditions . . . are surprisingly good." The *Times* answered its own question by pointing out that "a reason . . . is the discovery that the country's [stock market] values are no longer dependent solely, or even chiefly, upon economic factors." Rather "they [state legislatures] simply passed edicts that railroads should reduce fares." The editorial continued, "It is not the hostile legislation itself which is so alarming as the fact that it is based on no principle and therefore has no limit . . . but who can estimate the extent to which pure fiat will go?" The *Times* returned to the stock market weakness by saying, "No man can guess what anything is worth under such conditions."

The *Times* may have wanted to highlight an injustice—or to point out a flaw in Roosevelt's strategy—but investors were spurred to sell their stocks, and the Dow lost 8.3 percent that day to close at 76.23. It had lost 14.9 percent since the trial started just ten days earlier and was now down more than 19 percent for the year and more than 25 percent below its high point in 1906. Asked for a cause, E. H. Harriman declined, saying instead, "I would hate to tell you to whom I think you ought to go for the explanation of all this." Pressed for a name, Harriman again declined: "No, I cannot tell you. I would be criticized for doing so." He certainly meant Teddy Roosevelt.

Later that evening, Professor W. H. Lough Jr. of New York University addressed a group of bankers on the topic of "Conditions Favorable to Panics." He explained the economic and psychological conditions that had preceded previous stock market panics, and after some prodding by his audience, he admitted that "[a]lmost all the factors that make for a crisis are now actively at work."

The jury in Chicago got the case one month later, but only after Landis reminded them that Standard Oil didn't have to know the legal minimum rate, saying they had a duty to know and that would be enough to find them guilty. With that instruction, the verdict was as good as decided, and the jury was excused. By 9:00 P.M., after taking an hour for dinner and a single round of voting, they had reached a verdict. Standard Oil was guilty on every one of the 1,463 separate counts of violating the Elkins Act that had survived pretrial motions.

Roosevelt had occasionally picked at businessmen, sometimes in their presence, but he seized an unusual opportunity at the Gridiron Club dinner on Saturday, January 26, 1907. What was intended to be a lighthearted event—the club hired costumed actors who made light of Vice President Charles Fairbanks's height and future president William Taft's girth—turned ugly when Ohio senator Joseph Foraker, a potential presidential candidate, provoked Roosevelt to such an extent that Roosevelt lashed out at what he called the "malefactors of great wealth," to which it was assumed he meant J. P. Morgan and Henry Rogers, who were present. Roosevelt ended by warning "if you don't let us do this [presumably reg-ulate industrial trusts], those who will come after us will rise and bring you to ruin." It's no wonder that when Morgan later heard Roosevelt was going on an African safari, he announced his hope that the first lion Roosevelt met would do its duty.

Roosevelt wasn't done. Speaking on May 30, 1907—before Landis imposed sentence in the Standard Oil trial—at an India-napolis "Decoration Day" speech before 150,000, the president was expected to merely unveil a monument to Civil War veteran and Medal of Honor recipient Major General Henry Lawton and to praise all soldiers who had done their duty. But Roosevelt also said he felt compelled to do his duty and called upon the federal government to use its "full power of supervision and control over the railways doing interstate business." Speaking to those who were justifiably worried about the rights of property, Roosevelt cau-tioned "the rights of property are in less jeopardy from the Social-ists and Anarchists than from the predatory man of wealth." The next day the Dow lost more ground, to close at a new low for the year, 78.10. It had lost 17.2 percent since the end of 1906.

The Sherman Antitrust Act had been law for seventeen years. Combinations in restraint of trade like Northern Securities and Standard Oil not only violated that law but also disadvantaged all Americans by forcing them to pay more for goods like sugar and kerosene and services like railroad transportation. But it became clear that Roosevelt was looking for a battle, not just a means of doing right by the governed. In picking that battle, as he often had decades ago as a young assemblyman, he made it personal, which caused investors to wonder where he might stop. If he never stopped, the *New York Times* would have been right—no one could know what any stock was worth.

Standard Oil continued to wait for Landis to impose his fine, but for Roosevelt no amount would be high enough. On July 8, 1907,

Charles Bonaparte, Roosevelt's new attorney general and the great-nephew of the French emperor, and Milton Purdy, Roosevelt's "chief trust hunter," announced a new policy that they said would "do more to bring the trusts to bay than anything yet done by the Government." In an attempt to bring the trusts into compliance with the law, the trusts would be issued injunctions that would be followed by the appointment of receivers, who would run the trusts in the way the government dictated. One newspaper called the policy a "new line of warfare" necessary "because the infliction of fines was all that the Government could obtain, and fines, while inconvenient, were not fatal." The government had created a policy of confiscation. The Dow, which had rallied as Roosevelt's "predatory men of wealth" speech faded, fell 2.3 percent to 80.61 over the next two days and was now down 14.6 percent for 1907 to date.

Roosevelt wasted no time. Two days later, a *New York Times* headline declared that the "War on Trusts Will Open Today," as Bonaparte and Purdy readied plans to file injunctions and demands that receivers be appointed immediately. Later that day, a suit was filed against sixty-five companies and twenty-nine individuals, charging that the American Tobacco Company was an illegal combination working in restraint of trade.

The *Journal of Commerce* spoke for many when it suggested on July 12, 1907, that Roosevelt was playing politics and his "new line of warfare" was "calculated to raise apprehension and alarm in widely extended business interests of the country. It will throw into doubt and confusion calculations for the future in matters in which great corporations are concerned and they are so widely and deeply concerned in the larger industrial and commercial operations of the country that it may have a paralyzing effect upon activities, involving a large share of the capital and labor of the people. Nobody can tell where the line is to be drawn or where the 'trust smashing' process is to stop." The Dow lost 1.9 percent in July and was now down 16.4 percent for the year.

*   *   *

When court reconvened on August 3 to hear Judge Landis impose sentence, he wore a light gray suit and a white carnation as a boutonniere. Despite the finery, Landis was brutal. Calling the defendants no better than thieves, he fined Standard Oil the maximum, $20,000 per offense, a total of $29.24 million. He then shocked the courtroom by calling for a special grand jury to meet eleven days later to consider the facts as a criminal conspiracy that could result in jail for executives of both the railroad and Standard Oil. Roosevelt had already suggested this, but it was a new tactic from the judiciary, and it rattled a stock market that had gotten overextended during the fabulous performance in 1904, 1905, and the first months of 1906 and was now teetering due to the earthquake and the resulting spike in interest rates. The investors who had been buying heavily, the ones Jack Morgan had mentioned early in 1906, were already nervous; the Dow had finished 1906 little changed despite that outstanding start and closed at 78.48 on the day Landis read his decision, down 16.8 percent for the year. The verdict seemed to underscore the *New York Times*' contention that no investor could know the value of anything if the rules were going to keep changing.

John D. Rockefeller was playing golf when he heard the news, and he continued his round without commenting. But other investors were stunned, and predictably, the stock market weakened again. The Dow lost ground on seven of the ten days following the ruling, including a 2.9 percent loss on August 12 and a 3.8 percent loss on the fourteenth. In the ten days after Landis imposed his fine, the Dow lost 11.2 percent, and at 70.32 was now down 25.5 percent for 1907. While the year was disappointing, the stock market remained 60 percent above where it had ended 1903, leaving stocks still fully valued and vulnerable to any weakness in earnings or further increase in interest rates. The market didn't realize it yet, but most of the important pieces were already in place for the Panic of 1907.

On August 20, 1907, Roosevelt went to Provincetown, Massachusetts, to lay the cornerstone for a Pilgrim memorial. Strangely, with the stock market obviously weak, the president decided to again stick his thumb in the eye of Wall Street and take aim at the businessmen he thought were responsible for America's ills.

The advance version of Roosevelt's speech distributed to the press was benign, but as he was delivering his remarks he ad-libbed what he later called "an amusing thing." The amusing thing was the return of the phrase he had used extemporaneously when so angry at the Gridiron Club event in January, this time suggesting that "malefactors of great wealth" had combined to "bring about as much financial stress as possible, in order to discredit the policy of the Government and thereby secure a reversal of that policy, so that they may enjoy unmolested the fruits of their own evil-doing." Roosevelt went on to say that the only thing keeping a few leaders of the predatory industrial trusts out of prison was the difficulty in getting a jury to see things Roosevelt's way. The Dow closed the day down 25.8 percent for the year.

Fritz Augustus Heinze was completing his move from Montana back to New York City. He had been born in Brooklyn and educated in Germany and at the Columbia University School of Mines before moving to Butte, Montana, in 1889, at the age of twenty. There he lived alone in a small log cabin while earning five dollars a day as a mining engineer for the Boston and Montana Consolidated Copper and Silver Mining Company. Butte was the center of the country's copper mining when Heinze arrived, and with the introduction of electric lighting—in 1882, J. P. Morgan's home at 219 Madison Avenue had become the first American home wired for electric light— the demand for copper for electrical wiring was exploding.

After laboring as an engineer for two years, Heinze raised $300,000 and went to work for himself by leasing Butte's Estrella mine from one Jim Murray, considered, to that time, "the shrewdest man in Butte." But Heinze was shrewder as well as unscrupulous, and all agreed that he was tough in an era when that really meant something. According to the terms of the Estrella lease, Murray would get all the ore Heinze mined that was more than 12.5 percent copper, while Heinze would be left with the remainder. When they executed their agreement, all the ore being mined from the Estrella contained more than 12.5 percent copper, and although Murray knew that, he didn't realize Heinze knew it as well. After taking control, Heinze instructed his miners to blast waste rock and mix it with the copper-bearing ore, bringing the copper percentage below the 12.5 percent threshold that would let him keep it all.

But Heinze's biggest profits came after he discovered the obscure Montana "apex" mining law, which said that any vein that surfaced, or "apexed" aboveground, could be mined by the owner of the land where it apexed, regardless of where the vein led, even if it reached under neighboring properties. Heinze began acquiring rights adjacent to producing mines and managed to "discover" that those ores apexed on his newly acquired property.

The most frequent target of Heinze's apex strategy was his first employer, the Boston and Montana Company, and later the Boston and Montana's acquirer, Amalgamated Copper Company, a trust created by Henry Rogers and William Rockefeller. Amalgamated, created in 1899, had been modeled on Standard Oil, and Rogers's goal was to control all the copper-producing properties on Butte Hill. If Standard Oil's kerosene was going to give way to copper wires and electric lights for illumination, as it already had in J. P. Morgan's home and thousands of others, then Standard Oil, through Amalgamated Copper, wanted to control copper production.

Rogers saw Heinze and his apex lawsuits as a "nuisance," and in 1898 Rogers offered him $500,000 for his Butte properties. Heinze's natural contrariness led him to refuse, and he redoubled his efforts to antagonize Rogers and Amalgamated. Their war would spread on several fronts.

Heinze's most effective tactic was also the easiest—he bought a judge. William Clancy was "illiterate but cunning," and he had participated in only one case in district court before being named to the bench, and that one case had led to disbarment proceedings against him. Clancy admitted his guilt during the disbarment hearing, but the complaint was dismissed with a reprimand when Clancy blamed his failure on his ignorance of the law. This man, regardless of his legal shortcomings, was Heinze's most valuable legal asset. During the years of dueling lawsuits between Heinze and Amalgamated, Judge Clancy routinely sided with Heinze and frequently granted apex-law-related inspection orders that permitted Heinze to enter Amalgamated mines to observe their operations, while refusing to let Amalgamated do the same to Heinze.

Clancy's help extended even beyond civil matters. In a murder case against one of Heinze's foremen the prosecuting attorney excoriated Clancy in open court for giving jury instructions that essentially required an acquittal. After Clancy's reelection to the bench he was quoted as saying, "I've got these shuttle-headed Amalgamated lawyers where I want 'em now. I'll fix 'em. I'll make bumpin' posts out of 'em." Clancy proceeded to do just that, making Heinze an even bigger irritant to Amalgamated.

After his initial $500,000 offer to Heinze was refused, Rogers continued to consolidate the smaller firms in Butte into the Amalgamated Copper trust and would occasionally attempt to negotiate with Heinze, but those attempts resulted in nothing but "exasperation." Rogers eventually sent an associate, Thomas Lawson, to meet with Heinze to discuss a potential sale, but Lawson came back unsuccessful and frustrated, saying that Heinze was "akin to genius of the order that wins eminence in bunco and confidence operations." Lawson said Heinze's offices looked like a place where "one instinctively felt for one's watch" to make certain it hadn't been filched.

In 1899, Rogers offered $5 million for Heinze's properties, ten times what he'd offered just months earlier. Heinze continued to stall, having deduced correctly that Amalgamated was being pressured by Standard Oil to get the copper trust sewn up and dispose of Heinze's lawsuits.

In 1902, Heinze, still independent, merged his copper interests into the publicly traded United Copper Company, which he also controlled. While rumors continued that Heinze was selling out to Amalgamated, he kept mining and smelting copper, filing apex lawsuits and remaining a thorn in the side of Henry Rogers.

Finally, Standard Oil had had enough at just the moment its grinding power and financial resources, brought to bear through its ownership of Amalgamated, were eroding Heinze's ability to fight. Once negotiations resumed early in 1904, they continued for fifteen exasperating months—Heinze drew out talks to convince Rogers that he neither needed nor desired a deal. In February 1906, Heinze and Amalgamated reached an agreement—Heinze would pull his Butte holdings, by far his most valuable, out of United Copper and sell them for $12 million to Amalgamated in a convoluted transfer that left both Heinze and Rogers able to claim victory. Heinze had ridden into Butte seventeen years earlier as a young mining engineer making five dollars a day. He headed back east with $12 million in cash and the publicly traded shell that was United Copper Company.

Heinze had been born in Brooklyn but returned to Manhattan, opening an office at 42 Broadway, just two blocks southwest of Wall Street, in 1907. Heinze had settled near Wall Street because he wanted to do for finance in New York what he had done for copper mining in Montana. Heinze went shopping for a bank just at the time when weakness in the stock market had begun to spread.

In 1907 branch banking wasn't yet legal, so bankers practiced what was known as chain banking. Charles Morse, an acquaintance of Heinze, was the king of chain banking, in which a little cash would be used to buy just enough stock in a bank to gain control. That stock would be used as collateral for a loan to buy just enough stock in a second bank to again gain control, and the stock in the second bank would buy control of a third bank, and so on, theoretically infinitely, creating a daisy chain of interconnected and dangerously leveraged banking relationships.

By 1907, Morse was in complete control of three banks, had invested in thirty-one others, and was on the board of directors of seven. The *Wall Street Journal* commented that "to control a group of these banks means to have access to the very throne of American financial power." Morse was more succinct when he said, "Banks mean credit, and credit means power."

Today Morse would rightly be called a scumbag. He was at the unqualified center of three of the most disreputable episodes in the first decade of the twentieth century. A dapper man originally from Maine, Morse showed his earliest instinct for business when his father refused to send him to college and instead demanded that he work as a bookkeeper in the family business. The generous salary of $1,500 was supposed to placate Morse, but he simply hired a cheaper bookkeeper to serve in his place and used the surplus to finance his education.

Fritz Heinze, who had ready cash available but no influence, was drawn to Morse's method of gaining control of important institutions like New York City's banks. Heinze and Morse started working together, and at one point Morse took a stake in Heinze's United

Copper in exchange for shares in Morse's American Ice Company, with the understanding that both would retain the shares for investment. As their joint business dealings grew, Morse convinced Heinze in February 1907 to purchase a controlling interest in the Mercantile National Bank, a bank founded in 1850 and in which Morse already owned shares.

Heinze started buying shares of the Mercantile National early in 1907 at about $200 per share, but when it came to buying a bank, he displayed none of the patience and savvy he'd had when selling his copper mines. Eventually he had to pay as much as $325 per share to gain control.

In 1904, as Heinze was anticipating his return to New York, he paid $96,000 for a seat on the New York Stock Exchange and established his brothers Otto and Arthur in a stock brokerage business. Otto C. Heinze & Company had its offices across from Fritz's new office at 42 Broadway. With the purchase of Mercantile National Bank in 1907, Fritz Heinze was a fully fledged New York financier.

At the close of 1906, United Copper had been trading at $70 a share, but by the following autumn it had fallen to just $40. All of the decline could be blamed on fundamental factors—as early as July 1907, the *Wall Street Journal* reported that demand for copper was 30 to 50 percent below that of the previous year, and accordingly, by October 1907, the price of copper was half of what it had been earlier that year.

In an attempt to reverse the downward trend in the price of United Copper, Fritz's first move as a New York financier was to direct his brother Arthur to launch a stock pool. Arthur was to buy shares of United Copper, using as much borrowed money and as little of Fritz's $12 million in cash as possible, in an effort to lift the stock price. Since the shares Arthur bought were paid for with borrowed money, they had to remain on deposit as collateral with the brokers who had extended the loans. The pool was an extraordinarily risky play. If the price of copper kept dropping, if the value of United Copper shares kept falling, the brokers would demand more collateral in the form of cash from the Heinze brothers. Conceivably, if the share price of United Copper fell enough, the loans due could consume all the cash Fritz had received from Amalgamated.

As October passed, prices continued to fall, and as the pressure increased, Otto and Arthur wondered if the nearly 50 percent drop in the price of United Copper wasn't due to something other than the weakness in the price of copper or the share price of other copper concerns or the 28 percent year-to-date decline in the broad stock market; the brothers wondered if speculators were selling shares of United Copper short in a bet that the price would drop even further.

In a short sale, a speculator borrows shares from an investor who owns them, then sells the shares in the open market. Eventually the short seller will have to return to the open market, purchase the shares, and return them to the lender. Selling short is done in expectation that the price paid to purchase the shares in the future will be lower than the price received when the shares are initially sold. The difference in price is the short seller's profit or loss.

The risk in short selling is that the share price will rise after they have been sold short. When the lender of the shares demands their return the speculator's only recourse is to go into the market and pay whatever price is demanded for the shares, even if that price is higher than the price originally received. Theoretically, if no shares are available for purchase, the price would increase infinitely. This sort of appreciation is what had ruined so many speculators in Northern Pacific stock as Hill and Harriman fought for control and drove the price to $1,000 a share.

Not only is a short sale risky, but it is only possible if the speculator is able to borrow the shares, usually from someone who has them on deposit with a brokerage firm. If there are no shares on deposit, there are no shares to lend, and short selling becomes impossible.

On Wednesday, October 9, 1907, the first day the Dow's loss exceeded 30 percent for the year, Arthur did some calculations that convinced him short sellers were behind the drop in the price of United Copper. Otto assumed that between them, Fritz and Charles Morse, who had gotten his shares in the swap that saw him send shares in his American Ice Company to Fritz, owned the majority of the shares of United Copper, and that it was these shares, as well as the ones Arthur had purchased at Fritz's direction, sitting on deposit at various brokerages, that were being loaned to speculators in order to affect their short sales. Fritz's own stock was being used against him.

One potential solution was to pay off the loans Arthur had incurred when he started buying United Copper stock at Fritz's direction and demand delivery of every stock certificate on deposit. But the Heinze brothers, knowing how pressure exerted against Amalgamated Copper had worked to their advantage, believed that if they also bought even more shares of United Copper just as they were demanding delivery of the shares they already owned, they would pressure or "squeeze" the short sellers, forcing them to pay a higher price than they might have otherwise.

But demanding return of all the shares on deposit would require enough cash to pay off the loans that were secured by the shares, as well as cash to buy the additional shares that would squeeze the short-selling speculators. The simple stock-buying pool Arthur was running at Fritz's direction was risky. This plan would be an order of magnitude riskier.

The next day, Thursday, October 10, Otto went to Fritz, asking for the nearly $2 million he estimated would be needed to execute this plan. Fritz refused. During the previous four months, beginning just after he'd assumed ownership and taken control of the Mercantile National Bank, depositors, fearful of his new leadership in the era before deposit insurance, had withdrawn $4 million, a significant portion of the bank's deposits, and Fritz needed to preserve his capital. This "silent run" on the Mercantile National also meant the bank wasn't able to lend the money to Otto. But Fritz was sympathetic to Otto's plan. In an effort to implement Otto's scheme, Fritz arranged a meeting for them with Morse and Morse's friend and colleague Charles Barney, the president of the Knickerbocker Trust Company, the third-largest trust company in New York. Morse and Barney were longtime business partners in a variety of enterprises, including Morse's American Ice, where Barney was a shareholder and where he had been a director since 1900, as well as various other stock pools, even ownership of Broadway's Hotel Rossmoor.

When the four men sat to discuss United Copper, Morse said he believed Otto's estimate of $2 million was far short of the amount actually needed. Morse thought they would need $3 million. Two million had been too much to raise, and $3 million was out of the question.

On the next trading day, Saturday, October 12, United Copper's stock opened at $45.50 before dropping to $37.75 because, at least in part, that day's newspapers reported that a large producer was unsuccessfully attempting to sell several million pounds of copper at 13 cents per pound, which was below the cost of production. Miners were now losing money with each shovelful of copper ore they dug out of the ground.

Saturday's drop in the share price prompted more margin calls. The brokers who had bought United Copper shares on credit, at Arthur's direction, were demanding additional collateral for the loans, in the form of cash. It became obvious to the brothers that additional margin calls, which were certain to come if the price of

United Copper dropped any further, would wipe out the Heinze liquid reserves and result in the failure of Otto C. Heinze & Company. Knowing this, desperate for a solution, and illogically hoping that the downdraft in United Copper had been a result of short selling and not liquidation by owners of the shares in the face of that morning's news, Otto decided to execute his plan to corner the stock of United Copper and squeeze the short sellers without informing Fritz. He was going to put his plan into action, even if he had to go it alone without any capital.

Not only was Otto on his own and without capital, but also the broad stock market was working against him. The Dow closed that Saturday at just 62.34, down 33.9 percent for the year and 7.9 percent for the month as investors wondered what stocks were worth if there was no limit to President Roosevelt's attacks on business.

On Sunday, October 13, Otto gave orders for the brokerage firm of Gross & Kleeberg to buy 6,000 shares of United Copper at ascending prices when trading resumed on Monday. He also began to call for some of the shares of United Copper on deposit with various brokerage firms to be delivered to the offices of Heinze & Company. With this call for the shares, Fritz's loans would become due the moment the shares were delivered to Otto's office.

On Monday, October 14, United Copper stock opened for trading at $39.88, up $2.63 from Saturday's close, and as the pace of Otto's own buying increased, the price jumped to $40, then $41, then to $49.88, and eventually to $60. Before lunch, Otto had managed to drive the price of United Copper higher by almost $23, about 60 percent above where it had closed the previous trading day. After falling back a bit, United Copper closed that Monday at $52.88, a rally of $15.13, or 40 percent. Otto's scheme seemed to be working. The next morning's *Chicago Tribune* led its business coverage with the story of the stunning rally in United Copper; a headline reported that the Heinze brothers' buying "puts big crimp in those who sold stock short."

While Otto was buying, and would soon have to pay for, additional shares, the stock certificates he had demanded were arriving in his office, and he needed to make a payment of $630,000, which he did not have. But Otto's buying had potentially solved the problem for him; with United Copper trading at nearly $60, the total amount of cash needed for his plan was greatly reduced from his initial estimate of $2 million. When Otto went to Fritz at the end of the day on Monday, beseeching him again for capital, Fritz was more impressed by how well the scheme seemed to be working than he was angry at Otto's recklessness. Fritz gave in and arranged for the Mercantile National to cover any checks Otto wrote.

With the Mercantile National backing him, Otto sprang his trap and issued calls for all remaining United Copper shares on deposit with the various brokers before the market opened the next day, Tuesday, October 15. He was certain that the brokers would be unable to deliver the shares, as he assumed they had been loaned to the short sellers, and that he had all the available shares already sitting in his office or on their way.

United Copper opened for trading at $50 on Tuesday, just below Monday's closing price of $52.88, and during the morning it traded as high as $59 on heavy volume. But just as Otto was expecting to be notified of defaults by the brokerages not able to deliver the shares due, the shares he'd demanded instead started to arrive in his office. The trickle of stock certificates grew to a rush and then a flood just after lunch, as *every* share due was delivered. The flow became so great that Otto, not knowing how to stem the tide and unable to pay, began refusing delivery of the shares he had demanded just that morning. Otto, so certain that the short sellers were responsible for the drop in United Copper's price, so certain that the brokerages wouldn't be able to deliver the shares due, had gotten it completely wrong.

When the brokers for whom the shares had served as collateral realized that Otto wasn't going to take delivery and pay off the loans due, they became desperate. The only thing to do was turn to the market to get whatever they could. During the last hour of trading on Tuesday, as these shares hit the market, United Copper's price fell from $59 to $50 then $45 before closing at $36, down 31.9 percent for the day and below where it had ended the previous week. United Copper was now below the level that had moved Otto to act, and substantially lower than the prices he'd paid on Monday and Tuesday.

When the market opened on Wednesday, October 16, there was no place for the Heinze brothers to hide. Newspapers would report that copper prices reached an all-time low on this day, and that news crushed any remaining opportunity for Otto's plan to succeed. Shares of United Copper were thrown on the market at the open, and in a final insult, Otto refused to pay Gross & Kleeberg for the shares they had bought at his direction on Monday and Tuesday with the goal of sparking the short squeeze. Those shares were also sold for whatever they might bring.

United Copper opened for trading at $30 on Wednesday, another $6 below Tuesday's close. Three minutes later it was down to $20 as the wave of selling crested. At the close, it was trading at $10, making Fritz's stock in United Copper worth a fraction of the loans taken against it. Fritz Heinze, the copper king of Montana, was broke.

How had Otto and Arthur gotten it so wrong? What made them think that short sellers were active in United Copper, depressing the price in such a way that they were vulnerable? The selling hadn't been short selling. The fact that all the shares on deposit had been tendered as Otto demanded was proof that it had been an owner of a substantial number of shares in United Copper liquidating his holdings as copper prices fell.

One contemporary writer said there was a strange "fatality" about friendship with Charles Morse, and the Heinze brothers ultimately came to believe it was Morse, Fritz's friend and mentor, who was secretly selling the shares he'd received from Fritz, shares he was supposed to hold for investment.

Hill, Morgan, and Harriman's wild buying of Northern Pacific in 1901, as they tried to gain control, had caused the price to rise to $1,000 in a massive but inadvertent short squeeze that punished the broad market. The Heinzes' own buying of United Copper in 1907 hadn't led to a short squeeze, even though, ironically, that had been the goal. An inadvertent short squeeze in 1901 had punished the broad market; the unsuccessful short squeeze in 1907 would similarly punish the broad market.

When Fritz's self-dealing loans became known, he was forced to resign from the Mercantile National Bank on the evening of Wednesday, October 16, after less than nine months as its president. Friends tried to explain away the resignation by saying "he did not pretend to knowledge of the banking business and that he meant rather to learn the business as president of the Mercantile than personally to direct its operations." These friends didn't explain why he would be president of a bank if he had no knowledge of the banking business or why the president of a bank wouldn't be expected to personally direct its operations.

Fritz Heinze, who had $12 million in cash at the beginning of the year, was broke, as were the New York Stock Exchange firms of Gross & Kleeberg, which had done Otto's buying and not gotten paid, and Otto Heinze & Company. The smashing of the corner in United Copper stock wasn't merely a spectator sport for investors. On October 16, the day United Copper traded down to $10, the broad market fell in both fear and sympathy, with the Dow losing 2.6 percent to close at 60.46. The Dow was now down 35.9 percent for the year and 10.7 percent for the month.

The rumors promptly started in earnest. Fritz had been bankrupted, and he and Otto had taken Otto Heinze & Company and Gross & Kleeberg with them. If the damage had stopped there, the episode would have been merely an exercise in schadenfreude, as Heinze's former antagonists at Amalgamated gleefully watched his fortune evaporate. Instead, the questions of who else might be involved, who else might be exposed and overleveraged, were asked.

On Friday, October 18, the rumors were focused on Charles Barney, the fourth person at the original meeting with Fritz, Otto, and Morse to discuss squeezing the shorts in United Copper. Was Barney, and more important, was the Knickerbocker Trust, involved in the failed corner? With this question being asked, it seemed that the damage would extend beyond a small group of reckless speculators to the nation's bedrock financial institutions; stocks sank further, losing 2.3 percent on Friday, October 18, as the Dow closed at 59.13, its first close below 60 in more than three years. It lost another 0.8 percent on Saturday's shortened session, a day when the *Wall Street Journal* called the failed corner "one of the most absurd pieces of speculative jugglery ever attempted." The Dow was down 5.9 percent for the week, 13.4 percent for the month, 37.8 percent for the year, and 42.6 percent since making its all-time high in January of the previous year.

Fritz was out, and on Saturday, October 19, Morse was soon to be out as well. The New York Clearing House, the group that cleared checks and presented them to the proper bank for payment, had agreed to support the Mercantile National Bank with a loan, but the price of their support was the resignation of Charles Morse from any position of leadership in any bank with which he was affiliated.

One of Morse's closest friends was Charles Barney, which explains why Barney was at the original meeting to discuss cornering United Copper stock. Barney was attractive and courtly but high-strung. The son of a prosperous Cleveland merchant who moved his family to New York when Charles was six, Barney had returned to New

York after graduating from Williams College. Barney did well by marrying Lucy Collins Whitney, the sister of financier, secretary of the navy, and patriarch of the Whitney family William Whitney. Barney joined the Knickerbocker Trust Company in 1884, and by 1897 had become president.

In 1907 the Knickerbocker Trust had 18,000 depositors, and during the decade since he'd taken over, Barney had increased deposits by a factor of six. But despite the sober-sounding name, trust companies were new financial contraptions that were circling the edges of what the law allowed and testing the limits of what might survive in times of stress.

In the last half of the 1800s, traditional banks weren't able to accept trust accounts such as wills and estates, so those customers were directed to newly formed trust companies. With a large and expanding customer base, and unencumbered by many of the laws that constrained traditional banks, trust companies started to accept savings deposits. The trust company's primary advantage was the lack of a legal requirement that they maintain any reserves on hand to facilitate even the most basic banking functions. Meanwhile, the nationally chartered banks were required to reserve as much as 25 percent of their deposits in cash, in their vaults, generating no income. As such, the trust companies in 1901 were able to pay anywhere between 2 and 5 percent interest on deposit accounts, while most banks paid none.

The cost of this freedom was that trust companies operated outside the clearinghouse structure that allowed for direct clearing of checks drawn on other institutions and often provided temporary loans when a bank was under stress. Trust companies would instead have to clear through the courtesy of a member bank, a privilege that might be suspended at any time, and couldn't hope for any loan from the clearinghouse.

After 1900, as assets in trust companies grew, those assets were put to work in riskier ventures, including bridge loans for indus-

trial mergers, as well as the underwriting of stock and bond issuance, like a modern-day investment bank. Often these risks led to
others; the freedom to underwrite bond and stock issuance led to
an additional risk as the trust company would often hold unmar-
keted securities they had underwritten in their own portfolio,
hoping that the price of the securities would climb but liable for
losses if the price fell. One contemporary observer remarked that
the trust companies were "generally regarded as unsafe and even
piratical." Trust companies had come to combine the worst elements of two modern-day financial institutions: the savings and
loan and the hedge fund.

While trust companies were novel, insecure, and untested in
a crisis, their management continued to press expansion. The
Knickerbocker Trust had been founded in 1884 by Fred Eldridge,
an old friend and classmate of J. P. Morgan's, and by 1907, with
Charles Barney entering his second decade as its president, it stood
in quiet elegance at the corner of Fifth Avenue and Thirty-Fourth
Street, across from the original Waldorf-Astoria. Once depositors
got inside the Knickerbocker Trust building, clad in marble and
fronted by four massive columns, they saw more marble, bronze,
and mahogany woodwork. The main banking room soared to con-
sume three of the building's four stories, and though the result was
impressive and reassuring, it wasn't enough. In August 1907, the
Knickerbocker announced plans for a twenty-two-story building
at the corner of Broadway and Exchange Place, in the heart of the
Wall Street district. On Sunday, October 6, 1907, the *New York
Times* reported the building would cost $3.5 million, and the top-
floor penthouse would be devoted to "dining rooms, kitchens and
serving rooms solely for the use of officers and employees."

Not everyone was blind to the dangers of trust companies. As
early as 1874, bankers were warning that trust companies had
been converted into "stock-jobbing concerns apparently for the
benefit of stock operators." Alexander Dana Noyes noted in 1901

that the trust companies were not designed for the function they now served and that "the phenomenal rise of these institutions has occurred in a series of years of great prosperity. No institution or system can be pronounced entirely safe which has not been 'tried by fire' in a financial crisis, and the trust company system, as now conducted, has not been thus tried." Three weeks later, the Knickerbocker Trust would be tried by fire and would fail.

Just as every modern stock market crash has an external catalyst, each collapse has been fueled by a new, poorly understood financial contraption that introduces leverage into a system that is already unstable. In 1907, that contraption was the trust companies that were essentially ungoverned and "piratical." In addition to the absolute lack of reserves, much of the collateral securing trust company loans was illiquid and couldn't be easily sold to pay off the loans. It might take months to liquidate raw land, and if so, it could be at a substantial loss. This explains why banks were prohibited from owning land, unless it was through foreclosure. The facilities and machinery securing a bridge loan to allow for an industrial combination might have no value outside the businesses that used it, and if it did have value, it might similarly take months to sell and relocate before the loan could be satisfied. As is true with all the financial contraptions that have led to modern stock market crashes, the trust companies worked beautifully when the sun was shining, but once storm clouds formed and a gale started to blow, the trust companies weren't able to drop their sails. Instead the leverage inherent in their unreserved structure meant that they became more exposed as the storm worsened.

Leverage means that a $1 decline in a stock price might generate $2 in losses for shareholders using leverage. Those losses might force investors to sell, driving the price down another $3 and generating $6 in losses for the remaining levered shareholders, some of whom are now forced to sell, driving the price down another $9, again producing outsize losses for the remaining shareholders, some of whom will be forced to sell for whatever they can get.

But leverage isn't necessarily financial; it can also be behavioral. One depositor, knowing that the trust companies are able to pay higher rates of interest because they keep less in reserve and more in illiquid assets, might demand the return of his deposit and warn friends to do the same.

As word spreads, the price of the stock cascades lower or the line of depositors demanding their money overwhelms the system—not because it can't handle their reasonable demands but because an unstable system, made unstable by a massive rally in asset prices, an external catalyst like an earthquake, a belligerent change in government policy, and a poorly understood, poorly designed financial contraption like 1907's trust companies, injects leverage suddenly. The system can't handle the chain reaction of their cascading demands simultaneously. Friction never overcomes tension, so the tremor becomes an earthquake.

As Heinze and Morse were losing their jobs and as the stock market was panicking, J. P. Morgan was attending an Episcopal convention in Richmond, Virginia. Teddy Roosevelt was even more out of touch—just as he had been when McKinley passed—hunting an astonishing menagerie of animals in the remote canebrakes of Louisiana. Morgan was kept updated by wire and initially declined to return to New York early, fearing that doing so would lead to even more fear in the market. When he eventually decided on Saturday, October 19, that he would return the next day, he explained to the bishop, "They are in trouble in New York. They do not know what to do, and I don't know what to do, but I'm going back."

As Morgan was being updated, Roosevelt remained isolated. When asked on Saturday, in the middle of his hunting trip, about the financial chaos breaking out in New York, Roosevelt replied with a list of the animals he had just killed, including "three bears, six deer, one wild turkey, twelve squirrels, one duck, one opossum, and one wildcat."

The headlines on Monday morning, October 21, were reassuring: one on the front page of the *New York Times* promised "Banks Sound; Will Be Backed." After reporting with a slightly sinister tone that Heinze and Morse had been "eliminated" from all banking organizations in New York City, the paper of record and the "businessmen's bible" in the days before the *Wall Street Journal*'s rise to prominence went on to remind readers that depositors were expected to do their duty by meeting the situation "with coolness and calm judgement."

Despite this, on Monday, October 21, the "panic" of the Panic of 1907 set in. The stock market had lost 5.9 percent during the previous week and was now down 35.5 percent for 1907, but it was about to get much worse.

While most New Yorkers knew little about the relationship between Charles Morse, Fritz Heinze, and Charles Barney, the insiders at the city's largest banks were aware of their interlocking business connections—Barney was a director of Morse's National Bank of North America and the New Amsterdam National Bank, two of the banks Morse had daisy-chained together. Barney also served on the board of Morse's American Ice Company and was a large shareholder in his Consolidated Steamship Lines, which controlled steamship traffic along the east coast. Knickerbocker Trust also held sizable stakes in these companies, as well as Morse's American Ice Securities Company, the Clyde Steamship Company, and the Butterick Company. And all three were on the board of the Mercantile National Bank.

Although Saturday's newspapers proclaimed "Mercantile Sound," by Monday Barney's involvement in the scheme was well known among bankers, and questions about the viability of his Knickerbocker Trust had been whispered during the weekend. The National Bank of Commerce had been the Knickerbocker's agent with the clearinghouse, but rather than going down with Barney, the National Bank of Commerce announced it would no longer clear for the Knickerbocker. The Knickerbocker, which had been a financial island, was now completely adrift, unable to present checks drawn on other banks for payment. Despite this, but thanks to the reassuring headlines declaring the banks "sound," as well as J. P. Morgan's presence in the city, the market rebounded on Monday, gaining 3.7 percent to close at 60.81. It was still down 10.2 percent for the month and 35.5 percent for the year.

By the next day, Tuesday, October 22, it wasn't just banking insiders who knew about the connection between Heinze, Morse, and Barney and were questioning the Knickerbocker's survival; that morning's papers reported that Barney had resigned from the Knickerbocker late the previous day, and that he'd been forced out "because of his connection with Mr. Morse and the Morse companies." Asked if the Knickerbocker was in trouble, Barney scoffed, "Nothing could be more absurd . . . the company was never in a stronger position." Depositors weren't so certain.

With October 22's ambiguous headline "Knickerbocker Will Be Aided," but the certain news that Heinze, Barney, and Morse were connected, depositors took no chances. They lined up to withdraw their money. By the time the Knickerbocker opened for business at 10:00 A.M. on Tuesday, more than one hundred depositors were waiting in line. Fifteen minutes after the doors opened, the line reached from the tellers to the sidewalk as the tellers closed accounts and pushed stacks of bills across the marble counters, through the bronze gates inside the mahogany woodwork. Next to each teller were stacks of currency, bound into thousand-dollar lots. A stack would dwindle and disappear, and the teller would reach for the next stack to pay the next depositor. Soon every bit of the lobby was consumed by depositors waiting in line with bags to take away their cash as tellers slowed their counting in an effort to make the stacks last and get to closing time without having exhausted the cash.

After a check for $1.5 million drawn on the Knickerbocker was presented by Hanover National Bank, which was followed by a check for $1 million presented by a different bank, the demands of depositors who wanted their money back overwhelmed the Knickerbocker's small cash reserve. After returning $8 million to depositors in just three hours, the Knickerbocker Trust was forced to halt payments. Many of those already inside refused to leave. Those still outside rattled the doors, demanding information. Investors had lost faith in the Knickerbocker literally overnight, and a bank run that lasted just three hours forced the closing of one of the largest, most connected, best-known financial firms in New York City. The Dow lost 2.8 percent that day, to close at 59.11, and was now down 12.7 percent for the month and 37.4 percent for the year.

On Wednesday, October 23, the *New York Times*' front page featured a story about Ringling Brothers combining with Barnum & Bailey, but there was another story about another circus, the Knickerbocker Trust, and the news was bad for depositors. The Knickerbocker would not reopen after Tuesday's run. Despite the spreading panic, other news on the front page was good. The largest type of the edition was reserved for the headline reporting that the Trust Company of America (TCA) would be aided via loans from J. P. Morgan's syndicate.

In the era before the Federal Reserve Bank, J. P. Morgan was the unofficial but unrivaled leader of the country's financial community, and as such was the country's lender of last resort. Morgan was now seventy years old; he had turned sixty-nine on the day before the San Francisco earthquake. He was trying to untangle himself from his bank's day-to-day affairs—he wanted to get on with his collecting of art and antique manuscripts—and he was counting on his son, Jack, to take over. But just as Teddy Roosevelt had been the only Republican who could win the governorship of New York in 1898, J. P. Morgan was the only financier who might stop the Panic of 1907.

The headlines about the Trust Company of America were premature and counterproductive. As TCA depositors read of what had happened to the Knickerbocker Trust and that it wouldn't reopen, and that their own trust company was in need of saving, they decided not to take the chance. They lined up outside the TCA just as they had lined up outside the Knickerbocker the day before. J. P. Morgan's son-in-law reported that the line of depositors "extended down Wall Street and around the corner into William Street."

While it was certainly true that Heinze, Barney, and Morse were connected by joint business dealings, the extent of the connection was not yet obvious to outsiders. What was obvious was that Morse fostered a closer examination of the relationship that ousted Barney from the Knickerbocker and led to its failure—likely in a devious attempt to misdirect attention from his own banks to the Knickerbocker—in an even more extreme example of the sort of perfidy he had demonstrated by selling his shares of United Copper and then remaining quiet when the Heinze brothers told him they suspected short sellers were at work. While trying to explain away the troubles of his two largest banks, the Bank of North America and the New Amsterdam Bank, Morse told investigators from the New York Clearing House that they should "look around in other places too." Soon new concerns for the health of the Knickerbocker were being whispered.

As the Knickerbocker Trust was closing its doors, never to reopen, Morgan charged Benjamin Strong, a thirty-four-year-old man he barely knew, with answering a simple question. Morgan wanted Strong to spend Tuesday evening reviewing the Trust

Company of America's assets and liabilities, and then decide if the institution was solvent. Morgan had just met Strong, who had been recommended by Henry Davison, who had in turn been recommended by George Baker, president of First National Bank. Baker had Morgan's full confidence when Morgan gave Strong his assignment. In giving his report at 12:30 P.M. the next day, in the midst of the run on TCA, Strong tried to give a full picture of the TCA's situation. But Morgan wasn't interested in that. He simply wanted to know if Strong thought the TCA was solvent. Strong asked the assembled experts for their opinion of the value of several large loans TCA had made. When Morgan and his group said those loans were likely good, Strong said he believed the TCA was solvent and that any loans made by Morgan and his associates to prop up TCA were safe. Hearing this, Morgan was resolute: "This is the place to stop the trouble, then."

Morgan ordered TCA president Oakleigh Thorne to bring any securities the TCA had taken in as collateral to J.P. Morgan & Company at 23 Wall Street. Based on Strong's assurance, Morgan would loan as much as the collateral Thorne presented would allow.

At 1:00 P.M. the line outside TCA was growing, and the available cash had dwindled to $1.2 million. Thirty minutes later the cash balance was only $800,000. With forty-five minutes left in TCA's normal business day, the run by depositors had reduced TCA's cash to just $180,000, an amount equal to what Knickerbocker Trust had paid out every four minutes during its run the day before. But as Morgan added up the value of the securities Thorne had brought, he would occasionally stop, instruct that a loan be immediately made equal in amount to the value of the securities he'd just counted, then resume his counting. By TCA's closing time of 3:00 P.M., approximately $3 million in cash had been delivered and $12 million paid out to depositors, but TCA had survived. They were able to pay everyone who'd lined up, yet Morgan and

Thorne knew the run would continue tomorrow unless stronger action was taken.

As the banks and markets closed on the twenty-third, the Dow was at 58.21, down another 1.5 percent for the day and now down 14.0 percent for the month of October and 38.3 percent for the year. Morgan summoned the heads of all the New York trust companies after the market's close. Once they were assembled, he said what they all knew: the problem was a trust company problem and the trust companies would have to solve it. He then shared what they didn't know: the Trust Company of America would need another $10 million to see it through tomorrow and it was up to the trust companies to pledge enough capital to save their rival. Morgan then promised that if the trusts did their duty, the commercial banks and J.P. Morgan & Company would make up any shortfall. Bankers Trust immediately pledged $1 million, but the other trust companies balked. As they bickered, Morgan, so ill that some had recommended he not leave his bed that morning, napped in his chair.

When he woke up thirty minutes later, the trust companies were no nearer a resolution of their mutual problem. Morgan took a pencil and paper and announced that Bankers Trust had done its duty. He then twisted arms, recording each commitment until he'd raised a total of $8.25 million, at which point he committed the other banks and his own firm for the balance.

The next morning's newspapers announced that the Trust Company of America had been saved, although another $9 million would be withdrawn that day, requiring the loan against collateral Morgan had predicted. Benjamin Strong was forced to carry the securities down Wall Street to the National City Bank, where he exchanged them for as much as $1 million in cash, which he stuffed in his pockets before running to replenish TCA's tellers.

But as the trust companies had managed to save each other on Wednesday, on Thursday, October 24, the banks were trying to save themselves and reduce their risk by calling in loans. The result was to completely absorb the available money supply.

Stock prices were continuing to collapse. They had closed on Wednesday 43.5 percent below 1906's closing high, and as they did, the cost of short-term borrowing—already at obscene levels as the banks called in loans—reached 100 percent. The result was that any shares purchased with borrowed money were being sold indiscriminately. They were simply thrown on the market to bring whatever might be gotten for them, just as the brokers left holding shares of United Copper threw them on the market once Otto Heinze refused to pay. The stock exchange and all its member firms were in danger of failing under the torrent of liquidation.

Early on Thursday afternoon, Ransom Thomas, president of the New York Stock Exchange, left the stock exchange building at the corner of Wall and Broad Streets, but rather than heading to the nearby offices of the U.S. Treasury for help he crossed Broad Street and knocked on the door at 23 Wall Street. In this case, he was just another supplicant seeking an audience with the Zeus of Wall Street. Thomas walked directly to Morgan's office and interrupted Morgan's conversation.

"Mr. Morgan, we will have to close the Stock Exchange."

"What?"

"We will have to close the Stock Exchange," Thomas repeated.

"At what time do you usually close it?" Morgan asked.

"Why, at three o'clock," Thomas answered.

"It must not close one minute before that hour today!" Morgan said, according to his son-in-law, who later wrote that Morgan emphasized each word by keeping time with his right hand, the middle finger of it pointing straight at Thomas.

Thomas muttered some description of the difficulty faced by the exchange and its member firms, which were finding it impossible to borrow money as each stock quotation was 10 points lower than the one before.

Investors and speculators were rushing to sell their stock, some because they thought prices were going to weaken further, some because they simply had to. They had to because speculators had borrowed money from banks or their brokers and used it to buy stock, with the shares serving as collateral, as Otto Heinze had done with the disastrous United Copper pool. This is the simplest form of leverage.

These loans were not without conditions. If the value of the stock securing the loan dropped, as it was doing now, the lender might require the borrower to deposit more collateral in the form of cash. The borrower could deposit that additional cash or sell his shares. In a more extreme response, the lender could demand repayment in full, at any time, and lenders on October 24 weren't giving borrowers the option of depositing more collateral; they were demanding full repayment of outstanding loans immediately. Since borrowers didn't have the cash—they'd used it to buy stock—they had to sell their stock. It was as if every mortgage lender demanded every homeowner pay off their mortgage immediately; all those who couldn't raise the money would be selling their homes simultaneously.

There weren't enough buyers for all the stock being sold; there rarely are when everyone has to sell at the same moment. Thomas was there to ask Morgan, a man who abhorred stock speculation, for a loan that would allow stock speculators to pay off their original loans, extend the period in which they could liquidate their holdings, and end the panic.

Thomas told Morgan he needed $25 million or else "fifty" brokerage houses would fail. His only alternative was to close the exchange early.

Morgan knew that once a bank or trust company closed its doors early and told depositors it didn't have their money, the institution could never reopen. This is what had happened with the Knickerbocker Trust and what he had worked so hard to prevent for the Trust Company of America. Similarly, he knew that if the stock exchange had to close because of the selling, it might be a decade before it reopened.

Morgan acted quickly, summoning the presidents of the banks in the neighborhood. By 2:00 P.M. they were assembled, and Morgan was succinct. Unless the men in the room could commit a total of $25 million *in the next fifteen minutes,* at least fifty stock exchange firms would fail; also, the exchange would close and it might not reopen for years. Within five minutes the men had more than met their goal; $27 million had been allocated. When the announcement was made on the floor of the exchange that $27 million was ready to be loaned at 10 percent interest, a fraction of the 100 percent interest that had been demanded that morning, and an even tinier fraction of the 125 percent demanded by anyone with money to lend earlier that afternoon, one of the clerks responsible for recording names and loan amounts had his suit coat and vest ripped off in the chaos.

The New York Stock Exchange closed on Thursday, October 24, at its regular time. The Dow finished the day nearly unchanged at 58.18 and substantially above its low for the day, but it was still down by 38.3 percent for 1907 and 14.1 percent for the month of October.

While stock exchange firms would need an infusion of another $13 million the next day, Friday, October 25, the run on the Trust Company of America and the other trust companies slowed. In a two-week period, the TCA would pay out $34 million of its $64 million in deposits, a staggering percentage that was survived only because of the ability and standing of J. P. Morgan. When the stock exchange closed on Friday, the fever had broken. It had posted a small gain and would advance modestly again on Saturday. Calm would slowly return in part because Morgan quietly called on religious leaders to encourage it during their upcoming Sunday sermons.

When the closing bell rang on Thursday, October 31, the Dow was at 57.70; it had lost 14.8 percent for the month—about twice what it manages to gain in an average year—in the worst month it had ever had to that point and the worst single month it would ever have until the start of the Great Depression. During that month it lost ground on eight consecutive sessions and finished lower on nineteen of the twenty-seven trading days.

Concerns would continue to echo, and the Dow would display weakness during the remainder of the year before bottoming for good at 53.00 on November 15, down 43.8 percent for 1907 and exactly 50 points below the high made in 1906. When the stock market closed on December 31, 1907, the Dow Jones Industrial Average had lost 37.7 percent, by far its worst-ever annual performance until 1931, and still the second-worst loss ever.

CRASH
1929

The facade of the Bloomingdale Insane Asylum was strictly symmetrical, with mirror-image cupolas, windows, and patient rooms in matching wings, as if the intention was to not tax troubled minds any more than necessary. Michael Meehan arrived in the summer of 1936 and stayed until the next June. He had always been considered high-strung, even among other brokers on the New York Stock Exchange, where he had spent more than a decade. Some people said Meehan got the same thrill from his work on the trading floor that "stirs firemen in responding to a night alarm." He had been described at the end of one day's trading in March 1928 as being "at the point of nervous exhaustion." Maybe that was because people saw him as the "biggest man" among Wall Street's speculators. He would make between $5 million and $20 million that year.

But the 1929 crash would hit him hard, and seven years later, the market would break him mentally.

In 1935 Meehan had accumulated a large block of shares in Bellanca Aircraft Company at low prices and in his wife's name.

In a time when trade information, including price and number of shares, was disseminated on a ticker tape, he began "painting the tape" by making large prearranged trades at steadily higher prices, all between accounts Meehan already controlled, which meant that no change in ownership occurred. By painting the tape with substantial volume at ever-higher prices he expected to grab investors' attention and create the illusion that Bellanca was heading still higher and induce other investors to buy. Meehan drove the price from $1.75 per share to $5.50 over the span of a few months, at which point he sold his holdings to those investors he'd suckered. And without Meehan's machinations, the rally stopped, and the price per share fell back to its original level, with Meehan, and his wife, that much richer.

Matched sales, the large sales at ever-higher prices between accounts controlled by a manipulator, and the kind of stock pool Meehan excelled at, had been perfectly legal until 1934. This sort of dealing had helped push the stock market up 255 percent from the end of 1919 to its height in 1929, and then back down 48 percent in the next fifty-six trading days. It was the sort of thing Michael Meehan and men like him had done repeatedly, and Meehan had become famous and wealthy doing so.

Meehan didn't get his start on Wall Street but near it, as a twenty-year-old salesman at McBride's theater ticket agency on lower Broadway. Meehan's customers were the traders and brokers in the neighborhood, and he would give them the best seats in exchange for reliable stock tips, eventually building a respectable portfolio for himself. Realizing he was in the right part of town but in the wrong business, he went to work as a clerk on the Curb Exchange, so called because its dealings were literally executed on the curb of Broad Street. Clerks like Meehan would finger-wag orders from windows to brokers standing in a mob on the sidewalk, where the orders to buy or sell would be executed.

By 1918, Meehan had accumulated enough cash to buy a seat

on the Curb Exchange, and during his first month working for himself he cleared a mere eighteen dollars. To make ends meet, he once again spent his nights selling theater tickets. But he kept at it, and two years later paid $90,000 for a seat on the New York Stock Exchange.

Meehan and the NYSE would grow up together during the 1920s, when he started serving as a specialist. A specialist is given a lucrative near monopoly over dealings in a particular stock in exchange for a commitment to maintain an orderly market, even if it meant trading for his own account at a loss. By 1929 his brokerage firm, M. J. Meehan & Company, had four hundred employees and owned eight seats on the New York Stock Exchange, altogether worth $5 million, more seats than any other commission broker owned.

Meehan's greatest success came as the specialist for Radio Corporation of America (RCA), a company that didn't exist when he joined the New York Stock Exchange. It initially traded on the Curb market, and at the end of 1921, RCA was trading for $2.25 a share. RCA became the most famous stock of the decade, rallying from that puny beginning to trade as high as $570 a share in 1929 as radio went from a novelty to a luxury to a necessity.

Meehan's history would mirror that of the American stock market: finding its place in the world in the 1910s, then growing and getting wealthy in the 1920s, before despair and loss in the 1930s.

In 1914, the prospect of war in Europe shocked American business. As European political positions ossified and as the continent lurched toward war, the front page of the *New York Times* reported on July 31, "Closing of Stock Exchange Not Necessary," even though the Dow Jones Industrial Average had lost 6.9 percent the previous day.

The New York Stock Exchange never opened that day—one report mentioned NYSE president Henry G. S. Nobel's "discovery that the market was loaded down with big selling orders, and almost bare of buying orders"—and it didn't reopen until the middle of December. When trading resumed on December 12, 1914, the Dow Jones Industrial Average fell another 16.80 points, to close at 54.62, a loss of 23.5 percent since its previous close in July.

But the war turned out to be a boon for American business, because the European combatants needed to buy nearly everything America's businesses made or its farmers grew. It became nearly impossible to not make money during the war years, and as the United States resolutely avoided direct involvement in the conflict, the stock market surged higher. The Dow finished 1915 at 99.15, a gain of 81.7 percent for the year, still the greatest one-year gain the Dow has ever enjoyed. The rally eased as the United States became a combatant in April 1917 but resumed at the start of 1919, and the Dow closed that year at 107.23, a gain of 30.5 percent. The Dow had nearly doubled in the five years since the end of 1914, as America was beginning to understand its place in the world and Michael Meehan was beginning to find his way on the Curb Exchange.

In Paris they were known as "the Crazy Years," while in the United States they were "the Roaring Twenties." As 1919 ended, Babe Ruth still played for the Boston Red Sox, and he was still best known as a pitcher; he'd hit only forty-nine home runs sprinkled across his six previous major-league seasons. It was still legal to buy a cocktail or bottle of bourbon, and women still couldn't vote. Radio was still the province of hobbyists with crystal sets and headphones listening to Morse code from ships at sea. And the financial world was still dominated by bonds and by those who had become investors for the first time by purchasing Liberty Bonds, which had helped finance the war.

Change began slowly, then accelerated. By the end of the first week of 1920, baseball fans learned that Babe Ruth had become a New York Yankee. By the end of the first month, it was illegal to buy that cocktail or bottle of bourbon. By the end of the year, women could vote for president, and by the end of the decade, most investors would have turned their attention from boring bonds to sizzling stocks.

The war had turned Americans into investors in part because those who were trying to sell investments had become advertisers. The first Liberty Bonds were issued in April 1917, less than three weeks after the United States entered the war. While buying them was seen as a patriotic duty, the Treasury wasn't taking any chances. More than 10,000 advertisements urging Americans to buy Liberty Bonds appeared on billboards, buses, and streetcars in 3,200 cities. Mail-order powerhouses Sears, Roebuck and Montgomery Ward mailed two million Liberty Bond advertisements to farm families, while celebrities including Douglas Fairbanks, Mary Pickford, and Charlie Chaplin toured the country staging bond rallies.

But each bond had a face value and minimum investment of $50, two weeks' wages for the average industrial worker. So in addition to becoming an advertiser, the Treasury sold Liberty Bonds on the installment plan. A War Thrift Stamp cost only 25 cents; when sixteen stamps had been collected they could be exchanged for a $5 stamp called a War Savings Stamp. Ten War Savings Stamps would get you a $50 Liberty Bond.

Liberty Bonds were the first investment many Americans ever made, and by the end of the war, four different series of bonds worth more than $17 billion had been sold to 20 million Americans at a time when there were only 24 million American households.

Warren Harding had placed an inconsequential sixth on his party's inconclusive first ballot at the 1920 Republican convention. When no consensus candidate emerged, the likable, inoffensive Harding slowly gathered support, and on the tenth ballot he became the Republican nominee for president. After the first truly modern war, which had seen the introduction of both chemical weapons and the machine gun, Harding understood that Americans wanted a return to a simpler time, what Harding called "a return to normalcy." Harding even conducted a simpler, more chivalrous campaign by staying at home in Marion, Ohio, and letting proxies venture out to handle the barnstorming.

Harding was elected on November 2, 1920, with 63.9 percent of the vote. He became the first president elected when women could vote, the first who could not legally toast his victory, and the first to ride to his inauguration in an automobile. Once Harding started speaking after his swearing in, he returned to the theme that had gotten him elected, saying, "Our supreme task is the resumption of our onward, normal way."

One of the few things that didn't change was the Federal Reserve, which itself was new. The Federal Reserve System was part of the country's response to the Panic of 1907, when a single man, J. P. Morgan, with access to only private resources, stepped in to stop the chaos. The Federal Reserve Board in Washington, D.C., and the twelve regional Fed banks were expected to control credit and the flow of money while acting as the lender of last resort in a panic.

As American soldiers were returning from Europe, Benjamin Strong, president of the Federal Reserve Bank of New York since the founding of the Federal Reserve System in 1913, was not yet fifty years old. Strong was born in Fishkill-on-Hudson, New York, in 1872 to a respectable family of diminished financial circumstances. He had hoped to follow an older brother to Princeton University but was forced to take a job. Reportedly fired from his first position due to poor penmanship, Strong in 1891 joined the investment firm of Jessup, Patton & Company, where he thrived, evidently in spite of his penmanship.

Strong married Margaret LeBoutillier in 1895, and the couple moved to Englewood, New Jersey, where Strong enjoyed a bit of serendipity. Englewood was popular with the partners of J.P. Morgan & Company, and Strong became close to two of them, Henry Davison and Thomas Lamont. Strong joined the newly formed—and Morgan-controlled—Bankers Trust Company in 1904 after being recruited by Davison. Strong advanced steadily at Bankers Trust thanks in large part to the influence of his Englewood neighbors.

Unfortunately, life intruded. Shortly after the birth of their fourth child, a chronically depressed Margaret took a revolver that Strong had recently bought for protection from a string of burglaries and shot herself to death in May 1905. The next year Strong's oldest daughter died of scarlet fever.

In 1907, just months before that year's October panic, in which Strong would assist J. P. Morgan so ably, he married Katherine Converse, the eighteen-year-old daughter of the president of Bankers Trust, Edmund Converse. In 1909, Strong became vice president of Bankers Trust following the resignation of Thomas Lamont, and then president in January 1914 on the retirement of his father-in-law. Strong would step down himself just ten months later to become head of the newly formed Federal Reserve Bank of New York.

But again Strong's success was interleaved with tragedy. In 1916, Katherine abandoned him, taking their two children to California. That same year he was diagnosed with tuberculosis, requiring months convalescing in the pristine air of the Cragmor Sanatorium in Colorado Springs, Colorado. Strong's visits to Cragmor went on for years, which meant that the central architect of the country's interest rate policy was often away from work for months at a time during the 1920s, frequently leaving Federal Reserve interest rate policy in less capable hands.

During the war things had been simple enough—keep interest rates low to help finance military spending—but after the fighting stopped in November 1918, the Fed was often wrongheaded in its approach.

In November 1919 nearly a year had passed since the end of hostilities with Germany, and the Federal Reserve no longer needed to keep interest rates artificially low.

While a broad-based decrease in production was sure to follow the peace as business moved from a war footing, Strong and the Fed failed to realize that such a decrease alone would be a sufficient damper on the inflationary economic growth seen during the war years, when GDP had risen by more than 20 percent three years in a row. Instead of allowing that natural contraction to do its work for it, the Fed on November 3, 1919, increased the discount rate, the interest rate charged to commercial banks by the Federal Reserve (and at the time the Fed's primary means of influencing interest rates and economic growth), from 4 percent to 4.75 percent, saying that "the financial operations of the Government [that is, borrowing to finance the war] will cease to be the important factor in shaping Reserve Bank policies." The Dow closed that day at 119.62, its all-time high and a level it wouldn't revisit for more than five years, as prices fell and the postwar economy slowed. The Dow lost 12.9 percent that month, the worst month of the decade, with the exception of December 1914, when trading had resumed after the outbreak of war. One newspaper said November's slump was due to the "influence of credit restrictions upon speculation."

But the Fed wasn't done, and it didn't wait long to increase the discount rate again, raising it from 4.75 to 6 percent on January 22, 1920, and then to 7 percent on June 1, 1920, in another aggressive increase. The Fed had moved from 4 percent to 7 percent in just eight months and had done so in just three bellicose steps.

One observer said the increase to 7 percent on June 1 "supplied ammunition which professional traders seized . . . to attack stocks" as the Dow lost 2.0 percent for the day. During the eight months from the day the first increase became effective through

June 1, 1920, the day the final increase became effective, the Dow lost 24.2 percent.

Higher interest rates did more than just hurt the stock market; they throttled the entire economy. Agriculture was hit hardest by the slowdown. During the war, farmers had been encouraged to put every acre—even marginal land—into production. Now production overwhelmed the diminished demand. Between the summers of 1920 and 1921, cotton prices fell by nearly two-thirds, and corn prices fell by 60 percent to just 65 cents per bushel. One measure of overall producer prices fell by more than 40 percent between 1920 and 1921, as unemployment rose from 5.2 percent to 8.7 percent.

As unemployment grew and economic output shrank under the pressure of an economy weaning itself from war production and further burdened by rising interest rates, including the eleven poisonous months when the discount rate remained at 7 percent, economic output eventually declined by 16.7 percent in 1921.

Unfortunately, the Federal Reserve learned the wrong lesson from this tightening regime. Instead of realizing that a more moderate course of rate increases could safely temper an exuberant economy—the sort of economy they would face later in the decade—they believed that raising interest rates resulted in collapsing prices and a painful recession, not seeing that the pace at which they raised interest rates was crucial.

It wasn't just economic production and farm prices that were falling; wages were plummeting as well. In May 1921, U.S. Steel slashed the pay of furnace workers by 20 percent, and maritime workers were striking to prevent similar cuts. Recognizing their overreaction, and as the potential for war flared anew over German reparation payments, the Fed embarked on a course of rate cuts as wild as the hikes they'd instituted at the end of 1919 and throughout 1920. The first cut, to 6.5 percent, came on May 5, 1921, followed quickly by another to 6 percent in June, then to 5.5 percent in July and to

5 percent in September before cutting again in November, when the discount rate reached 4.5 percent. In June 1922 they cut again to 4 percent, the rate that had prevailed during the war. Immediately after the war the Fed had slammed on the brakes. Now they had the accelerator to the floor.

In response to this spasm of interest rate cuts, the Dow rallied 17.0 percent in less than fourteen months in an amazing recovery given 1921's downward momentum.

Surprised by the damage they had done, the Fed governors became reticent to exercise their mandate by raising the interest rates they controlled in an effort to modulate economic expansion and stock market speculation. Later in the decade, in the midst of what several contemporary writers came to call a "speculative orgy," the Fed put off raising rates and then did so only modestly, never again approaching the 7 percent reached in June 1920, despite a festival of public hand-wringing about the dangers of speculation and calls for somebody to do something. Even as the orgy got out of hand by 1929, the Fed's discount rate finally reached a post-1921 peak of just 6 percent in September 1929, less than two months before stocks crashed, much too late to restrain the speculation.

From 1921 to 1929, the Fed committed a grievous series of sins, and in doing so abdicated responsibility for managing the supply of money and credit in the American economy—the heart of its mandate—in an embarrassingly feckless display.

The Fed's raising interest rates to restrain the 1920s' decade-long stock market spree would have been good medicine if delivered in a moderate dosage years earlier. Delivered all at once after the disease had spread, it nearly killed the patient.

Americans thought it was magical that sound could move through the air to be heard on a radio.

In October 1919, the Radio Corporation of America was incorporated, and by the next month it had acquired the assets of American Marconi, with the help of the federal government and RCA's largest shareholder, General Electric. RCA started trading on the Curb Exchange in 1919 and closed the year trading at just $2.00 a share. In many ways it was the first consumer electronic start-up.

In February 1920, RCA fulfilled its strategic promise when it began offering transatlantic radio service, but another company, Westinghouse, would recognize the commercial potential for radio. Frank Conrad was a Westinghouse engineer with an eighth-grade education who was eventually responsible for more than two hundred Westinghouse patents, including the ubiquitous revolving electricity meter.

In his leisure hours, Conrad set up a radio transmitter in the loft above his garage near Pittsburgh. Conrad's station was a hobby, but the technology he'd invented was a vast improvement over existing designs, and soon he was broadcasting songs or reporting sports scores and local news. When listeners started requesting airtime, Westinghouse convinced Conrad to turn his hobby into a business, and on November 2, 1920, Election Day, Conrad's newly christened KDKA went on the air and announced to listeners from New Hampshire to Louisiana that Warren G. Harding had defeated James Cox for the presidency.

RCA joined Westinghouse in commercial domestic broadcasting on July 2, 1921, when it cobbled together a temporary station, known as WJY, in Hoboken, New Jersey, to broadcast the title fight between Jack Dempsey and Georges Carpentier; three hundred thousand listened as Dempsey retained his championship with a fourth-round knockout. In November, just one year after Conrad's first broadcast, Chicago's KYW became the seventh station to broadcast daily. With a steady stream of opera, it was also the first specialized radio station.

Cigarette smoking was doubling and car production was tripling, but radio was growing from nothing into the country's most important consumer product. Americans spent $60 million on radio equipment in 1922 as they started learning about the "radio music in the air, every night, everywhere. Anybody can hear it at home on a receiving set."

Nineteen twenty-two was also good for RCA stock and the stock market in general. Now that the Fed had reversed course and pushed interest rates lower, the Dow gained 21.7 percent to end 1922 at 98.73. Though RCA closed the year at just $3.88 a share, it had gained 72.4 percent after going nowhere in 1920 and 1921. The country had managed to shake off the effects of the war and of the Fed's ill-considered interest rate increases of 1919 and 1920 and the subsequent recession. The discount rate stood at just 4 percent at the end of 1922, the same level as the end of the war.

Now that the other Fed presidents had done an about-face on interest rates, Benjamin Strong started wondering if they hadn't gotten it wrong again. In a 1922 speech, he explained that he hoped to stop stock market speculators before they could "damage the economy." As the stock market ran dramatically higher, the Federal Reserve didn't have the fortitude to raise interest rates meaningfully for five and a half years.

Early in 1923 Warren Harding was preparing to run for a second term. Despite suffering from the flu, he embarked on what he called his "Voyage of Understanding," during which he visited more than a dozen states and became the first president to visit Alaska. But on returning to the contiguous United States, he experienced trouble. In a speech to fifty thousand in Washington State, he referred to Alaska as Nebraska and had difficulty maintaining his balance. He complained of shortness of breath and indigestion, which his physician blamed on bad seafood. Harding seemed to be recovering, but on August 2, 1923, he slumped over while in bed with his wife and couldn't be revived. Harding was the sixth president to die in office. Calvin Coolidge became president early the next morning when his father, a notary public, swore him in by the light of a kerosene lamp in the parlor of the family's farmhouse in Plymouth Notch, Vermont. Harding had been for "normalcy." Coolidge embraced it even more earnestly, adding deeply held beliefs in lower taxes and the sort of isolationism that he hoped would prevent another foreign war.

While 1923 would see the Dow lose 3.3 percent, from the day of Harding's death to the end of the year it would gain 8.3 percent while marking the start of what became known as the "Coolidge Prosperity," punctuated by the new president's proclamation: "The business of America is business."

The stock market rally continued in January 1924, with the Dow gaining 5.4 percent for the month and closing at 100.66. The next month radio went beyond opera music and boxing matches, developing into a tool for politicians. Harding had installed a radio in the White House in 1922, but on February 12, 1924, Coolidge became the first president to deliver a political speech on radio. Ten days later he went a step further and became the first to deliver a political speech by radio from the White House. It was carried on forty-four stations.

In 1924, money meant gold, and Great Britain was desperate to return to the gold standard. Abandoned in August 1914 as a reality of the outbreak of war, the gold standard before 1914 had meant stable exchange rates and a fluid international economy, with London at the center of the web and the pound sterling the world's reserve currency. The British knew that returning to the gold standard after more than a decade wasn't sufficient to restore Great Britain to preeminence in the mercantile and financial world, but they were certain it was necessary. They were equally certain that if they were to return to the gold standard, they would need the assistance of the United States Federal Reserve. The person asking Benjamin Strong for help was Montagu Norman, governor of the Bank of England since 1920.

Both sides of Norman's family had been bankers, and Norman's maternal grandfather, Mark Collet, had been governor of the Bank of England in the 1880s. Unlike Strong's family, Norman's was financially stable, and Norman was able to attend King's College, which he flunked out of after a single year. Norman joined his father's firm, Martin's Bank, in 1882, becoming a partner in 1900. Surprisingly, given his success as a banker, Norman displayed an astoundingly fragile grip on emotional stability throughout much of his life.

Regardless of his psychological trials, Norman was elected a director of the Bank of England in 1907 while continuing his employment at Martin's Bank. However, from 1911 to 1913 he didn't work at all, because he was suffering from what was likely a bipolar crisis. This breakdown established a pattern—at moments of emotional distress, Norman would abruptly abandon work for months at a time to travel in disguise and under a pseudonym. Despite this, or maybe because of it, he left Martin's and joined the Bank of England full-time in 1915. By 1920, he was governor.

Norman, profoundly troubled of mind, and Strong, profoundly weak in body with tuberculous, became best of friends once they were thrown together by their work at their respective central banks. The two would vacation together, alternating between Maine and the South of France, and maintain a constant stream of letters when apart.

In 1924 Norman was the greatest advocate for Great Britain's return to the gold standard, with the exception of the chancellor of the Exchequer, Winston Churchill. To accomplish this, the Bank of England would have to entice gold to return to the country, and Norman knew how to do so. Just as the Bank of England had raised interest rates in 1907 to make England a more attractive place to deposit gold and keep it from leaving for San Francisco, Norman, as head of the Bank of England, now asked Strong to reduce the Federal Reserve's discount rate to make London a relatively more attractive place to deposit gold. The mechanism was so strong and Norman's longtime goal so well known that when the Fed's discount rate had temporarily exceeded that of the Bank of England in 1923, causing gold to flow into American vaults, Strong had felt forced to rationalize the higher U.S. rate in an apologetic letter to his friend: "The results [the American stock market lost ground each of the next five months and fell 16.4 percent during that period] convinced me that our action was required. . . . Of course we must not close our eyes to the bearing this may have upon Europe."

Having shown a willingness to cut the discount rate when it could in 1921, and anxious to help the friend Strong had felt the need to apologize to a year earlier, Strong and the New York Fed cut the discount rate by 0.5 percent in May 1924, and then cut again forty-two days later on June 12, and again in August, in an effort to make England a better place for the world to deposit its gold.

By August 1924, the Fed had cut the discount rate to just 3 percent, matching the lowest discount rate the Fed had ever set, as well as the rate in effect when the United States entered the war. It was lower than the 4 percent rate that stood when the war ended. In short, it was an emergency rate, expected only during the most dire economic circumstances.

While the Fed would raise the rate by 0.5 percent in February 1925 in response to domestic considerations, that move was accompanied by a 1 percent increase by the Bank of England, thereby increasing the interest rate differential to again strengthen the flow of gold headed toward London. In May 1925 the goal was achieved. Britain returned to the gold standard with the passage of the Gold Standard Act of 1925.

The original charter of the Federal Reserve spoke to its responsibility to America and Americans. It was silent as to any responsibility to help another country return to the gold standard, but cutting interest rates was easy. Unfortunately, the Fed wouldn't show a symmetrical willingness to endure the hard work of raising rates or tolerate their vicissitudes even in the face of the manic stock market speculation these lower rates generated, until well after this cowardice had led to the unrestrained speculative frenzy that ignited the Great Depression. Perversely, and at Strong's insistence, the Fed would again cut rates three years later, with the lone goal of helping the British—American interests be damned.

When the Fed cut interest rates in 1924, it predictably ignited a furious stock market rally. With money now cheap, stock ownership was easier to finance as well as more attractive in comparison to owning bonds, and the stock market went on a fabulous run, with a 7.2 percent gain in June, when the discount rate was cut to a six-year low of 3.5 percent; a gain of 6.0 percent in July; and a gain of 3.0 percent in August, when the rate was cut again to just 3.0 percent, matching its lowest rate ever. The rally continued with gains of 7.0 percent in November and 8.2 percent in December, as rates remained low and as Coolidge established himself in office. At the end of 1924, the Dow had gained 26.2 percent, the best annual gain since the end of the war.

Born on Independence Day in 1872, Coolidge came from a prosperous but not wealthy family. Coolidge and his shopkeeper/notary public father shared a frugal nature and an abiding respect for personal industry. As president, Coolidge was confident that sound national economic principles that were consistent with personal frugality and honesty would lead to prosperity. He genuflected to both management and labor when he said, "The man who builds a factory builds a temple, the man who works there worships there, and to each is due not scorn and blame, but reverence and praise."

The Coolidge Prosperity would continue in 1925 with stock market gains of 2.2 percent in January and 2.8 percent in April, followed by a colossal rally of 8.3 percent in May, the best month the stock market had had since 1920. The Dow gained another 5.5 percent in August, and then bested May's performance with a gain of 9.1 percent in October.

The Dow would end 1925 with a gain of 30.0 percent as it closed at 156.66. The two years of 1924–25 resulted in a 64.0 percent gain for the Dow, its fourth-best two-year stretch to that point.

Those few who worried about the market were focused on the frenetic pace of the rally. In May, Benjamin Strong expressed his own concerns, citing "the ever-present menace of the stock exchange speculation." Privately he was frustrated that his efforts to help his friend in London were resulting in the unwanted side effect of excessive stock market speculation. In a letter to Norman, Strong complained, "It seems a shame that the best sorts of plans can be handicapped by a speculative orgy, and yet the temper of the people in this country is such that these situations cannot be avoided." Strong understood how dangerous such an orgy was, but as his health deteriorated, he would not be able to control the nation's speculative urge.

Strong wasn't the only one in government worried about the dangers of unrestrained speculation. Herbert Hoover became Coolidge's secretary of commerce after a distinguished career in business that had left him well traveled, well known by international business leaders, and splendidly wealthy. After an even more impressive stint leading the effort to provide food aid to a devastated postwar Europe, Hoover was famous to the world at large. In July 1922 the *New York Times* had named him one of the "Twelve Greatest American Men" for his relief work.

In 1925, during his term as commerce secretary, and as the stock market was climbing furiously thanks to a Fed discount rate of just 3.5 percent, Hoover turned to his friend Adolph Miller. Miller was one of several governors of the Federal Reserve. (The Federal Reserve had, and still has, several governors in addition to the presidents of the regional banks and is led by the chairperson, while the Bank of England had a single governor, who served as its most senior official. Montagu Norman was that single governor during the 1920s.) Hoover urged Miller to get the Fed to limit credit. After a single increase in the discount rate to the current rate of 3.5 percent on the last business day of February 1925, the Fed hadn't budged, likely because a 4.9 percent loss in the stock market in March was believed to have resulted from February's rate increase.

Since the founding of the twelve regional Federal Reserve Banks, each had been able to independently set the discount rate that prevailed in its particular region. In an era when capital was relatively immobile, this independence was intended to draw money to those portions of the country that needed it—for example, to finance agriculture. As 1925 ended, every one of the regional banks had their discount rate at 4 percent, with the exception of Strong's New York bank, which held its discount rate at just 3.5 percent, despite his concerns about stock market speculation. Strong finally raised the New York Fed's rate to 4 percent in January 1926 because, as he explained, "[w]e have had a dangerous speculation develop in the stock market with some evidence that it is extending into commodities."

Strong's hawkishness didn't last long. After a broad-based selloff in March 1926 when the Dow fell 9.1 percent and lost ground seventeen of twenty-seven trading days, he again gave way to his profound inability to stomach bad news from the stock market, even when it had gained 117.7 percent in the previous five years. He cut the New York Fed's discount rate back to 3.5 percent on April 23, 1926, though every other regional Fed bank held its rate steady at 4 percent. At about the time Strong cut rates in New York, he left for England. After he returned in October, he was stricken with flu and then pneumonia, dangerous conditions for a man already weakened by tuberculosis. Strong would leave for Colorado Springs to convalesce and would be absent from New York for a full year at a time when interest rates were historically low and speculation continued to run dangerously hot.

After the Dow had consolidated the gains of 1924 and 1925, it rallied just 0.3 percent in 1926, though the financial outlook for 1927 was rosy. One newspaper on January 1 described "the extremely favorable diagnosis of the existing position." Economic growth was strong if volatile. The stock market was also strong; even when it fell back it recovered its losses reliably and quickly thanks to low interest rates. Conditions certainly didn't call for the Fed to cut rates further.

Conditions were very different in Europe in 1927, as gold once again was leaving the vaults of European central banks. Normally those central banks would raise interest rates to slow the exodus or, at best, reverse it. Instead they were all trying to manage their currencies in relation to other European currencies, as well as to the dollar, in order to attract gold deposits while avoiding rate hikes that would inevitably slow their economies. For some time, Montagu Norman had been pressing for a meeting of the principals of the four leading central banks. He wanted to discuss their mutual dilemma, and in June Strong called such a meeting in the hope that they could reach a common solution and ease the tension developing between England and France.

No record was kept of the proceedings, and the participants refused to confirm that they were meeting, but once their conference broke on July 7, they left New York together to report to the Federal Reserve Board in Washington, D.C. Three weeks later, the rate-setting arm of the Federal Reserve, the Open Market Investment Committee, met and was joined by Strong. The committee's focus was obvious from the minutes, which said, "The most important consideration . . . was undoubtedly the fact that the differential between the rates in New York and the rates in London was not today sufficient to enable London, and therefore the rest of Europe, to avoid general advance in rates this autumn unless rates here were lowered."

The minutes further confirmed that the committee knew that helping London might have dangerous consequences at home: "It was felt that the only possible adverse development resulting from a general lowering of discount rates would be in the speculative securities markets, but that this possibility should not stand in the way of the execution of an otherwise desirable policy." So the Fed ignored the danger and lowered rates in the United States, even though money was plentiful and the economy was robust; they did so to help Strong's friend in London, knowing that they risked creating a speculative bubble.

Adolph Miller was the only member of the Federal Reserve Board to dissent. He would later call the Fed's course of action "the most costly error committed by it or any other banking system in the last 75 years." Economist Liaquat Ahamed would call Strong's supremely misguided course "the spark that lit the forest fire."

In a bit of misdirection, Strong convinced the Kansas City regional bank to serve as the vanguard for his scheme, with their first discount rate cut coming on July 29, 1927. Seven of the regional banks, including New York, followed during the first half of August, though Philadelphia, Chicago, Minneapolis, and San Francisco refused to participate. Despite the history of regional bank independence, in September the Federal Reserve Board, in an unprecedented move, forced the four recalcitrant banks to lower their rates, matching the rate that Strong had dictated from New York. The Fed also entered the public market, buying government securities in huge volume, driving interest rates even lower and leaving the sellers with cash they used to buy stocks.

By one measure, Strong's plan worked. Gold did flow out of the United States in substantial quantities as it searched for the more attractive interest rates that were now available in Europe. But as one professor from the London School of Economics described it a few decades later, "From that date, according to all the evidence, the situation got completely out of control."

Miller was not the only person in government who feared the course Strong had plotted. Hoover also recognized the danger, and he urged President Coolidge to intercede, calling Strong "a mental annex to Europe." But Coolidge was disengaged, and he refused, placing his confidence in Andrew Mellon, who was entering his seventh year as secretary of the Treasury and who had just been quoted as saying, "The stock market seems to be going on in a very orderly fashion, and I see no evidence of over-speculation." If Hoover had heard Mellon make this observation, he might very well have replied, "Not yet, but just wait."

A total of $500 million in gold left the United States in 1927. As a result, money for short-term loans to businesses and stock market investors, "call money," the same call money that had gotten so expensive at the depth of the panic in 1907, became scarcer as the outflow of gold shrank the money supply and kept banks from filling the demand for capital. Despite the decrease in the discount rate, this temporary scarcity in call money drove up the cost to those seeking to borrow, which meant that as 1927 ended, the cost of call money was at its highest level of the year, 4.4 percent.

This spread between the discount rate and the amount stock market speculators were willing to pay for call money created a new and supremely dangerous phenomenon. Prior to this moment, banks generally had been the providers of call money. But beginning in 1927, individuals, foreign entities, and American corporations, disappointed by the measly interest rate paid by banks that could get all the money they needed cheaply from the Fed, put their money into the call market. At the end of 1926, call loans had totaled $3.3 billion. One year later, they totaled nearly $4.5 billion. Call money available to stock speculators would explode over the next two years, driven by a differential in interest rates, and this expansion in call money would fuel a legendary stock market rally.

Calvin Coolidge decided that someone else would have to preside over whatever came next. In August 1927, while the president was vacationing in South Dakota, he summoned reporters and handed each a slip of paper with a single sentence: "I do not choose to run for President in nineteen twenty eight." Coolidge was leaving office even though he was governing during an age of astonishing affluence.

Despite having a devout capitalist leaving the presidency, the stock market continued its advance in large part due to low rates and the flood of call money. The Dow closed above 200 for the first time on December 19, 1927, gaining 21.8 percent during the last six months of the year thanks to Strong's latest efforts to help Europeans. It would close on December 31, 1927, at 202.40, an all-time high, with a gain of 28.8 percent for the year.

While new lenders were financing the stock market speculation through the call money market, there were also new vehicles for speculators. The investment trust idea was not new. Small investors in England and Scotland had been pooling their small investments into larger ones, managed by investment companies, since the 1880s. The manager would hold stock in several hundred companies—many more companies than an individual investor of modest means could hope to invest in—and provide diversification along with the promise of superior returns thanks to professional management.

When the concept made its way to the United States, it went by the august name of investment trust. Despite the logical value of investment trusts, relatively few existed in the United States before 1921. One observer put the number at about forty.

One reason there were so few investment trusts was that it took World War I and Liberty Bonds to turn Americans of modest means into investors. Fully half the bonds sold had the lowest possible face value, $50. Another third had a face value of just $100. After the last Liberty Bond issue was floated in October 1918, the majority of American households were investing, and after Harding's "return to normalcy," many of these small investors turned from bonds to stocks early in the 1920s. Others, having watched the stock market do so well in 1924 and 1925, were similarly enticed to join, and by 1926 another 139 investment trusts had been created. As the stock market continued making new highs, another 140 investment trusts were created in 1927 alone.

The growth in investment trusts wasn't due purely to their willingness to accept investments of just a few dollars. It was driven by the economics of the trusts themselves. The sponsor of the trust would receive a management fee in perpetuity and could enjoy other fees, such as commissions for buying and selling stock on the trust's behalf. Driven by the sort of advertising the Treasury Department had perfected when selling Liberty Bonds, investors' thirst for investment vehicles in the mid-1920s meant the pools were often selling for more than the cumulative value of the stocks they contained. An investment trust could assemble a pool with $50 million in stock and sell shares in it for $55 million, with the difference going directly into the sponsor's pocket. The growth in investment trusts was understandable; given the economics, it's only astonishing that more of them weren't created.

The amount of assets managed and the premium that a particular investment trust enjoyed were a function of the prominence and reputation of its sponsor. Advertising helped, but one certain way for a sponsor to enhance its reputation was to hire men of letters; university economists in the 1920s washed onto the shores of Wall Street in a migration that would be repeated in the 1980s by Hayne Leland and Mark Rubinstein, and two decades after that by David X. Li with his "Gaussian copula function." The stock market would pay the price each time.

The famous Princeton economics professor Edwin Kemmerer, known as the "Money Doctor," became one of these reverse refugees when he joined the board of investment trust sponsor American Founders Group, along with another well-known economist, Rufus Tucker. Another sponsor went one better, hiring three distinguished economists, one each from Stanford, Michigan, and Yale, advertising that in the same way that diversification of stocks was good for investors, diversification of the points of view generated by academics from three different institutions was good as well.

But there were only so many economists in the world. The sponsors would need a second point of differentiation—and tragically, that became leverage. The logic was that if the investment trusts guided by their resident academics were good, then a little leverage would make them even better. And that was how leverage came to the formerly sober world of investment trusts.

The leverage was easy to accomplish. An investment trust in 1927 might pool $50 million from many small investors, and instead of buying a like amount of securities, the trust's first act would be to borrow twice that amount. With a total of $150 million in hand, it would invest it all in stocks, and the shares would serve as collateral for the loans, just as the United Copper stock Otto Heinze bought at Fritz's direction had served as collateral for those loans. The financial alchemy was intoxicating. If the pool's value doubled, the value of an investor's stake would increase sixfold. And if such wonderful leverage could be enjoyed by investing $150 million in stocks, even more could be generated by investing the $150 million in investment trusts that were themselves already levered. Several sponsors did just that.

The leader in enjoying the reflected academic glory of the professors it added to its staff, the American Founders Group, also embraced leverage, and eventually had levered investment trusts nested inside levered investments trusts, like so many financial matryoshka dolls. Many American Founders Group funds were larded with $8 of debt for each skinny $1 of customer capital. At that rate, a drop of just 11 percent would topple the pyramid. The Dow had come close to that, losing 8.0 percent in October 1927, including a single day, October 8, when it lost 3.7 percent. The decline was blamed largely, and ironically, on the gain in value of the British pound versus the dollar caused by the differential in interest rates Strong and Norman had engineered. But investors in levered investment trusts seemed unconcerned, because the Dow more than bounced back with a gain of 9.1 percent the next month.

As 1928 began, America's new infatuation with investing and the stock market was about to turn to rapture. The Dow had gained 28.8 percent in 1927. RCA had ended the year at $90.50, up 68.4 percent for the year and up more than nineteen-fold from where it had ended 1923. The year 1928 would be even better, thanks in large part to Michael Meehan and William Durant, the genius behind the conglomerate that became General Motors.

William Durant came from a wealthy Boston family, and his maternal grandfather, a former mayor of Flint, Michigan, had served as governor of Michigan in the 1860s. Durant dropped out of high school in the 1870s and went into business selling horse-drawn carriages, before paying $1,500 for the company that owned the rights to an ingenious springed seat that offered a vastly more comfortable ride than the old rigid carriage. Durant moved the factory to Flint and grew his renamed Durant-Dort Carriage Company into the largest horse-drawn carriage firm in the country. Initially horrified by the automobile, which he considered dirty and dangerous, Durant eventually turned his expertise from the horse-drawn carriage to the horseless one.

In 1904 Durant acquired the struggling automobile works of David Dunbar Buick, and later a company that was the industrial residue of one of Henry Ford's early, failed endeavors, an auto manufacturer named for the French explorer who had founded the city of Detroit, Antoine Cadillac. Durant incorporated his conglomerate as General Motors in 1908. Durant could be wildly profligate when spending GM's money to acquire new nameplates in a rapacious desire to create a holding company that would outdo industry leader Ford. Durant would often get the company dangerously overextended, and as a consequence of one of these episodes, in 1911, the General Motors board of directors fired him. After joining forces with Louis Chevrolet, a celebrated engineer and race car driver whom Durant had met while Chevrolet was racing for Buick, the two founded the Chevrolet Motor Company in a Flint garage. Despite the failure of the first Chevrolet model, the Classic Six, to generate a profit, Durant brought about a reverse merger with General Motors and reassumed the presidency in 1918. When he was fired again in 1919, Durant left for Wall Street, where he engaged in speculation on an enormous scale.

By 1928, RCA had caught Durant's eye, just as it had caught the eye of every other stock market operator. But unlike those other operators, Durant realized that most of RCA's outstanding stock was tightly held by General Electric, Westinghouse, and RCA itself and would never be available to the general market. This meant that a small proportion of the shares made up the float and a little buying could have an outsize influence.

Before the Securities and Exchange Act of 1934, it was common and perfectly legal for investors to create temporary partnerships to baldly manipulate the price of stocks. The partnership would be established by a manager who was expected to attract wealthy investors, who provided the capital, and to operate the pool profitably.

Once the pool began operation, the manager would quietly accumulate a sizable holding in shares of the target company. Once that stake had been accumulated, the pool would begin its more public work, executing large buy orders intended to make a splash and to acquire the last of the pool's position, after which the pool operator would execute matched sales of large numbers of shares at ever-higher prices between accounts controlled by members of the pool. As the price of the target stock rose on this increasing volume, the general investing public would take notice. Then the pool operator might enlist the help of a friendly journalist who would, in exchange for cash or stock, craft fawning reports of the company and its prospects.

A. Newton Plummer was the man in New York who could get such stories printed. Known as "Fixer," Plummer was writing on Wall Street as early as 1916, when he helped launch a biweekly magazine titled *The Lamb*, which was described as being "devoted to the humorous side of Wall Street." Soon the title took on a less innocent meaning when Plummer became a publicist for at least sixty-one of the most manipulative Wall Street pools that were out to fleece investors.

Although there's no proof Plummer worked for Durant's RCA pool, other pools would hire Plummer to bribe writers who would "boost" stocks, like firearm maker Savage Arms, which was the target of a pool in 1924. Plummer paid reporters from the *New York Herald Tribune, Financial America, Wall Street Journal, New York Evening Mail,* and *New York Times* sums between $50 and $209 (other odd amounts, such as $184 and $140.50, were common) to write glowing articles about the company and its prospects. For his efforts, Plummer would receive cash—he received $2,500 for one month's work in the Pure Oil Company pool—as well as stock and options on more stock.

And Plummer could get results. He reported to his retainers that in 1924, 605 positive articles about Savage Arms stock appeared in 228 newspapers, with a combined circulation of 11 million readers.

* * *

After recognizing that RCA was ripe for manipulation and after assembling his investors, Durant recruited Michael Meehan to run his pool in March 1928. As the NYSE specialist for RCA, Meehan would be closer to the trading than anyone else in the world. While a specialist might not participate in every trade, his responsibility included monitoring all trading. Durant had selected the perfect associate.

RCA had ended 1927 at $90.50 a share. On March 3, 1928, it was trading at $94.38, only marginally higher, around the time Durant and Meehan began accumulating the stock. They continued buying quietly until it was time to make a splash. That day was March 10, when RCA gained $12.75, or 11.8 percent, on huge volume of 398,500 shares, while total NYSE volume was only 2.2 million shares. The next trading day, March 12, it gained another 14.9 percent to close at $138.50. As one broker said, the action at the RCA post on the exchange floor "looked like a street fight." Meehan would later say this was really when he started operations, likely meaning this was the day he began to quietly sell the shares the pool had acquired. On Tuesday, March 13, RCA opened at $160.00, a gain of another 15.5 percent, before closing at $146.00 as the public continued to buy and Meehan continued to liquidate.

This perfectly legal, premeditated manipulation made $10 million for the pool, while the shareholders who had rushed in were now stuck with a loss on stock they had purchased at higher prices.

RCA pulled back as Durant completed his selling and as those who'd piled in took their losses. But low interest rates and the deluge of call money ready to finance buying were more powerful than even outright manipulation. As the broad stock market resumed its rally, RCA was leading the way higher. The *New York Times* explained it was "carrying in its train a large number of other stocks." The Dow gained 9.5 percent for the month of March 1928 to close at 213.35, just 1.10 below the all-time high made the day before. RCA closed at $186.00.

These gains came despite the efforts of the Federal Reserve, which had realized in February that—Montagu Norman be damned—the U.S. stock market was dangerously frothy, and it was time they did something about it.

The Fed had raised the discount rate from 3.5 percent to 4 percent on February 3, 1928, and the Dow lost 1.9 percent for the month before shaking off the damage and posting that huge gain of 9.5 percent in March. But the Fed had seen what low rates could do for speculation. Afraid that they were too late to correct the speculation and that the market was indeed out of control, they raised the discount rate to 4.5 percent on May 18 and then to 5 percent on July 13. The market barely slowed, gaining 3.9 percent in May and 2.6 percent in July. As if to punctuate the Fed's insignificance, the Dow gained 11.3 percent in August. The Fed had lost control. It had played with the discount rate to such a degree that the market had found other sources of capital.

The troubling aspect of the stock market rally in early 1928 was that institutions inside the Federal Reserve System, mainly commercial banks, were no longer the predominate provider of speculative loans. This rush of "others" to finance the broker loan or call money market was logical because they could get a vastly higher return by lending to speculators who would then leave the stock as collateral than they could by putting the money in a bank that had all the relatively cheap money it could get from the Fed. From the beginning of 1928 to the middle of June, providers from outside the Federal Reserve System increased their percentage of money available in the call loan market from 24 percent of the total to 41 percent of the total. And that total increased by another $500 million. The Federal Reserve had lost control of stock speculation by losing control of the money that fueled it.

Brokers were starting to worry because there was so much call money to be had. In 1928, there were no regulations regarding how much margin a customer had to post as a down payment for a stock purchase; a broker was free to demand as much or as little margin as they chose. Since the broker could be responsible for any losses in excess of the margin, brokers tried to demand enough to protect against losses without driving customers to other brokers with more lenient margin requirements. While much has been made of 10 percent margin in the 1920s, most brokers had always required more than 10 percent, and beginning in April 1928, nearly all brokers increased the down payment they required from customers to an absolute minimum of 25 percent. One major broker demanded at least 25 percent margin, with certain stocks, including General Motors, requiring 33 percent margin, and the market leader and most volatile, RCA, requiring 50 percent margin. Few brokerage firms failed during the crash of 1929, an indication that lax margin requirements weren't the cause of the bubble.

Although speculators were forced to put down more of their own money, there was still an ocean of financing provided by individuals and corporations outside the Federal Reserve System for speculators to draw from—and draw from it they did. The market gained another 3.9 percent in May 1928. The press of buying was so acute that on several Saturdays that spring, the NYSE was forced to remain closed so that clerks could catch up on reconciling accounts.

As the market was gaining that 3.9 percent in May, Benjamin Strong was sailing for France. Strong's tuberculosis was now at a critical stage, and despite his plans to recuperate in the fresh air of an Atlantic crossing before spending time with his friend Montagu Norman, Strong's physician told him plainly that he would have to cease working entirely if he hoped to stay alive. Strong had made mistakes in judgment during his tenure as president of the Federal Reserve Bank of New York, including the rate cutting in 1924 to help England return to the gold standard, and then the less abrupt cutting in 1927, again to help his European central-bank friends, with little regard for the American economy.

A healthy Strong, like the one who had assisted J. P. Morgan in 1907, would probably have recognized the trouble ahead. The stock market rally was such a force that it just as likely could not have been stopped without a disastrous break in prices, but now the one man who might have seen the impending trouble, and had the reputation necessary to prevent it, was leaving the stage. Benjamin Strong would die that October at the age of fifty-five.

On June 12, 1928, many thought the bull market had finally come to a halt. One newspaper called it "a day of tumultuous, excited market happenings, characterized by an evident effort on the part of the general public to get out of stocks at what they could get." The broad market bounced from its lows and lost just 1.5 percent for the day, but RCA lost $23.50, or 12.1 percent, explaining why brokers required so much margin from speculators.

More than 5 million shares traded on the twelfth, easily besting the previous record. Then the market continued a dangerous habit—it rebounded. It recovered 2.6 percent in July and then went on an even bigger tear, gaining 11.3 percent in August, its best month since 1920, as the Dow closed at 240.41, another all-time high in a month that saw twelve new all-time highs in the month's final fourteen trading days. Investors would learn the wrong lesson: rather than investing sensibly and occasionally taking profits or selling stocks when they showed a bit of weakness, they had learned to hold on, that the market would always come back, that the flood of call money that had peaked above $5 billion at the end of May would fuel more speculation, which would drive prices to new highs. While it took four months, by September 1928 the amount of call money in circulation had indeed reached a new all-time high of $5.5 billion, before jumping to $6.5 billion in November, two months when the Dow also made new all-time highs.

*　　*　　*

On Monday, November 5, 1928, the Dow closed at 257.58, another all-time high. The next day was Election Day, and when the votes were counted, Herbert Hoover had crushed New York's Al Smith, taking forty of the forty-eight states in the greatest electoral vote majority in fifty-six years. Hoover even won Virginia and North Carolina in the traditionally Democratic South.

While much of America might have liked Al Smith's promise to overturn Prohibition, Wall Street loved everything about Herbert Hoover. The Dow rallied each of the next six days and eleven of the next twelve. On November 16 the market gained 2.7 percent and trading volume reached 6.6 million shares, shattering the previous record as the Dow posted another new all-time high, the forty-eighth of the year.

From the day before the election to the end of November, the Dow gained 13.9 percent, to close at 293.38. Total volume for the month was 114.8 million shares, another new record in a month that had six days with volume of more than six million shares, including the twenty-third, when volume was a previously unthinkable 6.9 million shares.

Hoover had been worried about the Fed fueling uncontrolled speculation during his time as secretary of commerce. He had even pled with President Coolidge and Adolph Miller to rein in Strong. He had been ignored. He wouldn't become president for another four months (prior to 1937, the inauguration was held in March), and during those four months, the speculative bubble would expand, along with Hoover's fear of it and enmity for those inflating it for their own ends. Hoover would eventually write about the speculators, "There are crimes far worse than murder for which men should be reviled and punished."

While the bull market hadn't come to an end in June 1928 as some had thought, that was in part because at the end of the year just over $6.5 billion was waiting to be put to work by speculators, another all-time high. And in a supremely dangerous display, the stock market lost 12.3 percent for the month early in December and gained it all back and more before the end of the year.

One newspaper called 1928 "the greatest year in the history of Wall Street speculation." And why shouldn't it be? The Dow ended 1928 at the nice round number of 300.00, another new all-time high, just as 1927 had closed with an all-time high. In 1928 there had been fifty-eight of them, more than one a week.

As 1928 ended, 12.3 percent of Americans owned stocks or bonds, either outright or through an investment trust, possibly one of the 186 new trusts formed that year. One reason that so many Americans had become investors was that there seemed to be little risk and much reward; investors had convinced themselves that the market would always bounce back, as it had in June and December. It seemed that getting out was for weaklings and suckers.

The Dow had gained 48.2 percent in 1928 and a combined 90.8 percent during 1927 and 1928, still the second-best two-year run the Dow has ever had, trailing only the 95.9 percent gain made during the two years ending in 1905, just before the San Francisco earthquake and the resulting Panic. The *Baltimore Sun* wrote on January 1, 1929, "The market is now its own law. The forces behind its advance are irresistible."

The first trading day of 1929 was a continuation of the rally. The Dow gained 7.01 points, or 2.3 percent, to close at another new all-time high on the second-busiest day in the history of the NYSE, and newspapers were reporting that investors were trusting in the adage, "As goest the first day, so goes the year." On January 4, the *Wall Street Journal* proclaimed, "One cannot recall when a New Year was ushered in with business conditions sounder than they are today." Alfred Sloan, the president of General Motors, opined in January, "Personally I believe it is going to be a very prosperous year—I do not see how it could be otherwise." The *New York Times* got it right, albeit unwittingly, when they reported during the first week of 1929 that "the Street as a whole expects 1929 to be one of memorable record."

In January the market gained 5.8 percent on huge volume after 1928 had ended with monthly gains of 5.3 percent, 16.3 percent, and 2.3 percent. Before 1928 the NYSE had never seen a single 4-million-share day; the average daily volume in January 1929 was 4.3 million shares. It all seemed to make sense when the country learned that the amount of call money available to speculators in January had reached another new all-time high.

In September 1927, Benjamin Strong had answered the critics who wanted the Fed to throttle stock market speculation, with a simple question: "I am wondering what will be the consequences of such a policy if it is undertaken and who will assume the responsibility for it." Clearly he had been worried about what Federal Reserve interest rate increases would do to the stock market. Strong was gone now, but early in 1929, the Fed was still reticent to act. During the first week of February, in the sort of half measure that was more a triumph of hope over experience than an intrepid approach to the specific problem, the Fed chose not to use its most straightforward tool, raising interest rates. Instead it sent a letter.

The letter was addressed to the regional Federal Reserve banks and explained that "a member bank is not within its reasonable claims for rediscount facilities [that is, to borrow money] at its regional Federal Reserve Bank when it borrows either for the purpose of making speculative loans or for the purpose of maintaining speculative loans." The Fed was telling private banks that their access to cheap money from the Fed was predicated on them not going overboard in making loans for stock market speculation.

Five days later, the Fed made its position public and stated clearly its concerns regarding speculation, saying it felt compelled to use its power to reduce the use of credit for speculative ventures in the stock market.

The Fed was trying what became known as "direct pressure," and this new strategy was flawed. Senator Carter Glass, who in the next decade would coauthor the sweeping regulation of American financial institutions in order to erect an impenetrable wall between commercial banks and investment banks, warned now that it was nearly impossible to create a legal distinction between loans made for business investment and loans made for stock market speculation. Glass understood that money is fungible. He also likely recognized that commercial banks, such as the ones with access to the Federal Reserve, were no longer the primary suppliers of loans for speculation. As Glass understood, the Fed was using the wrong tool against the wrong people.

Strong's replacement as president of the Federal Reserve Bank of New York also understood this. George Leslie Harrison had degrees from both Yale and Harvard and had joined the Federal Reserve Board in 1914. Harrison would later say he "got his education in central banking from Mr. Paul Warburg at the [Federal Reserve] Board and from Mr. Benjamin Strong at the New York Bank." In 1928 Harrison had been the unanimous selection to replace Strong.

After receiving the frustrating "direct pressure" letter from the Federal Reserve Board in Washington, Harrison traveled from New York to remind the board that every market rate of interest was higher than the Fed's discount rate, meaning all one had to do was borrow at a low rate from a private bank with access to the Federal Reserve's discount window and lend that money back out into any one of the markets willing to pay a higher rate, including the call money market. Harrison was forthright in his discussions with the Federal Reserve Board, telling them that the best way to align rates and limit speculation was to raise the discount rate.

But the Fed had a familiar reason to pursue the path of moral suasion and not raise rates directly. Montagu Norman was back in Washington, and with Benjamin Strong gone, he was meeting with

Secretary of the Treasury Mellon. It was reported that the purpose of Norman's trip was "a general discussion of international financial conditions with the Secretary and members of the [Federal Reserve] Board." In reality high interest rates in the United States had once again started to draw gold from London, and Norman was in town to lobby Mellon to prevent the Fed from taking any action that might exacerbate that flow. Once again, to appease the British, the Fed fueled a runaway stock speculation, this time by refusing to tighten rates further.

In the wake of the Fed's letter and public announcement and subsequent withdrawal of banks from the call money market, the rate available to lenders of call money climbed to 10 percent, making it an even more attractive place to deploy excess funds for those outside the Federal Reserve System. The result of this temporary reduction in the amount of call money available was that even more eventually made its way to the market. During the remainder of 1929, Standard Oil would deploy an average of $69 million to the call money market each day. Electric Bond and Share Company, a holding company for electric utilities, would deploy even more, averaging a little more than $100 million each day. And in a virtuous circle, a few corporations sold new stock into the rising market and loaned the proceeds to speculators. After February 1929, the banks being pressured by the Fed weren't the problem. It was these corporations and wealthy individuals, a "shadow" banking system operating beyond the Fed's control, that were inflating the bubble, as a record amount of money, more than $6.5 billion, was available in the call money market at the end of January. The demand for call money was driving up the interest rate that speculators would have to pay, despite the stupendous increase in the amount of money available to them. That alone should have signaled the danger. Speculators were now in such a rush to buy stocks they gave little thought to the price they had to pay to finance their operations.

On February 14, 1929, Harrison, frustrated by the board's inac-

tion, took advantage of his new role, and the New York bank uni-
laterally increased its discount rate from 5 percent, where it had
been since July, to 6 percent. In response to this renegade move,
the board met for more than five hours and passed a resolution that
"moved that the Board disapprove of the action of the directors of
the Federal Reserve Bank of New York and determine the rate of
that bank to be five percent." The board had overruled the New
York regional bank and forced them to reverse their rate increase.
Continuing to prefer direct pressure, the Federal Reserve Board
would veto nine more attempts to raise the discount rate and curb
speculation before they finally allowed the New York bank to raise
its rate to 6 percent in August. By then it was clearly too late.

The Dow fell from 317.51 at the end of January to 317.41 during February, a loss of just 0.10 despite the Federal Reserve Board's
efforts at direct pressure. If the goal of direct pressure was to reduce
speculation, it had failed.

Profitable stock market speculation is partly a matter of pattern
recognition. And in March 1929, Michael Meehan recognized
that an opportunity was repeating itself. The RCA pool Meehan
had managed for William Durant the previous year had been
enormously profitable. Now Meehan saw that RCA was again
susceptible to manipulation.

On March 7, 1929, Meehan distributed a three-and-one-half-
page legal document titled "Radio Corporation of America, Common Stock Syndicate." The pool Meehan envisioned would operate
by acquiring up to one million shares of RCA stock, then posting
matched sales between accounts controlled by members of the syndicate to paint the tape and drive the price higher. Meehan would be
paid 10 percent of any profits, and his firm would execute the pool's
trades, generating additional income from commissions. By one
measure, the investors in Meehan's latest pool were getting a bargain;
most modern-day hedge funds demand 20 percent of any profits.

Even though the pool managers clearly intended to manipulate the price of RCA stock for the pool's benefit, the document assured investors that the pool would be managed "in accordance with and subject to the rules and regulations of the New York Stock Exchange," an expression of the freewheeling nature of stock market speculation in the 1920s.

The pool began buying on March 12 in small amounts. Soon Meehan engineered the first sizable order intended to attract attention: a purchase of 5,000 shares followed quickly by a purchase of another 1,000 shares. Word that someone was accumulating RCA was soon telegraphed around the financial world. By the end of the day, the pool had bought 392,600 shares and sold 246,000, accumulating a sizable position while also making certain the market saw substantial volume trading at steadily higher prices without knowing much of the trading was taking place between accounts controlled by Meehan. RCA, which had just been split five shares for one, closed the day at $91.75, up $1.63. The next day RCA gained another $2.25 to close at $94.00 on volume of 330,600 shares, just more than 10 percent of all trading done on the NYSE that day.

On Thursday, March 14, RCA gained another $6.50 to close at $100.50, a new all-time split-adjusted high, on volume of 562,400 shares, more than 12 percent of all trading that day. The next day it rallied again, gaining another $6.50 to close at $107.00. On Saturday, March 16, it closed at $109.25 and again accounted for more than 10 percent of all trading. The pool already had a profit of more than $2.5 million, just on the shares it had accumulated that first day. An additional 92,000 shares had been purchased on subsequent days, which would only add to the profit, and there were other shares Meehan had bought in an effort to drive the price higher and then sold at a profit when the buying activity brought in legitimate buyers.

Like all the pools, this rally had been spurred by fawning newspaper articles, some legitimate, some likely ginned up by the pool.

The first appeared on Saturday, March 9, when the *Wall Street Journal* reported that RCA "is financially better off than ever before in its history." On Monday, March 11, the *New York Daily News* column "The Trader," the newspaper column most likely to be subverted by bribery, touted RCA because "its original sponsors are behind it." Another positive article appeared in the *Wall Street Journal* on Wednesday.

The principals of the pool met that Sunday, after RCA had closed the previous day at $109.25, and decided they'd had their fill. They sold 238,600 shares the next day, Monday, March 18. While the stock dropped under the pressure of their selling, they managed to unload their holdings, and once the pool finished its business, it had cleared $4.9 million in profit in just six days of trading. Mike Meehan and his wife, Elizabeth, made $652,784, and Meehan's firm billed the pool an additional $580,000 for brokerage commissions.

On Friday, March 22, the *Wall Street Journal* reported the bad news for those still holding RCA shares. The pool had wrapped up its business and was out of the stock entirely. RCA closed that day at just $91.38, 16.7 percent below the high Meehan had engineered just a few days earlier.

In 1929 more than one hundred of the stocks on the NYSE were the subject of similar manipulative syndicates in which members of the exchange or their business partners were participants. They had not yet managed to undermine confidence in the broader market, which may be the best measure of how far that market had come from levelheaded investing toward outright gambling.

When the members of the Federal Reserve Board met on March 22, they were stunned to learn that despite their best efforts, the money deployed in brokers' loans had just increased by $166 million, generating a net increase of $124 million since they'd instituted their policy of direct pressure on February 2. The Fed's efforts had been thwarted by the public manner in which they'd proceeded, because they'd pointed out that those with money to lend could earn vastly more in the call money market than by putting it in a bank. Corporations, for example, now had $2.8 billion lent out in this manner.

The Federal Reserve Board in Washington, D.C., continued to resolutely refuse to raise rates during the summer of 1929. On May 18, they rejected another attempt to raise the discount rate to 6 percent. This came from the New York and Chicago banks working in tandem. On May 21, the Fed's Advisory Council, made up of one representative from each of the twelve regional Federal Reserve banks, joined in urging precisely this advance of the discount rate to 6 percent in an attempt to bring the regional banks' discount rates "into closer relation with generally prevailing commercial money rates." The council also pointed out that "the amount of the country's credit absorbed in speculative security loans" had not been meaningfully lowered, proving that direct pressure had failed. While one newspaper predicted that an "increase [in interest rates] would cause inconvenience in speculative circles," it was the consensus opinion that the council would finally compel the board to act. The *New York Times* even said, "Wall Street has become reconciled to an increase in the discount rate, many bankers indicating that such a course is inevitable," before saying what everyone knew: "It has been rather generally acknowledged that the present rate of 5 per cent of the Federal Reserve Bank of New York is ineffective and quite out of step with present money conditions."

In expectation of an increase in rates, the stock market lost 4.2 percent on May 22, but then, just when the Fed was expected to act, they did nothing. Despite the market having prepared itself for a rate increase that was desperately needed, the Fed abstained.

The market had been ready for the retreat that higher rates would cause. When the Fed instead did nothing, the market took advantage and charged ahead, retaking lost ground and gaining 12.2 percent in June, 4.2 percent in July, and 9.4 percent in August to close at a record level of 380.33. It seemed everyone was buying, and some of those buyers were in the middle of the Atlantic Ocean.

That spring, about the time Michael Meehan was planning his latest manipulations in RCA, he had read that during a single six-day Atlantic crossing, passengers aboard the Cunard liner *Berengaria* had traded 50,000 shares of stock by having the ship's radio room telegraph orders to their brokers. Meehan wanted his firm to be the one executing all those orders and collecting the commissions. When he offered Cunard $100,000 for the exclusive rights to run a stock brokerage from the *Berengaria,* Cunard was happy to accept.

Meehan celebrated with champagne—Prohibition notwithstanding—on the pier as the *Berengaria* pulled into New York Harbor on August 16. The newest Meehan & Company brokerage office was located in the *Berengaria*'s tearoom on B deck near the promenade. Its first live run had been an unqualified success; 10,000 shares had been traded on Monday, and double that was traded on Thursday. Customer orders were being executed and confirmed in just five minutes, and the only problem was that the onboard office was not large enough to accommodate the crush of customers, some of whom spilled into the passageway. The response to his floating brokerage had been so positive from the moment Meehan made his plans public that he was already working to expand to the liner *Leviathan.* Meehan wasn't alone in bringing the broker to the speculator. The next month the brokerage firm of E. F. Hutton pitched a tent near the practice tee of the U.S. Amateur Golf Championship at Pebble Beach, California, and established a temporary office for players and spectators.

There was now almost no place in the world where a speculator couldn't play the market. And why not? Nineteen twenty-nine was just eight and a half months old, and the Dow was already up 20.5 percent. The Fed had even managed to raise rates, finally doing so on August 9, without stampeding the stock market. Even though the *New York Times* explained that the market was "caught entirely off balance by the suddenness of the decision," and the Dow lost 4.0 percent that day, it regained half that amount on the next day and had regained all the losses just three trading days later, posting yet another all-time high on the sixteenth, a mere week after the anticlimactic increase and the same day Meehan was celebrating the arrival of the *Berengaria* with its floating brokerage office. Many investors wondered why the Fed had waited so long if the stock market was going to recover yet again.

Trading volume that month was the heaviest of any August on record and was the third-busiest month of the year so far. On September 1, the *Times* described the month's action: "The stock market last month gave another remarkable demonstration of its recuperative powers. After one of the sharpest breaks on record . . . the New York Federal Reserve Bank raised its rediscount rate to 6 per cent, prices rallied and not only regained all their losses but continued climbing to the highest levels on record."

Even though Labor Day, September 2, was supposed to mark the end of summer, the next day, September 3, was the hottest of the year in New York City. As laggards returned from Long Island and New Jersey beach towns, long lines leading to the bridges and tunnels into Manhattan led to overheated cars, blown radiators, and traffic jams. The stock market continued to overheat as well. The Dow closed that Tuesday at 381.17, up 0.2 percent for the day and up 27.1 percent for the year. It had more than doubled since the end of 1926, just thirty-two months before. It had nearly quadrupled during the 1920s. Nobody knew it yet, but this was the top. After a drop of 1.56 points the next day, it would take twenty-five years to regain the level reached on September 3, 1929.

The new all-time high on September 3 was just one of thirty-four posted that year, as Americans became investors at home, at sea, and on the golf course. Even children were getting involved.

During the Labor Day weekend, newspapers around the country had carried the story of an unnamed girl from the American South who had sent four dollars to Standard Oil Company of New Jersey, asking that the company "please sell me as little an interest . . . in your Oil Wells as four dollars to start with, and then take what it makes for me and add to the four dollars until it amounts to a fifty dollar share for me." The girl apologized for the small amount of her investment, explaining, "I would be glad to put more into your oil wells if I was able, but I am not able to put any more than that in it, as I am a poor girl and I work on a farm with my home people, and I hired out to work in Tobacco to get this money." The girl was certain Standard Oil would make her rich, as the stock market had done for so many others.

Economist John Kenneth Galbraith would later agree with author Frederick Lewis Allen that the "striking thing about the stock market speculation of 1929 was not the massiveness of the participation. Rather it was the way it became central to the culture," as it had for this girl. The crash began two days later, on September 5, 1929.

Roger Babson was an investor, entrepreneur, and businessman with the estimable habit of founding universities. Having graduated from the Massachusetts Institute of Technology in 1898, Babson was also an erstwhile inventor; he was one of the first to work on what became the modern parking meter. Unfortunately, Babson's version was powered by a cable that the driver was supposed to plug into his car. When that predictably failed, Babson turned his attention to the stock market.

While in college, Babson had become enraptured by the work of Isaac Newton. Babson soon began to infuse his investing ideas with the teachings of Newton, with special emphasis on Newton's Third Law—"For every action there is an equal and opposite reaction."

Babson also relied heavily on the law of gravity, and beginning in 1927 he believed it alone would bring stocks back to earth, like Newton's apocryphal apple falling from a tree. Babson had spent most of 1927 and all of 1928 renewing his prediction that "any major movement [in the stock market] should be on the downward side." As the market rallied and Babson's predictions continued to be wrong, wags on Wall Street began calling him "the Prophet of Loss."

Despite his track record, Babson was asked to speak to the National Business Conference on September 5. He continued the bearish line he'd started more than two years before when he told those assembled, "Fair weather cannot always continue. . . . More people are borrowing and speculating today than ever in our history. Someday the time is coming when the market will begin to slide off, sellers will exceed buyers, and paper profits will begin to disappear. Then there will be an immediate stampede to save what paper profits exist." Babson continued: "I repeat what I said at this time last year and the year before; sooner or later a crash is coming which will take in the leading stocks and cause a decline from sixty to eighty points in the Dow Jones barometer."

Babson's warning made its way to investors over the news ticker and reached Wall Street with one hour left in the September 5 trading day. The Associated Press reported the story with the flash headline "Economist predicts 60 to 80 points stock market crash," though it did not say who the economist was or what he'd been saying for the past two years. Radio stations getting the news interrupted their programming to share news of Babson's prediction, again without context.

More than two million shares traded in that final hour, and the Dow lost 2.6 percent on what had been a quiet day until the Babson story hit. It would become known as the "Babson Break." While one paper described Babson as one "to whom Wall Street has not in past years paid any particular attention," it pointed out that the market was likely overextended after gaining 9.4 percent in August.

The stock market lost 3.2 percent during the five days ending on September 10, 1929, and on the eleventh the *Wall Street Journal* printed its thought for the day. It was Mark Twain's advice: "Don't part with your illusions; when they are gone you may still exist, but you cease to live."

Clarence Hatry was a fastidiously dapper man, consumed by appearances and his personal dress, which he attended to as a way of distracting from the limp that had resulted from an early bout of rheumatic fever. Hatry lived in a mansion on Park Lane in London's Mayfair neighborhood, where he had a dozen servants, including a valet.

Hatry had made his first fortune, which he subsequently lost in a cycle that would repeat itself several times, by charging Eastern European emigrants for transportation and entry to the United States. During the war he was a profiteer, and afterward he formed British Glass Industries. But like William Durant, Hatry tended to overextend his companies when trying to buy up smaller players and combine them into a larger holding company to generate economies of scale. British Glass would fail in 1926, but by then Hatry had larger plans.

In the summer of 1926, Hatry was working on a scheme to acquire United Steel Companies, which produced 10 percent of Great Britain's steel and iron. Hatry wanted to combine United Steel with several smaller producers and "rationalize" the entire British steel industry in the sort of combination that twenty years earlier had been known as "Morganization."

But after the failure of British Glass, Hatry, unlike Morgan, had little access to large-scale financing. Even so, he staked his ready cash of approximately one million pounds on a tender offer for shares of United Steel in the sort of attempt to acquire the company that would become popular in the United States in the 1980s. But Hatry needed more than his million pounds, and an expected line of credit evaporated during a business and political crisis following the general election of May 1929. Facing the loss of both his money and his prestige, Hatry agreed to an expedient but fraudulent stopgap that he would later self-servingly say had been suggested by a subordinate. Hatry would borrow money using certificates from another Hatry holding as collateral.

Unfortunately, the value of the other holding wasn't sufficient to support a large enough loan, and Hatry had to duplicate legitimate certificates and pledge the bogus certificates to multiple banks for multiple loans. His hope was that the United Steel shares being tendered would trickle in slowly, giving him time to arrange additional financing to cover the shortfall and reclaim the bogus certificates. But when one of the banks involved hired accountants to perform elementary due diligence, the extent of Hatry's fraud became obvious; he had pledged counterfeit certificates supposedly worth £810,000 to just this one bank. In total, the fraud reached £20 million, and the news reached Wall Street on September 20, 1929, when the Dow lost 2.1 percent.

Unfortunately, that wasn't the full extent of the damage, because as certificate holders in New York became aware of the size of Hatry's fraud, they started to wonder about the authenticity of their own certificates. The market lost ground five days in a row ending on the twenty-fifth, and then lost another 3.1 percent on September 27.

Every crash has a catalyst. Most have little to do with finance, but this moment was the catalyst for the stock market crash of 1929, as three London brokerages collapsed and every shareholder in every company around the world started to wonder about the value of the certificates they held. If Hatry could so easily defraud banks and brokerages in London, they wondered, who was doing so in New York? The American stock market started falling when

Babson reiterated his warning. It would gather speed as Hatry led investors to question the market's basic veracity.

When the market stabilized briefly on September 26, it was already 6.6 percent below its high for the year, made just twenty trading days earlier. But one hour after the market closed, the news hit that brokers' loans had increased by another $192 million in the previous week, to reach a new record that was so high it was "received with considerable surprise in the financial district."

September had begun with the Babson Break and ended with the Hatry turmoil. Predictably, it was a horrible month; the Dow lost 9.7 percent to close at 343.45. Many remembered the lesson the market seemed to have been teaching since the previous June: that lower prices were buying opportunities; it would bounce back and make yet another new high, and selling now would be a mistake. Immediately after the Babson Break, it was reported that "several large investment trusts were continuing their policy of adding to their holdings in a selected group of issues," and "the managers of several trusts said . . . that they had utilized the opportunity presented by the break to increase their commitments in some of the higher priced issues."

The sheer number of new investment trusts and the amount of money pouring into them demanded this sort of buying. In August, new stock issues totaled $383.3 million, of which $381.3 million, more than 99 percent, was issuance of new investment trusts that now needed to buy stock to put their cash to work. Babson had allowed them to buy at what must have seemed discount prices. Thanks to Hatry, prices were now even lower, and since so many investment trusts used leverage, they had little leeway when prices started falling. At the end of September, the worst of the crash was still twenty-nine days away. Any leeway these trusts had was soon to evaporate, and then the only thing to do was what Babson had suggested: sell stocks for whatever could be gotten for them.

On October 1, 1929, brokers' loans totaled $8.5 billion, having nearly doubled since the beginning of the previous year. During the first half of the decade, less than one-third of the capital funding brokers' loans had come from corporations and individuals, with the vast majority coming from banks. In October 1929, more than three-quarters was coming from these "other" sources. On this same day the *Wall Street Journal* noted that the phenomenon of investment trusts was not without its worries: "The rapid advances in prices of some trust stocks to substantial premiums above liquidation values have injected a new complication into an already involved security market."

Some readers understood "involved" was the euphemism for overextended, and they started selling stocks. The market had opened little changed on October 3 and sold off only gradually until the last ninety minutes of the day. Stocks cascaded lower when Britain's new chancellor of the Exchequer tried to offload blame from Hatry, and the new government that had been the undoing of his plans, saying that the cause of the emerging problems were "[a] year's orgy of speculative finance 3,000 miles away." Never mind that the orgy had been orchestrated at the request of Montagu Norman, while he was governor of the Bank of England, and Winston Churchill, his preceding chancellor, to suit the British government's purposes.

At the close of trading on October 3, the Dow had lost 4.2 percent, almost all of it in the last hour and a half of the day, to close at 329.95, in the worst single day of the year. It was already 13.4 percent below the high made exactly one month before. Some stocks lost much more that day: Montgomery Ward and Westinghouse both lost 7.3 percent. RCA lost 4.7 percent and was now 27.7 percent below its all-time high. One observer described the market succinctly: "Fear is in the saddle." The next day the Dow lost another 1.4 percent.

Many of the investors taking this ride were new to the game. The same day newspapers were reporting the chancellor's remarks, the *Wall Street Journal* was pointing out that nearly fifty investment trusts had been launched during the three-month period ending that September, and the total invested in these companies neared $1 billion. During the first nine months of 1929, the amount invested in new investment trusts neared $2 billion. Not only were many of these investment trusts leveraged, but also the advertising touting them and the academics on their staffs had encouraged investors to buy the trusts without regard to their value. For example, shares of Financial and Industrial Securities Corporation were trading for about double the value of the securities contained in the trust. This was a demonstration of the great faith in the trust's leadership—or of how outlandish the bubble was.

The market rebounded once again, gaining 5.0 percent on October 5, nearly as much as it had lost during the two previous days. The *Wall Street Journal* called it a "spirited rally" on the same page that spread the news that Chevrolet had sold more than 1.2 million six-cylinder cars in the first nine months of the year, surpassing the company's record total for all of 1928, as Chevrolet continued "the biggest fall production program ever undertaken." Next to the Chevrolet news was a notice that Auburn Automobile Company had shipped 1,867 luxury cars in September, more than doubling shipments made in September of the previous year; the company planned on shipping another 2,300 cars in October. With yet another bounce from the market and auto production setting records, there seemed to be little reason for worry. In the column titled "Broad Street Gossip," the paper promised that "[i]n time the people will pay less attention to brokers' loan fluctuations. That will be when they are convinced that the huge expansion over the last several years has been due to a new order of things."

The good news seemed to continue as investors read on the morning of October 11 that brokers' loans had decreased by $91 million the previous week, the first drop since August 14. But on the same day investors were getting this good news, the Massachusetts Department of Public Utilities was giving shareholders of the Edison Electric Illuminating Company of Boston the worst possible news, and the slide was about to reach its climax.

On August 1, Boston Edison had called a shareholder meeting to authorize a four-for-one split of the company's stock. While stock splits should have no net impact on the stock, they are often considered bullish. After Boston Edison's announcement, the stock reached $440 a share; it had ended 1928 at just $275.

Utility stocks had enjoyed even better returns in 1929 than the rest of the market. At one point in September they were up 68.9 percent for the year, and as a result of that rally Boston Edison was trading for nearly three times its book value, the best measure of its real value. This furious rally in the price of utility stocks also made them a larger-than-normal portion of the broad market. On September 1, the utilities trading on the NYSE had an aggregate value of $14.8 billion, or 18 percent of the value of all the shares listed. Utilities were also favorites of the managers running the new investment trusts.

Boston Edison's primary reason for requesting commission approval to split its stock was "it is the fashion." On October 11 the Massachusetts Department of Public Utilities Board unanimously denied Boston Edison's request to be fashionable and split its stock, saying the price of the stock was too high and that any split would only increase the speculative buying: "It is likely to encourage the belief in the minds of many innocent people that it is the forerunner of substantial increases in dividends, with the consequent result of their investing in stock at a very high price without their hopes being realized." Then the board said any split should "be left until the selling price on the . . . exchange more nearly approximates its real value." The commission had approved each of the forty-two requests from utilities to split stock since 1922, when it received veto power. This was the first instance of the commission refusing. The commission had become stock market analysts and found Boston Edison stock wanting: "The higher the speculative price of the stock the more embarrassment to this department, as if we fix a price higher than $215 a share, we are fixing a price much in excess of the real intrinsic value of the stock." The commission was saying Boston Edison had been inflated as part of a speculative bubble. "[D]ue to the action of speculators or other interests, the price of its stock has risen . . . to such a point that no one, in our judgment, viewing it from the standpoint of an investment on the basis of its earnings, would find it to his advantage to buy it."

The state of Massachusetts had decreed that Boston Edison was worth just $215 a share. It had closed the day before at $375.

Boston Edison and all the utilities saw their stock punished. Boston Edison lost 4.0 percent that day, to close at $360. The next day it opened at $330, down another 8.3 percent, and closed at $325 after trading as low as $299. American Power and Light fell 14.7 percent from October 10, before the board's decision was made public, to October 16. American Superpower fell 12.0 percent, and Electric Bond and Share, the company supplying so much capital to the call loan market, was down 12.9 percent during those five trading sessions. But the worst was still to come for the utilities. On October 15 the governor of Massachusetts announced he would investigate the utility's rates and dividends. On that same day, the Boston City Council began proceedings to seize ownership of Boston Edison, and the next day it announced it would investigate the utility's rate structure. The state Public Utility Commission advised Boston Edison to "reduce the selling price [of electricity] to the consumer" and warned that if rates weren't lowered, "the public will take over such utilities as they try to gobble up all the profits available," a threat oddly reminiscent of Teddy Roosevelt's warnings to the industrial trusts that resisted his attempts at regulation. The weakest stock market investors were using the most levered vehicles, investment trusts, which were heavily invested in what was now the most hated sector of the market, utilities.

The Dow lost 3.2 percent on October 16. The next day the *Wall Street Journal* blamed the weakness on the utility sector, saying, "The price structure of several leading active utility issues crumbled under a combination of professional attack and liquidation." Regulators recognized that utility shares were trading at multiples of their fundamental value because of the speculative power of the investment trusts: "Mention of the influence of the investment trust on utility securities is too important for this committee to ignore." On the same day, the Committee on Public Service Securities of the Investment Banking Association urged investors to avoid "speculative and uninformed buying" and warned them to take "care in buying shares in utilities."

Benjamin Strong had inflated an enormous stock market bubble. Roger Babson had pointed out the danger and was heeded only through happenstance. Charles Hatry led investors to question the basic soundness of the market, and now utility regulators in Massachusetts were finishing the job of undermining the market by stating plainly that it was too high. The crash was now inevitable.

The newspapers that Sunday reported the market's weakness and predicted that more was likely to come because brokers were starting to send out margin calls for additional collateral now that the market was down 15 percent from the high made just seven weeks before. If margins had stayed at 10 percent, the level common before 1928, many brokerage houses would have simply sold investors' stocks, and many would have been wiped out. With margins of at least 25 percent and as much as 50 percent for the most volatile stocks, like RCA, investors had to decide whether to send more margin or sell their stocks for whatever they would bring. Those who wanted to hold on did see some reason for hope. While brokers' loans had declined by $91 million during the week of October 9, they climbed by $88 million the next week.

But the flood of call money wasn't enough to save the market, because stock market premiums were starting to evaporate. First the premium at which utilities traded over their intrinsic value started to shrink, and that caused a drop in the value of investment trusts holding utility stocks. The pell-mell selling of investment trusts also drove down their premium over the value of their holdings. If Boston Edison fell from its current market price to the price the state of Massachusetts had assigned it—just $215—the stock would drop by 42.7 percent. If Boston Edison stock was inside an investment trust that was trading at a 100 percent premium to the net asset value and then that premium was halved, the drop would be even greater, 57.0 percent. If the investment trust was one of many that were levered, it would be even worse.

The trusts faced another problem. On October 20, the *New York Times* reported that in the face of leverage, many trust managers were completing the transition from sensible investment vehicle to craps table, and that "leading American investment trusts have indicated that the principle of wide diversification of holdings, which was one of the distinguishing characteristics of the British trust, is being abandoned by many units in this country." Customers of the trusts were forgetting the rationale for the investment trusts: the diversification that was supposed to reduce risk. And they were doing this at the worst possible time.

Things didn't get any better on Monday, October 21, as the Dow lost 0.9 percent to close at 320.91. Even the 1.7 percent gain posted on Tuesday was disappointing, as prices slipped badly near the close and "many of the bigger gains were quickly lost." The blame was placed on Roger Babson, who again warned late that day that stocks should be sold.

Things got substantially worse on October 23, as those who hadn't heard Babson's warning the previous day reacted. The Dow lost 6.3 percent, to close at 305.85. The value of all stocks traded on the NYSE fell by $4 billion, and the Dow was now 19.8 percent below its high from the previous month. RCA lost 14.6 percent, more than double the loss in the broad market; that summer's stock market darling was now 40.3 percent below its high for 1929.

The next day's *New York Times* described this second Babson Break with the front-page headline "Prices of Stocks Crash." The market opened that morning "like a bolt out of hell," according to one trader. The flood of sell orders was overwhelming, not merely because of their number but also because of their size. The first order to sell General Motors was for 20,000 shares, for Westinghouse 10,000, for Packard 13,000, for Sinclair Oil 15,000. Then the smaller orders followed. During the first half hour, 1.6 million shares traded on the NYSE, an amount about equal to the average volume for a full day in 1926.

By late morning one broker's clerk warned, "The whole place is falling apart," as the Dow reached an intraday low of 272.32, an 11.0 percent loss for the day and 28.6 percent below the high reached on September 3.

As word of the debacle spilled into the street, police were deployed throughout the financial district "in case there's trouble." At 12:30 P.M. the NYSE closed its Broad Street visitors' gallery to save investors the agony of watching their accounts dwindle.

Stocks across the list were being punished. RCA traded as low as $44.50, 35.0 percent below the previous day's closing price and 61.2 percent below its high for the year. Even 50 percent margin hadn't been enough. Montgomery Ward was down as much as 39.9 percent on the day and 68.1 percent below its high for 1929. And utilities continued to get some of the worst of it. Standard Gas and Electric was off 21.0 percent on the day when it hit its low and 44.9 percent below its 1929 high.

Private rescues were supposed to be unnecessary after the creation of the Federal Reserve, but just about the time the visitors' gallery was being closed on October 24, five private bankers were meeting in the offices of J.P. Morgan & Company, across the street from the NYSE, to fashion a rescue. Thomas Lamont took the place of the departed Mr. Morgan. Lamont was joined by Albert Wiggin, chairman of Chase National Bank; Charley Mitchell, chairman of the National City Bank (later known as Citibank); Seward Prosser, chairman of the Bankers Trust Company; and William Potter, president of the Guaranty Trust Company. Between them they had more than $10 billion in resources to support the market.

None of the five, not even Lamont, had the credibility of J. P. Morgan, who'd died sixteen years earlier. But as they attempted to divine what "Zeus" would have done, they all realized action was needed, and they also knew that a bureaucracy like the Federal Reserve Board could not move quickly enough to stop the butchery. Fortunately, just the news that the five were meeting was enough to ease much of the tension outside their doors and across Broad Street on the trading floor. Once the meeting broke, Lamont contradicted the regulators in Massachusetts by saying, "It is the consensus of the group that many of the quotations on the Stock Exchange do not fairly represent the situation," and that many stocks were trading below their fair value due to "air holes" in which buying interest had disappeared. The same sort of "air holes" would appear in 1987 and 2010, but in 1929 Lamont and the other four would provide some buying interest.

Richard Whitney had started his career at the New York Stock Exchange in 1912, and by 1929 he'd risen to the post of vice president, thanks in part to the influence of his older brother George, who was second in command to Thomas Lamont at J.P. Morgan & Company. At 1:30 P.M. on Thursday, October 24, with stocks at their lows of the day and with bellwether U.S. Steel trading at just $193.50, 26.1 percent below its high for the year, Richard Whitney walked onto the trading floor and headed for the U.S. Steel post. Whitney announced he was willing to buy stock, a lot of it, and was willing to pay vastly more than the current price. Whitney bid $205 a share for 25,000 shares of "Steel," and despite the panic selling of earlier that morning, the meeting at J.P. Morgan headquarters and this expression of confidence had calmed fears so much that Whitney wasn't able to buy enough to fill his order. He left instructions to buy the balance of the shares with another broker and went to the next post to similarly bid up that stock.

The Dow finished the day at 299.47, down just 2.1 percent. It was the first time it had been below 300.00 since June 1, but the support of Lamont and the other four had relieved the pressure. At its lowest point, the Dow had been down 11.0 percent, and the next day's *New York Times* called the break before the recovery "[t]he most disastrous decline in the biggest and broadest stock market of history." One Treasury official said the losses were inconsequential because they were "paper losses" rather than losses of real cash. They seemed real enough to investors, who counted themselves lucky that the market had once again rebounded. The Federal Reserve Board did not comment. The five men meeting in J. P. Morgan's old office seemed to have saved the day.

On the next day, Friday, October 25, the market continued its rebound, with the Dow closing at 301.22, a gain of 0.6 percent that still didn't recoup the week's losses, though this small rally was a hopeful sign, given the desperation evident the previous morning. Then, in Saturday's shortened session, the market gave back all that gain and more, with the Dow closing at 298.97, even lower than Thursday's close. Investors and traders would have Sunday to contemplate the best course of action.

During the weekend, news broke that Massachusetts regulators were expanding their investigation beyond just Boston Edison to all of the state's utilities, and that worried Europeans were shipping gold stored in American vaults back home. At the end of the weekend, investors would have decided to sell.

Monday, October 28, was a disaster. The Dow lost 38.33 points to close at 260.64, a loss of 12.8 percent, and this time stocks didn't bounce back, because the Whitney brothers were unable to muster the sort of support the market needed. Boston Edison lost 13.7 percent, and its shareholders were some of the lucky ones. RCA closed at $40.25 after a loss of $18.38, or 31.3 percent. RCA, which Michael Meehan had managed to manipulate above $100 that March, was now 64.9 percent below its high for the year. AT&T lost 12.8 percent. Montgomery Ward lost 20.5 percent. Volume on the NYSE was 9,212,800 shares, second only to the previous Thursday. The Dow was now 31.6 percent below the high made just forty-seven trading days before, as speculators scrambled to get what they could.

The five bankers who'd met the previous week gathered again ninety minutes after the market closed on Monday. It was obvious there was little they could do. At the same time, the Federal Reserve Board met and decided no action was called for. Over the previous decade, much of the Fed's actions were taken for the wrong reasons, and it had failed to act when it was appropriate. Now they were helpless.

Throughout Monday's trading, most investors believed that this was as bad as it could get. They expected stocks to stabilize and then rally as they had so many times in the past. One newspaper reported, "That the storm has now blown itself out . . . appeared certain last night from statements by leading bankers." The *New York Times* reported on Tuesday morning "that heavy banking support would come into the market today was the consensus of leading bankers last night." The paper's second page sported a six-column headline, "Huge Funds Expected in Market Today for 'Bargain Buying.'" Even if the funds wanted to go bargain hunting, they couldn't. Their leverage meant they had to sell stocks, regardless of the price, rather than buy them, regardless of the discount. All those times the stock market had bounced back previously had imbued the wrong lesson; the market wouldn't always bounce back, no matter how regular the recoveries of the past.

Those looking for good news on Tuesday, October 29, found it in the story that the little girl who wanted to invest her four dollars had gotten her stock certificate through the generosity of readers who added to her four dollars until she had accumulated enough for a single share of Standard Oil of New Jersey. Sentimental readers learned that "a few days ago a crisp new certificate for one share of stock was delivered to her." If she had received it the previous Monday, her investment had already lost 14.7 percent, and it would lose another 10.8 percent that day.

Tuesday's market faced the same problem it had experienced the Thursday before. The number of sell orders was enormous but the size of those orders was even greater. These were not individual investors getting out of the stock market. It was institutional investors, including the investment trusts whose leadership and resident academics were supposed to have known better and were expected to have seen this coming.

A total of 630,000 shares were sold in just the first twenty-six transactions. More than fifty different NYSE stocks opened with sell orders of at least 10,000 shares. The first trade in Anaconda Copper was a sale of a block of 45,000 shares at $80. It had closed the previous day at $96. Standard Oil opened down $7.75 on a sale of a block of 50,000 shares. RCA opened with an order to sell 30,000 shares, which was filled at $30. It had closed the previous day at $40.25. Three million shares were sold in the first thirty minutes. Eight million shares were sold in the first two hours.

The investment trusts had assumed that as exchange volumes increased over the previous years, their ability to sell sizable chunks of their holdings would increase as well. It was an understandable mistake, but as investors must relearn from time to time—as they would in 1987, 2008, and 2010—liquidity, that ability to sell sizable holdings without driving down the price precipitously, evaporates when it is most desired.

The public gallery was again closed on Tuesday after visitors watched one trader run screaming from the floor, and more police were dispatched to the corner of Wall and Broad Streets. The physician on staff at the exchange was the fifty-one-year-old Dr. Francis Glazebrook. He had treated shell-shock cases during World War I, and saw the same symptoms among the assembled traders as prices fell and fortunes evaporated on October 29, 1929.

The five-man bankers' consortium met around midday, and though they wanted to support the market, the selling was so wanton that talk was the only weapon they had. They issued a statement that they would be buyers if the "air holes" Lamont had mentioned the previous week materialized, but there was little else they could do.

One person knew what to do. White Sewing Machine Company had closed the previous day at $11.13 a share. When it opened on Tuesday morning at just $2 a share, a boy working as a messenger on the floor put in an order to buy 100 shares at $1 a share when there were no other orders to buy at any price. His order was filled; the messenger was happy to pay a total of $100 for 100 shares that had been worth $4,800 earlier that year and that were worth $987.50 later that day. No one would have expected that bid to be filled. Eighty-one years later, similar "stub quote" bids would be filled in a similar liquidity vacuum when dozens of stocks traded at the absurdly low price of one cent a share.

Few were as fortunate as the messenger boy. One NYSE security guard said the traders were "like a bunch of crazy men. Every once in a while . . . you'd see some poor devil collapse and fall to the floor."

The Dow closed on Tuesday, October 29, at 230.07, a loss of 30.57 points, or 11.7 percent, as 16,410,030 shares traded, by far the most ever. The Dow had lost 23.0 percent in just two days, and it was 39.6 percent below the high reached less than two months before. The rout was complete. RCA traded as low as $26, or 77.3 percent below its high from earlier that year. U.S. Steel closed at $174, a loss of just 6.5 percent for the day, but 33.5 percent below its high for the year and well below the $205 a share the bankers' consortium had paid. Westinghouse lost another 14.6 percent. Montgomery Ward lost 9.7 percent. Boston Edison closed at $250. Two months earlier it had been at $395.

George Leslie Harrison again recognized an immediate danger to which the larger Federal Reserve Board was blind. Before the market even opened on Tuesday morning, Harrison took the only unilateral action available to him that couldn't be undone by the Federal Reserve Board in Washington, D.C. Harrison let the world know the New York Fed would inject at least $100 million into the money market by buying government securities. He ended up injecting $132 million by the end of the day, replacing much of the call money frenetically pulled from circulation by those "others" who'd enjoyed the high rate of return they'd received but who now feared losses.

Monday, October 28, was the worst day the American stock market had ever experienced. Tuesday, October 29, was the second worst, although many say it did more long-term damage to the market, given the even greater trading volume. Neither day would be surpassed until October 19, 1987, and neither has been passed since. The Dow, which had been up as much as 27.1 percent, closed 1929 down 17.2 percent.

The Fed finally acted. On October 31, the Federal Reserve Board allowed the New York Fed to lower its discount rate from 6 percent to 5 percent, effective the next day. Brokers' loans dropped by $1.1 billion during the week, and after the market rebounded on Wednesday and Thursday, the NYSE was able to close in order to catch up on the mountain of unprocessed trades—the trading volume in October set a record that wouldn't be surpassed until 1965—without the threat of rumors spreading that they'd been forced to close by the selling.

While the crash was complete, the decline in stock market values wasn't. The Dow had gained a total of 90.8 percent in the two years before 1929; there was still much speculative exuberance to be wrung out of the market. Though the Dow would gain 8.0 percent from the close on October 29 to the end of the year, it would lose 33.8 percent in 1930, 52.7 percent in 1931, and 23.1 percent in 1932.

The Great Depression would follow, caused in part by the economy's unprecedented reliance on the spending of what would now be called the "1 percent," spending that was drastically reduced along with the financial circumstances of the wealthy. The government didn't help. Herbert Hoover, a man who had risen to global prominence through his work helping the poorest in Europe following World War I, didn't know how to help Americans impoverished in the wake of the crash. Hoover would later write that he'd relied too much on the advice of his Treasury secretary, Andrew Mellon, who was wealthy almost beyond understanding and therefore insulated from the worst deprivations of the crash and ensuing depression. Mellon was also an incredibly callous and moralist prig who believed the crash would "purge the rottenness out of the system" and that "[p]eople will work harder, live a more moral life. Values will be adjusted, and enterprising people will pick up the wrecks from less competent people."

The Federal Reserve System had been built in response to the Panic of 1907. The Crash of 1929 would lead to the Securities Act of 1933, which required that issuers provide disclosures about securities being offered for sale, and which prohibited market participants from willful deceit in the sale or trading of securities. The crash also led to the Securities Exchange Act of 1934, which created the Securities and Exchange Commission and empowered the commission with broad authority over nearly all facets of the securities industry.

The Dow, which had closed at 381.17 on September 3, 1929,

would close at 41.22 on July 8, 1932. It wouldn't make a new all-time high until November 23, 1954, more than twenty-five years after the crash.

Michael Meehan finally left the Bloomingdale Insane Asylum in 1937, and he had the perverse distinction of being the first person prosecuted by the new Securities and Exchange Commission for his antics in Bellanca Aircraft Company. He died in 1948 without seeing the Dow reclaim the all-time high he'd helped it make nineteen years earlier.

BLACK MONDAY

1987

Hayne Leland couldn't sleep. Despite a master's degree from the London School of Economics and a Ph.D. in economics from Harvard, he was worried about finances—his own.

The United States had been floundering in a recession from 1973 to 1975, with unemployment climbing to 9 percent as oil prices quadrupled. Leland, a thirty-five-year-old junior academic at the University of California, Berkeley, knew his salary was at risk as he tossed in bed that night. He would later explain, "Lifestyles were in danger, and it was time for invention." He had to figure out how to increase his income.

He had been forming the pearl of an idea for years, ever since a conversation he'd had with his older brother John, an executive at a money management firm. Shortly after the U.S. stock market bottomed out in 1974—a loss for the Dow Jones Industrial Average of 39.6 percent in 1973 and 1974, still the worst two-year performance since the Great Depression—John lamented at a family gathering that so many institutional investors had pulled their money out of the stock market with no intention of returning. "It's too bad there is no way you could buy insurance on your portfolio. Then people wouldn't have to sell out at the worst time and have no way to participate in the subsequent market rally." Hayne Leland was intrigued by his brother's complaint, but he also knew the issues involved were surprisingly complex, and other research topics were more pressing. He filed it away and planned to return to it "at a later date." This sleepless night in September 1976 was that later date.

Leland eventually got out of bed, sat down at his desk, and started to think. He later remembered that it took "something like two hours" to reach a solution.

What Leland's brother needed was a "put" option on the stock market. A put option works just like insurance. For a small up-front payment—both a put option and an insurance policy call this up-front payment a "premium"—one can buy protection against a stock's price dropping by purchasing an option to sell it at a predetermined price.

But these exchange-traded put options didn't exist. The Chicago Board Options Exchange had been launched three years earlier, but they traded only "call" options, the right to *buy* stock at a predetermined price. In 1976, put options, the right to *sell* stock at a predetermined price, were not available because they were considered dangerous and un-American.

Sitting in his darkened room, Leland remembered a paper published in 1973 that was gaining notice in academic finance. "The Pricing of Options and Corporate Liabilities" was the work of Fischer Black, a professor at the University of Chicago, and Myron Scholes, of MIT, and though the title promised solutions to a range of problems, the paper's important nugget focused on figuring out how to calculate the value of an option, and not just its price. Leland realized that inherent in Black and Scholes's work was the revolutionary concept that it was possible to replicate the investment results of a put option even if put options weren't traded. Black and Scholes's paper demonstrated that the investment results for a put option could be constructed using a portfolio that included just cash and a continuously adjusted position in the underlying stock or portfolio. Leland recognized it was possible to synthesize the option his brother had pleaded for by trading tiny slivers of stock in a careful, regimented fashion such that as the market fell, and the insurance value of the hypothetical put option increased, he would have sold many slivers of stock, but if the stock price increased, making the insurance value of the put option less valuable, he would have sold no slivers of stock.

The morning after Leland's middle-of-the-night insight, he realized that the mathematical complexity that had caused him to initially put the problem aside intruded again in the light of day. Even though Black and Scholes had described theoretically how to do what Leland wanted to do, he was not able to perform the actual calculations required to create a protective option out of thin air. Leland decided to approach Mark Rubinstein, a colleague at Berkeley, with his idea for insuring a stock, or a portfolio of stocks, and Rubinstein responded by saying, "I'm surprised I never thought of that myself!" As the two settled into a discussion, they sketched a rough outline based on Black and Scholes. It would begin with a portfolio of stocks and would require continuously adjusting the amount of stock held, selling small slivers of stock if prices dropped, then buying them back if the stock rallied, and repeating the process endlessly. If the stock continued lower, they would sell more slivers as the price fell—all in the mathematically rigorous and "unthinking" manner dictated by Black and Scholes, which would define exactly how many shares to sell at exactly what price—until eventually the synthetic option had expired. When the synthetic option expired, the profit or loss in the original position, combined with all the subsequent trading, would match that of a hypothetical portfolio with a protective option position. The concept wasn't really insurance; it simply offered a payoff that was supposed to mimic that of an insured portfolio.

That day, Leland and Rubinstein decided they would be partners in the creation and marketing of what they called "dynamic hedging," and what the rest of the world came to call "portfolio insurance."

Leland and Rubinstein had taken similar paths to academia. Both had undergraduate degrees in economics from Harvard and master's degrees from top schools, the London School of Economics for Leland and Stanford for Rubinstein. Rubinstein had received his Ph.D. in economics from the University of California, Los Angeles, and had gone straight to Berkeley, while Leland returned to Harvard for his Ph.D., after which it was his turn to go to Stanford, where he served as an assistant professor. In 1976 they were both professors at Berkeley. Physically the two were incredibly different. Leland was dapper, with a high patrician forehead, coupled with an easy smile. Rubinstein was dark and would sometimes sport a mustache that bore an unfortunate resemblance to a black caterpillar.

Progress was slow. There were daunting problems to be solved in the creation of portfolio insurance, and Leland and Rubinstein also had to take into account certain assumptions Black and Scholes had made about how the financial world worked. Black and Scholes had called them "ideal conditions," and the most glaring was that stock prices moved smoothly, without jumps or gaps, an idea that anyone who's watched the stock market at all would find laughable. A second was that interest rates and the volatility of the stock were constant through time. A third, also laughable to market participants, was that there were no transaction costs. Leland and Rubinstein knew this first assumption was a giant weakness, and they would later warn potential clients that portfolio insurance could not work if an exogenous event caused the stock market to fall discontinuously—the analogy Leland used was the Soviets invading Iran and cutting off Middle Eastern oil supplies.

Some of the assumptions were inconsequential—for example, that the cash held in the portfolio earned a fixed rate of interest for the term of the synthetic option. This clearly wasn't the case, as short-term interest rates are constantly changing, but the changes, even over a fairly long time frame, are relatively minor, and the effect of these changes on the theoretical price of an option is very small.

One assumption that Leland and Rubinstein inexplicably trusted was that their own regimented trading would not affect the price of the underlying stock even if the volume of their selling increased. They failed to accept that if liquidity were poor, just as it might be on the day the Soviets invaded Iran, their own selling might drive the stock's price down in a cascade. But the two dismissed this concern, believing the market would realize their selling was "uninformed," that it was purely mechanical and without any special insight, and that the market would do its own analysis; smart, disciplined investors would recognize value and happily snap up what Leland and Rubinstein were selling. The idea that other investors would remain rational and buy stock as Leland and Rubinstein were selling it, thereby preventing it from cascading lower despite knowing more portfolio insurance selling was likely to come, wasn't just an assumption inherent in the Black-Scholes formula and portfolio insurance; it was fundamental dogma in all finance theory. Black and Scholes's assumptions were necessary to keep the math from becoming unmanageable, even if they were occasionally completely divorced from reality. Since Leland and Rubinstein were hitching a ride with Black and Scholes, portfolio insurance would rely on these "ideal conditions" and would fail when reality intruded.

Finally, in 1979 Leland and Rubinstein had a product they were pleased with, essentially a series of rules dictating how much and when to sell, and their dynamic hedging promised to establish a floor under which the value of a portfolio could not fall, regardless of the steepness of the drop in the broad stock market, as long as their assumptions held.

Now that Leland and Rubinstein had decided to rely on uninterrupted rational behavior by the stock market as the solution to their tactical concerns, there were strategic decisions to be made. Would the partners themselves sell this insurance to investors—an idea that could be wildly lucrative if they were successful in synthesizing insurance but an astonishingly risky proposition if the insurance didn't work as expected—or could they simply charge the consulting fee Leland hoped for? Eventually they chose a middle path: they would serve as investment advisers for their customers by charging an asset-based fee while managing the actual trading required by their scheme inside client portfolios. As the assets protected increased, the fees they received would increase.

The history of modern stock market crashes invariably includes some theoretically sophisticated yet poorly understood financial contraption that mutates when stressed, pushing an already weakened system closer to the cliff. In 1907 it was the trust company, a hedge fund dressed as a savings and loan. In 1929 it was the levered investment trust, a massive stock market wager with little room for error. Portfolio insurance was another of these contraptions, though it would take more than a decade to metastasize. What Hayne Leland and Mark Rubinstein had devised led to, and was largely responsible for, the worst day the United States stock market has ever had.

With a letter from a respected Bay Area money manager vouching for the methodology they had developed, Leland and Rubinstein began marketing it actively, focusing on bank trust departments and other fiduciaries in the East and Midwest. They believed their product offered these institutional investors the best of all worlds: superior returns and lower risk.

But as is common when selling novel financial products, particularly complicated ones—and at its heart, portfolio insurance was stupefyingly complex—Leland was welcomed in to explain what they had developed. He would later brag that meetings often ran hours over schedule, but he always walked out without having closed the sale. When he sat by his phone waiting for the business to roll in he was astonished to find that, "by God, no one ever called." The fact that his meetings ran so long should have convinced him that he needed help explaining such an intricate product.

Help arrived in the autumn of 1980 when Leland and Rubinstein met John O'Brien at a finance seminar at Berkeley. As Leland and Rubinstein explained their concept of portfolio insurance, O'Brien instantly recognized its value and commercial potential. He quit his job to become chief executive of the renamed Leland O'Brien Rubinstein (LOR) in 1981. O'Brien could speak the language of finance and was able to break portfolio insurance down into manageable and understandable pieces. He landed their first client almost immediately, and soon LOR was protecting $135 million in assets. By the end of 1982, they were insuring portfolios for Honeywell, Gates Rubber Corporation, and the Auto Club of South Carolina, together worth more than $250 million. It turned out that LOR's timing was exquisite, because investors were searching for the products that would provide them with protection and allow them to venture back into the stock market at just the moment LOR had created portfolio insurance.

The 1970s had been dismal, given that horrible stretch in 1973 and 1974, and the decade ended with the Dow Jones Industrial Average a measly 38.38 points, or less than 5 percent, above where it had ended the 1960s. While the Dow gained 14.9 percent in 1980, it had another pathetic performance in 1981, when it lost 9.2 percent. Things only got worse when the Dow closed at 776.92 on August 12, 1982, a trading session that marked eight straight losing days, nine losing days in the previous ten, fifteen losing days in the previous seventeen, and a loss of 11.2 percent for the year to date. The Dow was now below where it had ended the 1960s, and was even below the closing level from 1964.

Investors didn't know it at the time, but August 12, 1982, was the bottom; the Dow Jones Industrial Average has never again closed as low as it did that day. The 1980s bull market began on Friday, August 13, when the Federal Reserve lowered the discount rate by 0.5 percent, the third such rate cut in six weeks, leaving interest rates at their lowest level in nearly two years. These lower rates finally made stocks attractive enough for those who had fled eight years before, and the Dow gained 1.4 percent that Friday. The gains continued, with the Dow climbing eight of the next ten days, including consecutive daily gains of 1.1 percent, 3.7 percent, and 2.5 percent. The Dow ended the month with a gain of 11.5 percent and closed above 900 for the first time in more than a year. Nineteen eighty-two ended up being a pretty good year, with the Dow Jones Industrial Average eventually posting a 19.6 percent gain, with a 34.7 percent gain in the 141 days following the August bottom in the strongest sustained rally since the Great Depression. Investors felt President Ronald Reagan could point to the second half of 1982 as the turning point when he would later say, "It's morning again in America."

Just before the stock market bottomed in August 1982, and before most institutional investors learned about the promise of portfolio insurance, two investors saw a deal that was too good to pass up. Gibson Greetings was an also-ran maker of Christmas and birthday cards. In 1982 Gibson was best known for its dubious invention decades before of the "French fold" card—one sheet of paper folded in half and then folded in half again—and for the cartoon star of its newest line of greeting cards, a lazy, obese, sardonic cat named Garfield.

Gibson had been acquired by a middle-market lender in 1964, and in 1980 the lender was in turn acquired by RCA—the same RCA that was such a stock market darling in the 1920s—which wanted the lender's financial services and business assets. Gibson was surplus, and RCA had been trying to unload it for some time. William E. Simon was a former partner at the investment bank Salomon Brothers who had served as secretary of the Treasury under Presidents Nixon and Ford, and Ray Chambers was a tax accountant who'd done several small buyouts in the 1970s. Together they formed Wesray Capital Corporation, taking the name from Simon's initials and Chambers's first name, and they happened upon Gibson while acquiring another RCA divestiture—Tactec Systems, RCA's portable radio business. While the two businesses, portable radios and greeting cards, could not have been more different, Wesray bought Gibson Greetings from RCA in January 1982 for $80 million. What made the Gibson transaction unique was that Simon and Chambers each contributed a mere $330,000 to the purchase price, and Wesray's total commitment was only $1 million. Simon and Chambers levered their capital 79 to 1 by borrowing the rest.

Wesray kept existing management and made them partners. As a result, Gibson's profit in 1983 was half again what it had been when Wesray acquired it just the year before. As Gibson hummed along and the stock market strengthened, Simon and Chambers realized they might sell off a portion of the company in an initial public offering (IPO).

When Gibson Greetings went public at the end of May 1983 at $27.50 a share, the company Simon and Chambers had bought for $80 million just seventeen months earlier was worth $290 million. Simon and Chambers each took home $70 million on a deal that cost them $330,000.

What struck Wall Street was not that greeting cards could be so profitable but that there were undervalued companies ready to sell and bankers ready to lend. One observer said it was the equivalent of finding "gold at Sutter's Mill," the discovery that launched the California Gold Rush. This began an era of the leveraged buyout, or LBO, when investors could commit a small amount of capital and borrow a mountain of money to do a takeover.

The Gibson deal had been friendly because RCA was only too happy to sell off "noncore" businesses, but friendly deals were rare. If the targets weren't willing to sell, there were ways to force the issue and liberate the value trapped within. Friendly buyers were about to become raiders.

When Thomas Boone Pickens Jr. was a twelve-year-old newspaper boy in Holdenville, Oklahoma—a flyspeck of a town in the dead center of the state's red clay hills—he grew his route from 28 customers to 156 customers by finagling a second route and then a third and learning the value of expanding rapidly. He would later become the best known of these raiders.

Pickens bounced around hardscrabble Oklahoma and Texas after leaving Holdenville, starting college at Texas A&M before transferring to Oklahoma A&M, where he earned a degree in geology. Pickens's father was a landman at Phillips Petroleum, serving as the connection between oil companies seeking mineral rights and property owners willing to sell. His son, known as Boone, started at Phillips as a geologist in 1951, before setting out on his own in 1955 as a wildcatter. The company Boone built, Mesa Petroleum, was eventually one of the largest independent oil companies in the world, but in 1968 Pickens was still in a hurry. Remembering the lesson he'd learned from expanding his newspaper routes, Pickens attempted to merge with Hugoton Production Company, even though Hugoton was thirty times larger than Mesa. Hugoton owned a sizable portion of the Hugoton gas field, a massive bulb of natural gas fifty miles wide and more than one hundred miles long that builds in southwest Kansas before spilling across the panhandles of Oklahoma and Texas. At the time it was the nation's largest natural gas field. Pickens saw value, but Hugoton management considered Pickens nothing more than an upstart.

Two decades before such a thing would become common, Pickens launched a hostile tender offer, a promise to give existing Hugoton shareholders 1.8 shares of Mesa for each share of Hugoton they wished to sell, or "tender," directly to Pickens, who assured them they'd be better off with him than with current management. Shareholders tendered nearly one-third of all Hugoton shares, which meant Pickens had to be taken seriously. In April 1969, Pickens got the merger he was seeking and control of the combined company, and he saw that it was sometimes easier to find oil and gas by buying companies than by working a drilling rig. In 1982, about the time Wesray was buying an undervalued gem in Gibson Greetings, Pickens was again looking to buy an undervalued asset much larger than his own company, and he was proceeding in a much less decorous manner than Simon and Chambers had.

Cities Service had started in 1910 as a natural gas and electricity supplier to small public utilities in Texas and Oklahoma before it eventually started producing crude oil, refining it, and selling the gasoline at its CITGO stations. Pickens had been eyeing Cities for decades—his second wife said he'd been talking about Cities and its underappreciated mineral rights for as long as they'd been married, and Boone and Bea Pickens were set to celebrate their tenth anniversary. Cities Service in 1982 was more than twenty times larger than Pickens's Mesa Petroleum, but he wanted Cities Service for its ten million acres of untapped minerals. Pickens was convinced that, in his hands and with his wildcatter's luck, they were worth vastly more than the stock market said they were. Pickens had called Cities management "a case study in what was wrong with big oil's management" because they seemed to be more interested in keeping their jobs than driving the stock price higher. Pickens easily understood why they seemed to care so little about the stock price: they had such little personal stake in the company—one longtime member of the board of directors owned just 300 shares, another owned 392, a third owned all of 450, and the newest member of the board owned just 60 shares of Cities stock, worth barely $2,000. But Mesa owned 4 million shares of Cities stock, about 5 percent of the total, which they'd accumulated over the previous two years at an average price of $44.00.

On the last trading day in May 1982, Cities Service stock had closed at $37.00 a share. Pickens was running out of patience with a recalcitrant management team that didn't want to deal with him. When the Cities CEO was asked about the possibility of a take-over, he said Pickens "should buzz off," without naming him. In response Pickens formally offered $50 a share for enough Cities stock to bring his stake to 51 percent in a deal with a total value of $3.8 billion.

Newspapers disparaged Pickens, calling him a raider, and he indignantly wrapped himself in the flag of "shareholder rights," but at the core of the deal, Pickens saw value in Cities stock. Even with the huge premium he was offering—35.1 percent above Cities' price just before his offer became public—Pickens figured he was trying to buy Cities at just one-third of the value of its underlying assets. The price he offered for Cities stock translated to just more than $5 per barrel of crude oil reserves, even though industry-wide "finding cost" was about $15 a barrel and oil was trading for more than $30.

On June 17, less than three weeks after Pickens had formally put Cities Service "in play" and alerted the world to the idea that the cheapest place to find oil was Wall Street, the company agreed to be acquired by Gulf Oil for $63.00 a share. Pickens didn't get Cities but Mesa made a profit of $45 million.

*   *   *

Carl Icahn could not have been more different from T. Boone Pickens. Pickens had been born in Oklahoma to an oilman, while Icahn had been born in the Far Rockaway neighborhood of Queens, New York, to a Jewish opera singer. After Carl graduated from Princeton with a degree in philosophy in 1957, about the time Pickens was hitting his stride in the oil business, Icahn enrolled in the New York University School of Medicine. He eventually dropped out of medical school because of what he called "slight hypochondria."

Despite their differences, Pickens and Icahn seemed to be reading from a book that no one else understood. Icahn had excelled as an investor and trader in the 1960s. During the 1970s, he began taking significant stakes in smaller companies in order to exert more control, and in 1980 he started agitating for a seat on the board of directors of Saxon Industries, a copier manufacturer of which he owned 9.5 percent. Rather than give him that seat, management offered to buy his stock back at a premium to the going price. Icahn pocketed $2 million in greenmail—the premium above market value paid by entrenched management, with shareholders' money, so a potential acquirer will go away and leave existing management alone—before the term *greenmail* even existed. One year before Pickens's 1982 raid on Cities, Icahn had made $9 million by taking a stake in Hammermill Paper, threatening a proxy fight for control of the board, and then happily selling his stock back to the company at a premium unavailable to other shareholders. A few months later, he earned a profit of more than $30 million by acquiring a stake in the Marshall Field department store chain and then intimidating management into selling to a competitor at a price that was $12 a share lower than a friendly offer they'd rejected four years earlier. From there he'd moved to profits in Anchor Hocking, American Can, and Owens-Illinois.

As Pickens was counting his profits from Cities and Icahn was counting his profits from Marshall Field, August 1982 came to a close after its miraculous U-turn. In October the Dow gained

10.7 percent, then gained another 4.8 percent in November. Drastically lower interest rates were helping, but raiders like Pickens and Icahn had shown just how undervalued the stock market could be.

As the stock market strengthened, Pickens figured 1983 was time for the "fireplug to piss on the dog."

Gulf Oil was one of the legendary Seven Sisters of the oil business, a consortium that controlled 85 percent of the world's crude oil reserves prior to the rise of OPEC in the early 1970s and a group that still looked down on firms like Pickens's Mesa. Founded by Andrew Mellon's nephew, William Larimer Mellon Sr., Gulf had started propitiously with the largest oil strike in history, the legendary Spindletop well near Beaumont, Texas, a gusher that rose 150 feet into the southeast Texas sky and produced nearly 100,000 barrels of oil a day once it was brought under control. By 1983 Gulf was the world's fifth-largest oil company, with $20 billion in assets, $30 billion in revenue, and 40,000 employees. It was a giant and, according to Pickens, it was even more undervalued than Cities Service.

Mesa started buying Gulf stock on August 11, 1983, when it was trading near $39, with Alan "Ace" Greenberg, chairman of investment bank Bear Stearns, handling the trading personally. By September 28, just forty-eight days later, Mesa owned 8.5 million shares of Gulf.

On Monday, October 17, Mesa owned almost 9 percent of the company. It had become Gulf's largest shareholder, eclipsing even the remaining members of the founding Mellon family. Gulf stock closed that day at $47.00, and Mesa's average purchase price of $43.45 meant the group already had a profit of more than $50 million. Gulf was up more than 11 percent for the month and 58 percent for the year in the sort of levitation that was helping the entire stock market.

One week later, Mesa had amassed another slug of stock and

now owned 10.8 percent of Gulf. Gulf executives expressed no interest in selling to Pickens; shareholders would be enriched by such a deal, but executives would lose their prestigious jobs, enormous salaries, and regal perks.

With 1982's 19.6 percent gain, the Dow had added 43.9 percent in the two years that ended with 1983. While not nearly as impressive as the 95.9 percent return for the two years ended in 1905 or the 90.8 percent return for the two years ended in 1928, it was still the thirteenth-best two-year stretch to that time.

Nineteen eighty-three was one of the best years the Dow would enjoy, as the entire market was pulled higher by takeover battles, including those waged by other raiders who were fighting to buy companies in the same way Pickens was waging a battle for Gulf. Although December was disappointing, with a loss of 1.4 percent, the Dow managed a new all-time closing high of 1287.20 on November 29, 1983, one of thirty new highs in a year that set one about every nine trading days and finished with a gain of 20.3 percent.

Pickens wasn't the only oilman who saw that it can be cheaper to buy oil than to drill for it. By March 5, 1984, he had accumulated 21.7 million Gulf shares at an average price of about $45 per share when Chevron announced it would acquire the entire company, with the support of Gulf's management, for $80 a share. Pickens would not own Gulf, but he had made $760 million for himself and Mesa and nearly $5.5 billion for other Gulf shareholders by unleashing assets that had seen their value increase with inflation in the 1970s and 1980s, even if the price on the stock market failed to keep up.

Pickens, Icahn, and Wesray had vividly demonstrated how the game could be played, and that it didn't matter if a bidder ended up acquiring its target. In June 1984 Disney paid investor Saul

Steinberg $60 million in greenmail to go away and quit trying to accumulate a stake in the company. Steinberg had pulled Disney's stock price from $52.75 at the end of 1983 to $64.00 when he sold his holdings less than six months later, a rally of 21.3 percent. The week before the Steinberg deal, Disney had tried to thwart him by agreeing to an acquisition that required extensive borrowing, which would foil Steinberg's plans. Disney's acquisition target? Gibson Greetings, for which they'd agreed to pay $337.5 million.

Nineteen eighty-four was disappointing for most investors, with the Dow giving back 3.7 percent despite the previous two years' momentum, but T. Boone Pickens was not a mere investor. He was playing a different game, and in December, as the mediocre year came to an end, Pickens had found a new target with assets that outpaced its stock price: his former employer, Phillips Petroleum.

Phillips had been in business for three generations, and two generations of the Pickens family had worked there. In 1984 Phillips Petroleum was safely cocooned in Bartlesville, Oklahoma, and kept its old-fashioned trade name, Phillips 66, a name coined by two engineers when a 1930s road test of gasoline from a new Phillips refinery allowed them to reach a top speed of 66 miles per hour on a stretch of Route 66 that ran near Bartlesville.

Pickens found Phillips appealing because he was looking for crude oil and natural gas reserves he might take advantage of, and cash flow he could use to pay the debt he would take on to effect any acquisition. Having picked its target, Mesa had accumulated 8.8 million shares of Phillips, 5.7 percent of the company, at an average price of $44, when Pickens announced on December 4, 1984, that he wanted to pay $60 a share for another 15 million shares. And realizing that he would have a credibility problem if the stock market thought Pickens was in it just for the greenmail, Pickens cemented his hero status among investors by pledging that he would not sell any shares "except on an equal basis with all other shareholders." But now the game had gotten tougher. Targets like Phillips and their law firms had gotten better at fending off unwanted advances, even the ones that juiced stock prices and enriched shareholders. Phillips succeeded in getting an Oklahoma district court judge sitting in Washington County, the seat of which just happened to be Bartlesville, to stop Pickens from moving forward.

Pickens called it getting "hometowned," and with the Oklahoma courts thwarting his effort to take a bigger stake in Phillips, Pickens realized he needed to get out of Phillips while the getting was good. Two days before Christmas in 1984, Mesa and Phillips agreed to end their fight, and Pickens would accept $53 a share in a convoluted swap engineered to allow Pickens to say he hadn't taken greenmail (similar to the swap between Augustus Heinze and Amalgamated Copper that had allowed both sides to claim victory). Investment banks First Boston and Morgan Stanley would buy Pickens's shares at a premium and sell them at market prices, with Phillips covering any difference between what Pickens got and what the banks ultimately received. Phillips had started the month at $43.75. On the last trading day before Pickens threw in the towel, Phillips was trading at $54.88, a gain of 25.4 percent.

Pickens was making money by terrorizing incumbent management, but LOR's portfolio insurers were making money in 1984 by trying to put institutional investors at ease.

The Chicago Mercantile Exchange (CME) had introduced a futures contract on the S&P 500 index in 1982. Futures contracts are standardized agreements made on an exchange to buy or sell an asset, such as the S&P 500, at a price agreed on today but with delivery and payment made later. Since delivery and payment is pushed to a predetermined later date, only a small payment is initially due, making futures the perfect instrument for speculation or hedging. LOR immediately realized that selling futures instead of the specific stocks in a client's portfolio made it much easier to execute portfolio insurance. Futures were the slivers of the market LOR could buy and sell to replicate a protective put option on the S&P 500 index.

LOR ended 1984 with nine employees, $850 million under management (up from just $350 million the year before), and nearly $1 million in revenue. But problems had started to appear for portfolio insurance despite the ease of operation offered by futures. Early in 1983, after watching an LOR sales presentation, Bruce Jacobs, a Wharton Ph.D. who worked in Prudential Insurance Company's Pension Management Group, pointed out several problems with portfolio insurance, which he called "portfolio insulation." The problems included higher fees, inferior long-term performance, and, distressingly, the worry that "if a large number of investors utilized the portfolio insulation technique, price movements would tend to snowball. Price drops would be followed by sales, which would lead to further price depreciation. Market prices would not be efficient, and it would pay to not use portfolio insulation." Despite these concerns, the assets protected by portfolio insurance would grow about ninety-fold by October 1987, when the snowball started downhill.

Even though targets like Phillips, and their law firms, had gotten better at fending off unwanted advances, raiders had gotten better at making them. With Phillips weakened by its payment to Pickens, but with the oil it had in the ground still fundamentally undervalued, Carl Icahn announced less than two months after Pickens had walked away that he was taking Pickens's place and offering $55 a share for Phillips, a total of $8.1 billion.

Unlike Pickens's previous offer, which was financed by Mesa's profits from the Gulf deal and capital from bank loans and partnerships, Icahn was using a new tool: the "highly confident" letter. The investment banking firm Drexel Burnham Lambert had entered the 1980s in the second tier among banks until Michael Milken explained to the world that the bonds of companies that had fallen on hard times were mispriced. Even with a few defaults, these bonds would generate more return for the risk assumed than traditional investment-grade bonds, and this made them a relative bargain. Twenty years later, investment banks selling mortgage-backed securities would make an identical argument.

But in the early 1980s, there were relatively few of these distressed bonds, so Milken had difficulty investing the amounts of money he wanted to. He had two alternatives: he could wait around for the occasional "fallen angel," or he could get Drexel to underwrite and sell lower-grade, speculative bonds for companies that had never been able to sell bonds before because they weren't considered "investment grade." Milken understood these new bonds could support the sort of speculative takeover that was fueling the stock market's rise.

In July 1984, Milken and Drexel managed to sell $100 million of these lower-than-investment-grade, or "junk," bonds for Nelson Peltz's Triangle Industries. The cash proceeds went into a blind pool, cash that Triangle would keep to have on hand for raids on targets they hadn't identified yet. By the summer of 1985, Milken was selling a similar $750 million blind pool for Ronald Perelman, and just one year later, the junk bond market Milken had created was so large that he was able to sell a blind pool of $1.2 billion of bonds, the largest ever and more than ten times what he'd dared to sell just two years earlier. Pickens had been forced to fly around the country, scraping together the financing he had needed to bid for Cities Service. Now all a raider needed to do was call on Mike Milken, sitting atop Drexel's massive junk bond franchise in Beverly Hills, to get nearly any amount of financing desired.

Icahn was one of Milken's best customers. Now that Pickens had softened up Phillips Petroleum, Icahn again turned to Milken and Drexel to finance his $8.1 billion bid. Drexel had shown an uncanny ability to sell junk bonds for all sorts of takeovers, and Icahn was asking them to sell more than they had ever sold. He needed Drexel in his camp because without financing, there was no way Phillips would take him seriously, and without that there was no way Phillips could buy his stock back at a premium, particularly after they'd stretched themselves to get Pickens to go away. Drexel's fee for selling junk bonds was nearly extortionate, but without financing, a raider wasn't much of a raider, and Milken and Drexel offered one-stop shopping, although at a price. In exchange for underwriting the $100 million blind pool for Triangle, Drexel had received warrants, essentially long-term options, that effectively gave Drexel ownership of 12 percent of Triangle.

With the financing for Phillips, Icahn tried to strike a bargain. He wanted Drexel to commit to raising the money he needed without actually raising it, because if they actually raised it, Icahn would incur that huge fee. Just as Leland and Rubinstein had managed to synthesize an option out of thin air with their portfolio insurance, Icahn was asking Drexel to spin a takeover threat out of thin air. When Icahn and his attorney met with Leon Black of Drexel, Black suggested, "Why don't we say we're 'highly confident' that we can raise it? It's really different. It hasn't been done before." When Icahn asked his lawyer what he thought, the response was forthright: "Leon's full of shit. It's not legally binding, what good is it?" The meeting broke up with Icahn, apparently taking his lawyer's advice, saying he was no longer interested in doing the deal. But overnight Icahn realized that Black's idea was just what he'd been searching for; the next morning he revived the "highly confident" letter. Icahn had his credibility, Drexel got the $1 million they charged Icahn for writing the letter (Icahn got an even bigger bargain than he realized, because just two months later a "highly confident" letter would cost $3.5 million), and the stock market had another reason to rally. In the span of just ten weeks, Phillips's share price rallied from $44.75 to $50.13. Icahn made $52.5 million for his ten week's work, and though he'd taken a page from Pickens's playbook and sworn off greenmail to add legitimacy to Drexel's "highly confident" letter, a little more than half his profit came from the 12 percent rally in Phillips shares, while the remainder, $25 million, came not from a greenmail premium but rather from the reimbursement by Phillips of certain "expenses."

Raiders now had the tools to make any one of them credible in nearly any takeover battle, and not only did raiders bid up the price of all number of stocks, dragging the Dow and the S&P 500 with them, but they also improved all companies by making them leaner and more focused on results and less focused on perks for leadership.

With Ronald Reagan safely reinstalled in the White House in January 1985, and Pickens, Peltz, Perelman, Icahn, and a raft of others running around scaring stocks higher, the Dow Jones Industrial Average resumed the march that had started in 1982. However, an ominous feeling started to creep into the stock market. Doubters worried that investors were bidding up stocks, paying more than they might otherwise, simply because they believed so many companies were takeover candidates and some raider would come along to force their stock dramatically higher. When a company was indeed bid for or taken over, all the other companies in that industry almost immediately saw their stock rally in sympathy until their values matched that of the target company.

In early 1986 Milken told a group of pension fund managers that "the force in this country buying high-yield securities"—the polite name for junk bonds—"has overpowered all regulation." It had also overpowered critical thinking. Ted Forstmann, another takeover artist, called the junk bonds that funded buyouts, greenmail, and hostile takeovers "wampum" to show his derision. Politicians were still uncertain whether the takeovers that concentrated so much power in so few hands were good for the country and their constituents. They came to realize that the players, other than a few who were becoming folk heroes, made for handy villains, and thirty bills were introduced into Congress in 1984 and 1985 meant to regulate takeovers. None passed. The investment banks, led by Drexel, were making a lot of money, enough to lobby these bills to death.

By the end of 1985, the Dow had gained 27.7 percent, as interest rates and inflation continued to fall. One expert summed it up when he called 1985 "a super year." The Dow had closed above 1300 for the first time ever in May, then above 1400 for the first time in November, and above 1500 in December before ending 1985 at 1553.10, while posting thirty-six new all-time closing highs. Takeovers were largely responsible for the strength, even on the last day of the year, when Midcon, an operator of natural gas pipelines, rallied 4.7 percent on rumors it was to be taken over by Occidental Petroleum.

Nineteen eighty-six was nearly as profitable as 1985, and the good news began on January 2, with Occidental Petroleum confirming the New Year's Eve rumors as it formally bid $75 per share for Midcon, a company that had started the previous year trading at just $41.25. The Dow ultimately gave ground slightly in January, but from that month's low, it staged a nearly unbroken string of advances, gaining 8.8 percent in February alone, more than it would in the average year, and then 6.4 percent in March as the takeover premium ballooned, before finally weakening a bit and becoming more volatile in April over fears of Libyan terrorism. It lost 4.2 percent over a two-day period in July and lost 86.61 points, 4.6 percent, on September 11, 1986, the worst point loss ever to that day and the worst percentage loss in more than twenty-five years. It then lost another 1.9 percent the next day.

The SEC investigated September's price action and concluded that it was the typical "change in investors' perception of fundamental economic conditions," but Mark Rubinstein, who with Hayne Leland was the architect of portfolio insurance, thought the SEC was wrong and told them so. Rubinstein, one of the great minds in finance, believed, but couldn't prove, that selling by portfolio insurers on September 11, 1986, had led to the losses.

Even though portfolio insurance was growing large enough to speed the market's declines, there was no way to stop the flow of investors using it, even if LOR shut their doors. Rubinstein argued that LOR didn't have an exclusive on the math at the heart of portfolio insurance. Many clever financial minds had come to understand that the Black and Scholes model was a road map to creating the synthetic options LOR was using, and those clever minds went into business competing with LOR.

Rubinstein recounted that "we had one client come to us who had a huge pension plan. We wanted to tell that client that was too much money for us to handle. We were just too worried about the impact that the trading would have on the markets." But LOR knew that if they turned the client away, "he'd go somewhere else," to one of those competing firms.

By the time 1986 closed, the Dow had stabilized and gained 22.6 percent, despite losing 1.9 percent in April and 6.9 percent in September. It set a new closing record of 1955.57 and made a new closing high thirty different times, about once every nine trading days.

The two-year gain for 1985 and 1986 was 56.5 percent, even better than the gain during 1982 and 1983, and the tenth-best two-year gain to that time. The Dow had now gained more than 126 percent since the end of the dismal 1970s.

As 1987 began, it looked like the run would continue. The Dow Jones Industrial Average began the year by closing higher for thirteen consecutive trading days, something never accomplished before or since by the Dow in its current thirty-stock configuration, and the gain of 44.01 points on January 5 was the largest-ever point gain to that time. When 1987's historic thirteen-day winning streak ended it was with a whimper; the Dow finally finished in the red on January 21, losing 10.40 points, just less than 0.5 percent. The next day, Thursday the twenty-second, the rally resumed; the Dow gained 51.60 points, about 2.5 percent, and in doing so established yet another record for the largest point gain ever, just days after breaking the old record. After a minor pullback, it would take the Dow another five days to break this new record set on the twenty-second; it took five days only because a weekend intervened.

The Dow closed above 2000 for the first time on January 8, 1987. It closed above 2100 for the first time on January 19. It had taken the Dow all of 1986 to post thirty new all-time closing highs. It made fifteen in January 1987 alone, a month with only twenty-two trading days. It closed lower on only three of those twenty-two days, and it finished the month 13.8 percent above where it started, still the eleventh-best month the Dow's ever had and the sixth best if you ignore the volatile months during the worst of the Great Depression.

As the Dow was in the midst of its golden January, the raiders were still at it. In part, January was so good precisely because the raiders were still at it. But raiders weren't the only reason the market was climbing. Since the start of Ronald Reagan's second term, the American economy had created nearly 7 million new jobs. Money was being made and spent, and companies were reporting record profits. Reagan, a man whose primary credential for public office seemed to be an incandescent optimism about America, its place in the world, and the power of its economy, had helped the country feel good about asserting itself again. On June 12, 1987, he went to Berlin's Brandenburg Gate, and while speaking within sight of the Berlin Wall, so close that he was positioned behind bulletproof glass to shield him from East German snipers, he threw off the solicitous language of some of his predecessors, and instead of asking nicely, hat in hand, he demanded bluntly, "Mr. Gorbachev, tear down this wall."

While the bidding by raiders at times seemed madness, the takeover craze hit its peak on June 23, 1987. P. David Herrlinger was a small-scale Cincinnati-based investment advisor, described by his boss as "a great employee, very stable, solid and a good worker," who called the Dow Jones News Wire after telling that boss he was "going to make some money." Herrlinger announced that on behalf of Stone Inc. he was formally bidding $70 a share, a total of $6.8 billion, for retailer Dayton Hudson, parent of the Target chain of discount stores. After calling Herrlinger back to confirm his identity, Dow Jones shared the news of the takeover bid with Wall Street at 9:49 A.M. Rumors had been thick that Dart Group was interested in Dayton Hudson, and when news of a bid hit the tape, traders reflexively started buying the stock. They bought wildly until the New York Stock Exchange temporarily halted trading, and when Dayton Hudson reopened ninety minutes later, it was at $63.00 a share, up $9.00 from the previous day's close, in the sort of takeover-induced rally that had become common.

Unfortunately, Stone Inc. didn't exist. When Dow Jones dispatched someone to ask Herrlinger about his takeover offer, the interview was conducted with the reporter standing on Herrlinger's lawn—the would-be raider no longer had an office because he had been fired that morning when his offer became public. Herrlinger and the reporter talked through a closed window as Herrlinger explained that "an offer is really an intangible thing." Asked if his bid was a hoax, he explained, "It's no more of a hoax than anything else." At 12:37 P.M. Dow Jones reported the first doubts about the bid, and Dayton Hudson came back to earth, closing at $53.13 a share, down 87 cents for the day, but not before trading 5.5 million shares and becoming the second most active stock on the New

York Stock Exchange. Herrlinger's lawyer explained that his client "is not well today." Herrlinger wasn't available to comment after the close of trading because his wife had taken him to Cincinnati's Good Samaritan Hospital for observation.

Takeover bids had originally been attempts to recognize hidden value and were backed by temporary partnerships and bank loans before junk bonds and greenmail became the overpowering forces. When raiders balked at paying a fortune for Milken and Drexel to sell junk bonds, Drexel began charging a smaller fortune to craft a letter saying it hadn't raised a cent but was "highly confident" it could raise whatever was needed. As P. David Herrlinger was being driven away by his wife, it became obvious that he'd taken buyouts to their logical extreme, a bid backed by nothing, not even the "highly confident" letter that caused Carl Icahn's attorney to say its creator was "full of shit."

Although the stock market was up more than 40 percent by August 1987, fears were growing beyond Bruce Jacobs at Prudential and Mark Rubinstein at LOR about the lurking downside of portfolio insurance. In June 1987 Hayne Leland had calculated that in certain circumstances a stock market drop of just 3 percent would require that LOR sell S&P futures contracts in an amount that would be the equivalent of an entire average day's trading on the New York Stock Exchange. What had begun as an elegant idea had grown too large to work. Leland later said, "From the very first day I thought of portfolio insurance, I said, 'What if everyone tries to do it?' I didn't like the answer I came up with." It had taken LOR a year to find its first customer. As the Dow was making its high for 1987, everyone seemed to be employing portfolio insurance as covered assets increased fourfold in 1987. By October 1987, LOR had $5 billion they were protecting directly and $45 billion they were protecting through arrangements that allowed licensees to use their methodology. Another $40 billion was being protected by identical portfolio insurance products offered by other providers.

In August, William Silber, a professor at New York University, wrote, "Unlike earlier financial disasters, this one will emerge not because of too much speculation, but because of the inverse— too much hedging." With portfolio insurance the hedging was unthinking in that the number of futures contracts to sell and the price at which to sell them were strictly dictated by the math of the Black-Scholes model and the rules LOR had devised. The only human interaction was seeing what the model said to do and placing those orders.

Even though Silber would soon be proved correct, it wasn't just the amount of stock investments covered by portfolio insurance that was the problem; it was that institutional investors, emboldened by the promise of portfolio insurance, were investing more of their portfolios in stocks than they otherwise would have. At the beginning of October 1987, pension funds that were using portfolio insurance had 56 percent of their assets invested in stocks, while the entire universe of pension funds, those covered by portfolio insurance and those not, had just 46 percent of their assets invested in stocks, an enormous difference that translated to billions of dollars invested in stocks that would have instead been diversified across other asset classes if not for portfolio insurance. When the upward momentum in stock prices reversed—and it always does at some point—this extra money invested in stocks would leave the market all at once, its managers confident that the market would cooperate and let them out in the regimented way Black, Scholes, Leland, O'Brien, and Rubinstein promised.

On August 25, 1987, the Dow made its closing high for the year and of all time to that point, 2722.42, a gain of 43.6 percent for a year that was just eight months old. If the Dow could have hung on to that level, it would have been the sixth most profitable year ever for the American stock market, but the Dow started to slide, the upward momentum reversed, and portfolio insurance selling kicked in. Just thirty-eight trading days later, the Dow had lost all of 1987's 43.6 percent gain and more.

Interest rates had fallen with only a brief interruption since peaking in July 1981, when the interest rate on long-term Treasury Bonds had reached nearly 16 percent. When 1987 started, the yield was just 7.5 percent, less than half of what it had been six years earlier, and that decrease in interest rates was a tonic for stocks, making them more attractive and bonds less so.

But beginning in March, interest rates started rising. The enormity of the growing budget deficit drove interest rates higher, yet another deficit was a bigger concern. For years the United States had been buying all sorts of goods from overseas, particularly electronics from Asia and crude oil from the Middle East. As a result, the trade deficit mushroomed; in 1986 it was more than eight times what it had been in 1981. The January 1, 1987, *New York Times* reported that the trade deficit in November 1986 had set a record. The top economist at the Department of Commerce called the news "horrendous," and the dollar took a beating as a result. By the end of the month it was at a seven-year low against the West German deutsche mark and at the lowest point against the Japanese yen since the late 1940s, as Americans sent dollars overseas to buy stuff and the recipients sold those dollars back, driving down the dollar's value.

The trade deficit then set a new record in the first quarter of 1987 and then again in the second quarter, causing trading partners to sell back even more dollars, weakening it further. Now people were calling for the Federal Reserve to reverse the course it had set in 1982 and raise interest rates in order to get America's trading partners to keep those dollars and deposit them to earn that higher interest rate. When the value of the dollar fell to another new low against the West German deutsche mark on September 2, calls for the Fed to help the dollar started to drown out those worried that higher interest rates would spark a recession. Those asking for help didn't have long to wait. On September 4, the Fed raised the discount rate by 0.5 percent, to 6.0 percent. The Fed had fiddled with the discount rate once in 1984, raising it by 0.5 percent in April before lowering it by that same amount again in both November and December. But other than that single increase, which had been quickly reversed, September 1987's hike was the first increase since 1981, when the Fed had raised rates to stamp out inflation.

The Dow continued to be weak in September. It lost ground the first five days of the month and had another stretch of five losing days in the middle of the month before finally limping to a close of 2596.28, a loss of 2.5 percent for the month as all interest rates increased.

As October 1987 began, investors had their fingers crossed that one increase in the discount rate would be enough and that interest rates had reached their peak. Those hoping were horribly disappointed when Alan Greenspan, the newly installed chairman of the Federal Reserve, went on a Sunday morning news program on October 4 and warned that another rate increase might be needed. In labyrinthine logic, Greenspan warned that even with no sign that inflation was increasing, he was worried that "if everybody gets it into his head that inflation is inevitable, they will start taking actions which will create" higher inflation, forcing the Fed to raise interest rates to stamp out higher inflation because "if [higher inflation] happens then what has got to be done to preserve the economy and prevent it from breaking apart is dangerously higher interest rates. It would cause a tremendous contraction in the economy." Viewers who were able to follow Greenspan's tortured scenario realized he had adopted the philosophy used by the U.S. military in Vietnam: sometimes you have to destroy the village in order to save it.

The Dow had its worst point drop ever when, on Tuesday, October 6, two days after Greenspan's perplexing warning, it lost 91.55 points as interest rates reached their highest level in nearly two years. The drop amounted to 3.5 percent, and though Leland's June fears weren't realized, forces were beginning to converge against the stock market, and portfolio insurance was starting to overpower buyers. What was described as "waves of computerized selling" on the sixth was likely the manifestation in New York of all the portfolio insurance selling being done in Chicago.

Although much of the damage on October 6 was done by the hedging from portfolio insurance, it had been started by a warning. That morning Robert Prechter had published the latest edition of his popular newsletter the *Elliott Wave Theorist* and emphatically and unambiguously warned, "Both investors and traders should sell now."

After graduating from Yale with a degree in psychology, Prechter had joined Merrill Lynch as a technical analyst, one who studies a stock's past price patterns to divine its future course. Psychology was perfect training for a technical analyst like Prechter, because technical analysis applies psychology to how investors will respond when a stock gets back to a recent high and how investors might react when a stock falls in price.

Prechter had started his career as an obscure adherent to an obscure technical analysis tool, the Elliott Wave Theory, which seeks to identify market trends by identifying extremes in investor sentiment. Prechter eventually became known because of several high-profile predictions. He predicted the start of the appreciation in the stock market in 1982, saying a "super bull market" was under way. In 1984 he won the U.S. trading championship, a slightly hokey marketing gimmick run by a brokerage firm; but while trading in an audited, real-money account, Prechter used his wave theory to generate an annual profit of 444.4 percent, a then record for the contest. With each success, Prechter's prestige grew. Even *People* magazine profiled him in May 1987. In the article he deployed psychology to explain that when dark, unsettling rock music becomes more popular, it is a sign to buy stocks, and that the "shorter, puffier skirts" then in fashion were a market indicator.

Writing on the morning of October 6, Prechter warned in the psychology-laden terminology of a technical analyst that the small rally from September 20 to October 2 was a rebound in a larger decline rather than the beginning of a new upward "wave." He also pointed out that more stocks were declining than advancing and that investor sentiment was shifting based on the price action in stock index futures, the same stock index futures being sold by portfolio insurers.

In the middle of the October 6 volatility, exacerbated in part by Prechter, the new head of the Securities and Exchange Commission (SEC), David Ruder, gave his first speech as chairman. Ruder had been a professor at Northwestern University and had been confirmed as head of the SEC only that August, about two weeks before the Dow made its high for the year.

Ruder spoke in Chicago, his hometown and also home of the largest markets for the trading of futures and index options. Speaking while the Dow was having its worst day ever, Ruder made a mistake common to academics newly installed as regulators: he thought out loud. Wasting no time, he ruminated on a number of potential steps to reduce volatility, which he blamed on program trading, the automated delivery of sell orders for a basket of stocks, often the basket being sold by arbitrageurs to offset their purchases of futures on the S&P. The first step he suggested in response to a dramatic drop in stock prices was the most drastic, a total system-wide trading halt. What stayed with listeners and the media was that the new chairman of the SEC was most concerned about volatility and considered the most drastic option, a complete shutdown, a reasonable response.

The Dow ultimately fell 91.55 points, or 3.5 percent, on the sixth, partly due to Prechter's warning and partly due to higher interest rates and worries about the dollar. But what Prechter and Chairman Ruder had demonstrated was that the market was nervous, that a market tremor might not stop and might become a fully fledged earthquake, which is what would happen thirteen days later.

Another problem for the market was that the government seemed to have finally decided what it was going to do about restraining takeovers. Rather than try to outlaw them, Congress would propose making them significantly less attractive. The House Ways and Means Committee met on October 7 and 8 to discuss ways to trim the budget deficit, and soon rumors started circulating that they would limit the deductibility of interest paid to finance a friendly takeover and outlaw it for hostile ones.

The Dow lost 1.4 percent on both October 8 and Friday, October 9, as interest rates rose both days, reaching their highest level for the year as a painful stretch ended and the Dow closed at 2482.21, a loss of 6 percent for the week.

The worries about portfolio insurance had been limited to Ph.D.s and other academics until investors opened the *Wall Street Journal* on Monday, October 12. Beatrice Garcia, writing in the widely read "Abreast of the Market" column, introduced many readers to portfolio insurance. Garcia warned that portfolio-insurance-induced selling could drive stock prices lower, which would make even more portfolio-insurance-induced selling necessary in a cascade of steadily falling prices—exactly the thing that Leland and Rubinstein had worried about and that Black and Scholes had assumed wouldn't happen. Garcia suggested that the vicious cycle of selling might "snowball into a stunning rout for stocks," and she quoted a researcher who "envisions a scenario where selling stock-index futures to implement hedging strategies could start off what could be a huge slide in stock prices that feeds on itself." Those just learning about portfolio insurance as well as those already familiar with it were reading about how the financial apocalypse might play out. October 12 was also a day when the *Wall Street Journal* reported that "pressure is building for higher interest rates, both here and overseas." The Dow fell slightly on the twelfth, losing 10.77 points, but it was the third losing day in a row and the fifth losing day of the last six, which included that worst-ever loss of 91.55 on October 6.

The stock market bounced back a bit the next day, Tuesday, October 13, with the Dow closing at 2508.16, a gain of 36.72 points, about 1.5 percent, as the dollar strengthened and interest rates ticked down. But ninety-three minutes after the close of trading, Democrats on the House Ways and Means Committee met in a closed caucus and agreed to a series of tax increases that included a range of new taxes aimed at raiders. Takeover targets had been the darlings of the bull market, but not for long. Congress was about to close the funding spigot, and the era of the corporate raider was over. The era of the stock market rally headlined by names that were "in play" was over as well. The market just didn't know it yet.

The crash began the next morning, Wednesday, October 14, 1987. The first hint was the news of the Ways and Means Committee agreement to implement takeover-tax proposals as part of a total of $12 billion in new taxes. The agreement included proposals that would frustrate many friendly corporate takeovers and kill the hostile ones by eliminating deductibility of interest payments on debt, including junk bonds, that was used to acquire more than 20 percent of the stock of another corporation. It also proposed creating a "Corporate Raider Tax," a 50 percent nondeductible excise tax on greenmail payments.

The Ways and Means Committee made clear its goal when it said, "The committee believes that corporate acquisitions that lack the consent of the acquired corporation are detrimental to the general economy as well as to the welfare of the acquired corporation's employees and community. The committee therefore believes it is appropriate not only to remove tax incentives for corporate acquisitions, but to create tax disincentives for such acquisitions." The committee didn't mention shareholders.

The second hint that the crash had begun was the announcement at 8:30 A.M., one hour before the market opened, that the trade deficit for August was an atrocious $15.7 billion. Not only was the number huge, but it was larger than expected by about $1.5 billion. Long-term interest rates immediately rose above 10 percent for the first time in two years, and the dollar fell by 1 percent against currencies like the Japanese yen and the West German deutsche mark.

During the first half hour of trading, the Dow was down just 1.7 percent, a bad day but not horrible if that had been the totality of the damage. It wasn't, as the Dow lost another 1 percent in the hour around lunch and then more in the final ninety minutes to close at 2412.70, a loss of 95.46 points, 3.8 percent, in the worst point loss ever, displacing the 91.55 loss from Tuesday of the previous week. A portfolio made up of potential takeover targets, the stocks that had been propping up the rest of the market, lost half again as much. The *Wall Street Journal* would write, "It's hard to overstate the indiscriminate nature of [Wednesday's] selloff." Every one of the thirty stocks making up the Dow lost ground as the Dow closed more than 10 percent below its summer high.

The Dow opened trading on Thursday, October 15, down another 19 points, and the weak open coupled with the previous day's losses led portfolio insurers to sell $380 million worth of S&P 500 index futures in the first half hour of the day. The Dow wallowed until thirty minutes before the close, when it was off only 4 points. At that point many observers were thinking the worst was over; the market was nearly flat on the day, and it had absorbed substantial selling from portfolio insurers. But long-term interest rates ticked up again as the close approached, and optimists saw their hope disappear when the Dow started to tumble. It lost another 53 points in those final thirty minutes when $175 million in sell orders came from index arbitrageurs in the S&P 500 futures pits—the arbs had likely bought the futures from portfolio insurers.

Index arbitrageurs were the link between the portfolio insurers selling futures contracts on the Chicago Mercantile Exchange and the New York Stock Exchange, where many of the stocks that make up the S&P 500 basket traded. To get their futures orders executed, portfolio insurers had to sell them at slightly less than the basket of stocks they represented was worth. After buying the futures, the index arbitrageurs, known as index arbs, hedged away their exposure by selling all of the stock comprising the basket in the proper amounts and ratios. Once that was accomplished, any profit or loss on the futures contracts would be precisely offset by the basket of stocks. It was a bit like owning a one-dollar bill but owing someone one hundred pennies. The index arbs would then wait until the selling pressure in the futures had eased and the relationship had returned to normal when they would unwind the trade. The arb's profit was the discount received when the futures contracts were originally purchased. If the original purchase price for that $1 bill was just 97 cents, then the arb has made a profit of 3 cents. Not a massive profit until one realizes that arbs can do this repeatedly with millions of dollars' worth of stock and futures contracts.

The Dow closed Thursday at 2355.09, a loss of another 57.61 points or 2.4 percent; it was now down 5.1 percent for the week, with one more day to go. Congress wasn't going to be any help, and that evening the full Ways and Means Committee approved the anti-takeover tax provisions, including the Corporate Raider Tax.

The Dow opened at 2363.90 on Friday morning, a small gain from the previous day, and drifted lower as portfolio insurers who still had futures to sell from the previous two days fed them into the market slowly, trying to take advantage of the early gain and eroding it slowly until the Dow was trading slightly lower on the day. Selling slowly worked until 11:00 A.M., when portfolio insurers decided this was as good as it was going to get and turned more aggressive, selling S&P 500 futures contracts worth $265 million. Much of the selling but not all, approximately $183 million worth, was transmitted to the NYSE by index arbs, and the Dow fell 30 points. Then between noon and 2:00 P.M. it fell another 70 points. As 4:00 P.M. neared, the Dow was down 4.6 percent and Frank Cassar was climbing to the visitors' gallery overlooking the NYSE trading floor. Cassar wasn't a trader or a broker. He wasn't a disgruntled investor. Instead, he was a maintenance man at the exchange, and he was going up there to make certain the closing bell would start ringing when it should, exactly ten seconds before 4:00 P.M. In the past few days, the bell had failed to ring, and no one wanted this day to go on any longer than it had to.

The 108.35-point loss was the Dow's largest ever. The New York Stock Exchange set a volume record by trading 338 million shares on a day when seventeen stocks fell for each one that advanced, as the Dow posted its first-ever 100-point loss. Portfolio insurers had sold futures equivalent to $2.1 billion in stock, and index arbs had transmitted $1.7 billion of that to the NYSE. It was a rout, with interest rates once again higher at the end of the day than they'd been at the beginning (long-term interest rates had started the year at 7.23 percent and were now exactly 3 percentage points higher at 10.23 percent). Given that $400 million of futures remained in the weak hands of opportunistic traders who'd bought them from portfolio insurers and had not yet offset their position by selling them back or by selling the basket of stocks represented by the futures, there was likely to be substantial pressure on the stock market when it opened on Monday.

Friday's most distressing news was that despite the enormous selling by portfolio insurers, they hadn't come close to selling as many futures as they were supposed to and had fallen well behind their models. From Wednesday to Friday, the Dow had lost 10.4 percent, and those models dictated that, at a minimum, $12 billion of S&P 500 index futures should already have been sold, while less than $4 billion had actually been sold. Unfortunately, this wasn't portfolio insurers' dirty little secret. Any reasonably sophisticated market participant could do the math to calculate how many futures needed to be sold and could then compare that number to the published volume from the futures pit. Soon everyone would know that portfolio insurers had about $8 billion in futures to sell, the equivalent of approximately 228 million shares of stock, more than the average volume for an entire day, as Leland had prophesied. Stock market volatility was also changing the calculus of the models themselves. Over the weekend, one institutional user of portfolio insurance who'd scrupulously followed the guidelines of its adviser in selling, would be told that, based on Friday's close, it should sell 70 percent of its remaining holdings on Monday "to conform to parameters of the insurance model."

With the close on Friday and the Dow's three-day loss of 10.4 percent, the U.S. stock market had posted its worst three-day stretch since May 1940, when the German army broke through French defenses and began its march on Paris.

Then the United States attacked Iran. On Friday, a missile had been fired from the Iranian-held Fao Peninsula, which juts into the Persian Gulf, and had struck the *Sea Isle City,* a U.S.-flagged tanker operating in Kuwaiti waters and capable of carrying 300,000 barrels of gasoline or fuel oil. The missile had struck the wheelhouse and crew berths, wounding eighteen and blinding both the captain and a lookout. President Ali Khamenei of Iran had announced the attack at a prayer gathering that weekend, and though he stopped short of claiming responsibility, he did say, "Where the missile came from, the Almighty knows best."

The United States responded early on Monday, October 19, in what the military called Operation Nimble Archer. Four American warships fired hundreds of shells at two derelict Persian Gulf oil platforms that the Iranian military used for communications and surveillance. Eventually the platforms were set ablaze. President Ronald Reagan called the action "a prudent yet restrained response." As with the initial attack, details about our retaliation were limited, but no one could blame the Americans who woke on the morning of October 19, 1987, thinking we were finally at war with Iran.

Designated Order Turnaround (DOT) was the New York Stock Exchange's electronic system for cutting out the middleman. DOT would route orders electronically from brokers to the exchange post where the stock traded. Once at the post, the order would be printed and executed by humans. DOT also eased program trading, the simultaneous buying or selling of a basket of many different stocks. The basket might resemble the S&P 500, so index arbs could and did use DOT to execute program trades to offset their buys or sells in the futures.

On Monday morning, the NYSE opened DOT an hour early so brokerage firms would have plenty of time to enter orders. Firms used the extra hour to stuff "four or five times" the normal order flow into DOT, almost all of it orders to sell, and by the time the opening bell rang at 9:30 A.M., DOT had orders to sell a total of 14 million shares of a variety of stocks, worth about $500 million.

Fifteen minutes later, the Dow was reported to be down just 21 points. That might have been great news, but the calculation was made on incomplete information. Many stocks hadn't opened at all yet because there were so many sellers and so few buyers. Those stocks that hadn't yet opened were still reporting Friday's closing prices. The crush of sell orders was so great that 187 issues on the NYSE, 18 percent of all listed stocks, failed to open at or near the scheduled 9:30 A.M. start time.

Thirty minutes after the titular open, the market was looking worse; between 9:30 and 10:00 A.M., another $475 million in sell orders were loaded into DOT, making it even more difficult to open the stocks that hadn't yet opened because orders to sell overwhelmed what little buying interest there was. At 10:00 A.M., $140 million worth of futures had already been sold for portfolio insurance, and as the latest batch of sell orders was loaded into DOT, ninety-five of the stocks in the S&P 500, making up 30 percent of that index's value, still weren't trading. At 10:30 A.M., 175 NYSE stocks, including some of the largest and most important, such as IBM, Exxon, and Sears, Roebuck, hadn't traded a single share; eight of the thirty stocks making up the Dow Industrials hadn't managed to open because of the flood of sell orders. Even with the advantage of the Dow being calculated with so many stale prices from Friday's close, it was down 104 points, nearly matching Friday's 108-point loss, which had been the worst ever.

John Phelan had decided finance was not for him. He'd started his career as a clerk for his father's specialist firm, Phelan & Company, when he was sixteen years old and hated it. He told his father and went off to serve as a sergeant in the Marine Corps in Korea before giving finance another try in 1955. Phelan eventually decided to stay, and would spend years as a specialist himself, taking over his father's company in 1966 and then joining the exchange leadership. He was named to the unpaid position of vice chairman in 1975. In 1980 he became president, and then chairman and CEO in 1984. With a round face and receding hairline, Phelan in 1987 was the public personification of U.S. capitalism and an advocate for the spread of market economies to places that didn't understand the concept. In 1984 Phelan had gone to Communist China at the invitation of President Deng Xiaoping. In the customary exchange of gifts, Phelan was surprised to receive the first-ever stock certificate for a Chinese company, the Shanghai Feile Acoustics Company, a manufacturer of audio equipment.

On the morning of Monday, October 19, 1987, Phelan was an immensely powerful presence on Wall Street. At 10:45 A.M. he was hosting other Wall Street royalty in his office with the heads of Salomon Brothers, Merrill Lynch, First Boston, Prudential-Bache Securities, and Dean Witter. Phelan had just spoken by phone to the heads of Goldman Sachs, Shearson Lehman Brothers, and Bear Stearns. Despite the break in prices the previous week and that morning's selling pressure, Phelan believed that any exchange-wide trading halt would just deepen the emerging panic once the exchange reopened—if it could reopen, just as J. P. Morgan had feared eighty years earlier. Since only the president of the United States and the NYSE itself have the power to close the exchange—not even the SEC has that power—Phelan knew there would be calls for the exchange to close if Monday got much worse than Friday. But Phelan hadn't succeeded on Wall Street and then become chairman of the NYSE by demanding things from the men sitting in his office. Instead he knew how to co-opt them to his point of view. He asked for, and got, a consensus that the New York Stock Exchange would ride out the day and remain open, no matter how bad it got and no matter what others said.

At 10:45 A.M., about the time of the meeting in Phelan's office, IBM finally opened for trading at $125.00, down $10.00, or 7.4 percent, from Friday's close. At 10:48 A.M., Merck and Exxon opened down 14 percent and 8 percent, respectively, and once the rest of the Dow stocks were open, the extent of the damage could be understood. The Dow had fallen 104 points in the first hour, and in the next half hour, as most of the remaining stocks were finally being opened, it lost another 104 points. With the Dow down 208 points in the first ninety minutes, about double Friday's entire-day loss, the market finally found some footing, and the speculative trad-ers who had sold S&P 500 futures, thinking that the market might never be able to open, scampered to buy their positions back. Over the next thirty minutes the Dow cut its loss nearly in half.

At 11:30 A.M., not knowing that most stocks were now open and that the market was strengthening, SEC chairman Ruder stepped off the dais at the Mayflower Hotel in Washington, D.C., after giving a speech to an American Stock Exchange–sponsored conference. While desperate to get back to his office, Ruder knew he had to respond to the assembled reporters, and the first ques-tion was about a trading halt, which had made news when he'd mentioned it in the abstract after his first speech as chairman months before. Now he was more specific, saying he had been in touch with Phelan and that Ruder had given thought to such a halt. From that moment, the press was focused almost exclusively on the possibility of a trading halt.

Ruder didn't know that while he was giving his speech the mar-ket had started to rebound. Editors at Dow Jones News Service shelved Ruder's quote, questioning its relevance given the bounce, but other media outlets ran it, and eleven minutes later, the Ruder news hit the wire services under the headline "SEC Has Discussed Trading Halt. Not Now." Thirteen minutes later, there was a less definite and more worrisome headline: "Ruder on Halt: Anything Possible." But the market didn't need the second Ruder item before it started selling off again, which it did as soon as the idea of a trad-ing halt hit the tape.

At 11:45 A.M., about the time Ruder's quotes first reached trad-ers, the Dow continued to cut its loss slowly, but over the next sixty-eight minutes it dropped 87 points, as traders sold and as portfolio insurers returned aggressively; between 11:30 A.M. and 1:30 P.M. portfolio insurers sold another 10,000 futures contracts, worth $1.3 billion. Many of these futures contracts were bought by arbitrageurs who instantly transmitted sell orders to the NYSE via DOT in order to sell the basket represented by the futures they had bought. One portfolio insurer was also selling $400 million in stock.

The assumptions inherent in Black and Scholes's model, and by extension portfolio insurance, had now broken down. There might have been enough liquidity to support portfolio insurance when the market was trading normally, but with everyone wanting to sell at the same time, that liquidity had become a delusion. It was as if Leland's fear had come true. With everyone using portfolio insurance, he couldn't have liked the results. This same illusion of liquidity would cause the Flash Crash of 2010, when one hedging algorithm confused volume with liquidity, but the difference in 1987 is that some humans entering the orders came to understand the fundamental truth that liquidity vanishes as markets plummet. In LOR's offices, the trader responsible for executing sales of futures contracts dictated by the models eventually refused to relay the sell orders to the trading pit, explaining that "if I try to put on [sell] all the contracts [I'm supposed to] . . . I'm convinced the market will go to zero."

At 12:55 P.M., the Dow was at 2,053, down 194 points, or about 8.6 percent, and with the market weakening again, the Dow Jones News Service editor who had held the earlier story about Ruder and the potential for a trading halt realized the story was relevant now. At 1:09 P.M. Dow Jones reported the story without explaining that the quote was old and had been previously reported elsewhere. Investors, thinking this was a new statement and that a trading halt was again being considered, moved to sell before they were locked out of the market. Between 1:15 P.M. and 2:05 P.M., the Dow dropped to 1,969, a loss of 278 points, or 12.4 percent. This was the first time the Dow had traded below 2,000 since January 7 of that year. The Dow was still up 3.9 percent for the year, but it was 27.7 percent below August's high.

The likelihood of a trading halt was so muddled by now that

fear swamped greed, driving everyone to sell, and during the final two hours of trading, the Dow lost another 262 points. The Dow stopped falling only when the NYSE closed at 4:00 P.M.—its regular time.

The Dow had lost 508 points, a 22.6 percent drop that nearly doubled the worst daily performance to date, the 12.8 percent loss on October 28, 1929 (the two-day decline for October 28 and 29, 1929, was 23.0 percent, nearly identical to the October 19, 1987 loss). The Dow was down 8.3 percent for the year and was 36.1 percent below August's high. Six hundred four million shares worth $21 billion had traded on the NYSE, again nearly doubling the previous record. Only 52 stocks that trade on the NYSE finished the day higher—mostly gold and silver miners that were seen as a haven from the chaos—while almost 2,000 stocks fell. During the crash, from the close of trading on Tuesday, October 13, before the anti-takeover-tax bill and the horrible trade deficit report, to the close on Monday, October 19, the Dow had declined by nearly one-third, and total stock market losses equaled $1 trillion. NYSE specialists bought stock during the day in order to maintain orderly markets, but they now owned a combined $1.5 billion of stock, ten times what they would normally hold and nearly four times the amount they had ever owned before. Thirteen specialist firms, about one in every four, were at or under the exchange's warning level for capital reserves. Five firms, nearly one in ten, were in dire condition. At the end of Monday, only 58 percent of specialist firms were capable the next day of buying at least $5 million in stock, an unthinkably small amount.

Over the course of Monday, portfolio insurers had sold 33,000 S&P 500 futures contracts worth approximately $4 billion, and billions more in outright stock holdings.

As bad as the morning had been, the Dow lost 300 points, more than half its total loss, in the last seventy-five minutes of trading. The sheer velocity of the drop in those last seventy-five minutes meant that, despite all their selling early in the day and their best efforts during the final two hours, portfolio insurers once again lagged behind their models. That overhang of unexecuted selling, combined with a continued weakness in the futures after the NYSE close, meant no one was confident they'd seen the bottom.

John Phelan knew the press wanted to talk to him. He also recognized that if he came off as weak, it would terrify investors who were desperate to hear from someone in whom they could place their confidence. As he addressed the fifty reporters assembled in an overly ornate NYSE meeting room, Phelan was masterful. Asked if the day qualified as a "panic," he pushed back. He ran through the bull market of the previous five years to address how the market had gotten here, reinforcing the idea that the economy was healthy and that the market would be able to "work out of this on its own." He said the specialist firms were in good shape, even though many were not, and he explained the practical and perception problems inherent in a trading halt, channeling J. P. Morgan in questioning what it would take to reopen the exchange if it ever closed simply because of too much selling. Phelan spoke slowly, answered every question, and used less jargon than he might have, recognizing that this was a new cast of reporters, many of whom may not have known much about the exchange or the markets. One who did know was John Dorfman, a reporter for the *Wall Street Journal* who was so comforted by Phelan's performance that he later remembered "there was talk among the reporters about how assured and in command Phelan seemed to be. He just dominated that press conference." Phelan was a lonely bright spot, maybe the only bright spot, in the worst day the American stock market had ever had.

The American stock market had its worst day ever by nearly a factor of two, and the signs for the next day weren't good: momentum was clearly lower, and that momentum had increased in the final hour of the day; portfolio insurers were again woefully under-hedged; and selling had continued in the S&P 500 futures pit after the NYSE closed. Yet many of those who lived through both days would say that Tuesday, October 20, was worse, and at one point that day, all hope had vanished.

The first problem was that the losers in the S&P futures had to pay the winners. On a normal day, losers owe the Chicago Mercantile Exchange clearinghouse a net of about $250 million, and winners are in turn owed that amount. On Tuesday morning, the total was $2.5 billion.

The clearinghouse of the CME is ostensibly separate from the exchange, but ultimately the guy in charge of paying and collecting is a Chicagoan who'd been born Leibel Melamdovich in Bialystok, Poland. As a child he fled the Nazis with his mother and mathematics teacher father, reaching America via Lithuania and Japan. As a law student in Chicago in the 1960s, the renamed Leo Melamed needed a job as a law clerk. Believing that Merrill Lynch, Pierce, Fenner & Beane had to be a law firm, with all those names in the title, Leo applied for a clerk's job and was hired, as a trading clerk and runner, on the floor of the CME. Twenty years later, on October 19, 1987, Leo Melamed was chairman of the same exchange.

Melamed had always been particularly protective of the S&P 500 index futures, explaining that he felt like their "author." They had been a tremendous success for the CME and had increased efficiency in the entire financial arena. As chairman, he was proud that the CME was able to provide as much, or more, liquidity than any other exchange in the world, including the NYSE, but he wondered if the selling demanded by portfolio insurance was too much. He once called portfolio insurance "some fictional thing" and explained that when he first heard of the concept, he "laughed," realizing as most traders do that liquidity disappears when it's needed most. He'd even gone to government regulators earlier that year to ask about implementing limits on how far the S&P 500 futures price could fall in a single day. Melamed was fearful that something like portfolio insurance might snowball, leading to finger-pointing that would focus unfairly on the CME.

Like the rest of the exchange leadership, Melamed spent Monday night at the CME, making certain that the firms that owed the CME clearinghouse $2.5 billion were paying it so that those who were owed could in turn be paid. As the night wore on, it became obvious that one giant firm with exposure in S&P futures, exposure that might be offset elsewhere but that might be naked, owed the exchange $1 billion, and it was slow in paying. If a single clearing firm, the two hundred or so firms charged with presenting trades to the CME clearinghouse on behalf of customers and handling the bookkeeping for customer trading accounts, was unable to make good on its trades by the appointed hour early the next morning, the CME would not be able to open. The exchange's rules were strict: everyone pays and gets paid the next day, or the exchange doesn't open.

Alan Greenspan's question to Melamed when the two talked earlier that evening was simple: "Will you open tomorrow?" The only thing that could keep the CME from opening on Tuesday was if the firms that owed it money, those that had been long S&P 500 futures, didn't pay. Melamed's answer was less simple: "I do not know."

Melamed decided to face the biggest problem first, the $1 billion, and he went straight to the top, calling the firm's chairman. Later he marveled at the surreal nature of the situation, what must it have been like to wake up to a phone call from Chicago at 2:00 A.M. on October 20, from someone you don't know, who's saying, "You owe us one billion dollars, and we want our money."

Slowly, most of the money, including the $1 billion, dribbled in, and at 8:00 A.M. Eastern Time, twenty minutes before the CME's scheduled open for interest rate and foreign exchange futures and the deadline for all the money to be in, $100 million was still missing from the clearinghouse's account at Continental Illinois Bank. Continental Illinois and the other banks that worked with the CME often drew down a clearing firm's prearranged lines of credit to cover any shortfall. But when Leo got on the phone with Wilma Smeltzer, the banker at Continental Illinois handling the account that was short, he heard what he already knew: "Leo, we have $2.4 billion. There is still $100 million missing." But he also heard something he didn't know but feared: "And it does not look like it is going to make it." If the CME didn't open on time, it was unlikely to open at all, since rumors would fly that its clearinghouse was insolvent. It wouldn't matter, and the world wouldn't care, that it was just $100 million. It might as well have been ten times that amount or a thousand times that amount; the cascade would begin anew, and this time it was unlikely to stop.

Melamed shouted, "You mean you are going to let a stinking one hundred million dollars stand in the way? Just advance the money." Melamed knew that even if a clearing firm had exhausted its cash on hand and prearranged credit lines, Smeltzer's bank could extend additional credit in the form of a "daylight overdraft," which was to be satisfied during the course of that day.

"Leo, I cannot do that."

Now Melamed was pleading: "Wilma, we know the customer. They're good for the hundred million."

"I know that too, Leo, but I don't have that kind of authority." Melamed later learned that his $100 million ask was ten times the amount Smeltzer was authorized to advance.

The market had crashed—the *Wall Street Journal* said so on page one that morning—and it was due to a confluence of events, large and small. Raiders had come to understand the unseen value in some companies, then bid them beyond the sustainable value of their cash flows. Leland and Rubinstein had created portfolio insurance, and O'Brien had sold it despite its inherent weaknesses.

The market had rallied as the economy improved, and interest rates had come down; then the rally had shifted into another gear at the start of the year. The trade deficit got out of hand and the dollar got crushed, and the House Ways and Means Committee decided to kill hostile takeovers. But one small bit of serendipity occurred with about five minutes to spare: Tom Theobold, the chairman of Continental Illinois, happened into Smeltzer's office.

"Hold it, Leo, there is Theo. I'll ask him." A quiet moment later, Wilma came back. "Leo, Tom said it's okay to advance the money." Melamed later explained that Theobold happening into Smeltzer's office at the very moment he was needed was a "pure accident."

Now Melamed could return Alan Greenspan's call and report good news. When he was told that the CME would open, and would do so on time, Greenspan's reply was a simple but heartfelt: "Thank you very much."

The Chicago Mercantile Exchange opened, on time. About thirty minutes later Continental Illinois got back the $100 million it had floated, and though there were mumblings about whether the CME clearinghouse was solvent, once the exchange managed to open on time, the questions were muted.

Continental Illinois had taken a small risk in funding a clearing firm, but many banks seemed uninterested in joining them. E. Gerald Corrigan, president of the Federal Reserve Bank of New York and Alan Greenspan's right-hand man, was calling the nation's biggest banks and telling them to lend, particularly to other financial firms. One banker later described Corrigan's Tuesday morning message to bankers as "We're here. Whatever you need, we'll give you."

The first step in the Fed's campaign to assure banks and the market that while there might be problems, liquidity wasn't one of them, was the statement Greenspan had disseminated earlier that morning: "The Federal Reserve, consistent with its responsibilities as the Nation's central bank, affirmed today its readiness to serve as a source of liquidity to support the economic and financial system." The Fed had broadcast its willingness to be the lender of last resort. Bankers eventually took Greenspan and Corrigan at their word. On a normal day, Citibank had loans of $300 million outstanding to securities firms; at the end of the day on October 20, it had $1.4 billion.

DOT began accepting orders at 8:00 A.M. on Tuesday, and thirty minutes later sell orders marginally outweighed buy orders; but the tide started going out, and at 9:00 A.M., thirty minutes before the open, there were nearly twice as many shares to be sold as bought. In reaction, just before its opening, the NYSE asked its members to abstain from using DOT to execute "program trades," the consolidated selling (or buying) of baskets of stock made up of many different issues. Even though that morning's prohibition was presented as a request, everyone realized it was really a threat. DOT was now closed to index arbs, meaning that the link between the price of the futures contract in Chicago and the price of the stocks represented was broken.

Phelan's focus was on the specialist firms. He was not asking questions he didn't want answered, and he later said, "On Tuesday there wasn't any [specialist] firm that told us they couldn't open, otherwise we would have reallocated their stocks [to other specialist firms]. At a time like this, we just want to know whether they're in or not, we're not interested in the details." Many specialists were unacceptably weak, and for some the vulnerability was too much. A. B. Tompane & Company was typical. A sixty-year-old specialist firm that weathered the crash of 1929 and the resulting depression was in 1987 responsible for maintaining markets in twenty-seven different stocks, including Royal Dutch Petroleum, Chemical Bank, and USX, the former U.S. Steel. Tompane was already looking for help and would be acquired by Merrill Lynch at 3:00 A.M. on Wednesday.

In an effort to help firms like Tompane, the NYSE spread the word that specialists would have even more latitude than normal in setting opening prices on Tuesday morning. Phelan would be quoted later as saying, "We had two goals Tuesday morning. One, get rid of [the specialists'] inventory [that $1.5 billion of stock they owned]; two, but don't go too high [with the opening price] or you won't get rid of it."

Despite the weight of sell orders in DOT (those entered before the exchange's prohibition were executed), the orders that were hand carried to the specialists leaned slightly to the buy side, and the buy orders were market orders, telling the specialist to pay whatever was required. Buyers realized stocks were trading at a substantial discount to value, so rather than specify a maximum price they were willing to pay (a "limit order") and risk not buying the stock, their orders were to simply buy at the best available price the market offered (a market order).

With the preponderance of market orders, the specialists had a unique opportunity. They could essentially open a stock at whatever price they wanted. The imbalances between those wishing to buy and those wishing to sell were so severe in some stocks that opening of ninety-two NYSE issues was delayed. But for the stocks that did open, the specialists made the most, and sometimes too much, of the market orders to buy. Atlantic Richfield, one of the thirty members of the Dow, opened at $75.00, $10.00 or 15.4 percent above Monday's close. One particularly notorious specialist opened trading in J.P. Morgan Bank late, but they did eventually open at $47.00, which was $19.25, or 69.4 percent, above Monday's close and $5.38 or 12.9 percent above where it had closed on the previous Friday.

Coca-Cola opened at $40.00, up nearly $10, and almost precisely where it had closed the previous Friday, as if the specialist was trying to make it seem that Monday had never happened. Johnson & Johnson opened higher by an identical $10 at $75.50.

Even if stocks didn't open, the specialists tried to bluff their way to higher prices. General Electric had closed on Monday at $41.88. Though delayed, when asked at 9:52, twenty-two minutes after it was supposed to open for trading, the specialist for GE said he thought it would open between $45.00 and $65.00.

On the back of the specialists' best efforts and bargain hunting by investors, the Dow at 10:27 A.M. was at 1,936, a rally of nearly 200 points, or more than 11 percent. For those stocks that were open, the specialists didn't waste the opportunity. The SEC would later say specialists were "very heavy sellers on the opening transactions and during the first 30 minutes of trading."

The S&P futures also opened higher, up 10.7 percent. But while the Dow continued higher after the first thirty minutes, thanks to those stocks that were opened both late and substantially higher, the S&P futures were signaling trouble. Portfolio insurers had returned, but as they had on Monday, they were being patient, working to avoid overwhelming the market with the futures they still had to sell. However, at 9:50 A.M., they caught up more aggressively, eventually selling $500 million of futures in the first hour of the day.

Index arbitrage was the mechanism that kept the futures price in line with the value of the basket of stocks the futures represented, and the value of stocks in line with what the futures were saying. Restricting access to DOT eliminated index arbitrage, but it didn't mean the selling pressure wasn't transmitted in other ways.

At 10:30 A.M., with most stocks opened at unsustainably high levels and with portfolio insurers once again selling in the S&P futures, the rally was dead. General Electric, the stock that had been indicated as high as $65.00 before it opened, a price that would have been more than 55 percent above Monday's close of $41.88 and more than 28 percent higher than it had closed on Friday, a price that would have been less than $2 from the highest price GE had ever traded at, finally opened for trading at $46.50, up a much more modest, but still unsustainable, 11 percent. J.P.

Morgan, which had opened at an unrealistically high $47.00, was collapsing; it would trade at $29.00 later in the day.

Investors and traders—and specialists are the quintessential traders—deal with the tension between fear and greed every day, but on October 20, 1987, the greed to open stocks at high prices, greed that had been sanctioned by the leadership of the NYSE because it would allow specialists to unload their $1.5 billion inventory of stocks at acceptable prices, completely overtook the fear that stock prices would collapse from unrealistic levels before they could finish that selling.

During the next hour, everything plummeted. The Dow fell 225 points from its 1,936 high, made just before 10:30 A.M. Portfolio insurers continued selling in the S&P futures—between 10:30 A.M. and 11:00 A.M. they sold another $340 million worth of futures—and with DOT closed to index arbs, the futures fell well below the value of the basket of stocks, suggesting to traders that the smart money that had access to the futures pit was selling aggressively. Just before 11:00 A.M., selling in the futures market had driven the price so low it was trading at a 19 percent discount to the basket of stocks it represented, like being able to buy a one-dollar bill for 81 cents in spare change. The discount was a profoundly troubling signal that couldn't be easily narrowed, since DOT was closed. In New York, investors watching the S&P futures price decided that that must be the appropriate value of stocks and continued to sell the issues they could as specialists were inundated. Overwhelmed by the selling, the specialists shifted into slow mode—like the tellers at the Knickerbocker Trust in 1907—and trading volume evaporated. Phelan would later say, "The scary part about Tuesday morning was the vacuum developing. The volume slowed way down, and you had the idea of it just going into a 500-point free fall with absolutely no bids."

After the first hour's Pyrrhic victory, the second hour turned into a disaster as stocks fell to losses on the day despite, or due to, inexcusably high opening prices. Portfolio insurers denied access to DOT, and refusing to sell S&P futures at the giant discount to value that was demanded in Chicago, again did portfolio insurance the old-fashioned way, by dispatching NYSE floor brokers with paper orders to the specialists at their trading posts. Between 11:00 A.M. and 11:30 A.M., brokers dumped orders to sell 6.3 million shares of stock for portfolio insurers on the specialists. Another 1.1 million shares would be sold in similar fashion for other program traders, likely index arbs who were buying futures in Chicago at the massive discount. The selling by program traders in this half hour would be more than twice as much as any other half hour of the day. One specialist had a crowd of floor brokers standing in front of him with orders to sell a total of 500,000 shares of stock, while the specialist didn't have a single buy order in his book waiting to be executed at any price, no matter how low.

By 11:31 A.M., ten of the thirty stocks making up the Dow had halted trading because of the selling pressure. Those closed included giants IBM, Philip Morris, and Sears, Roebuck. Merck had opened for trading at 9:46 A.M. but was overwhelmed by selling pressure and closed just eight minutes later. DuPont never managed to open at all. Given the Dow's weighting scheme, stocks making up more than half the average were not trading. Though the Dow would continue to be calculated and disseminated, as it had been the day before, input prices were again stale and much higher than reality; the Dow was falling quickly, but it was also understating how bad things were.

With so many stocks closed to sellers in New York, the selling shifted back to Chicago, and between approximately 11:50 A.M. and 12:10 P.M., the S&P futures collapsed from 206 to 181, a price that translated to 1,400 for the Dow, which had started the month at 2596.28.

With so few stocks actually trading and the few that remained open falling precipitously, calls started for the entire New York

Stock Exchange to close. Phelan would later say that the exchange had been fully committed to staying open on Monday, but at noon on Tuesday, "It seemed like everyone wanted to close." The NYSE doesn't operate alone, and Phelan knew he had to call Leo Melamed in Chicago and let him know what he was thinking so Melamed could prepare to halt trading in the S&P 500 futures pit if it became necessary. On a conference call, Phelan explained, "Well, we don't want to close," but said it was something the exchange had to consider.

Melamed heard something else and said later that Phelan explained he was going to get board approval to close. Although the two men would subsequently disagree over the details of the conversation, Melamed was convinced that the closing of the New York Stock Exchange was imminent. Not only do CME rules require closing the S&P pit if the NYSE isn't trading, but Melamed knew that a closure of the NYSE would be the ultimate manifestation of fear, and that if the S&P futures remained open once the NYSE had closed, the entire world would try to sell S&P futures at any price. Yesterday the LOR trader responsible for executing sells in the futures pit had been afraid he'd drive the price down to zero. Believing the NYSE was set to close, Melamed was now afraid of the same thing.

At 12:15 P.M., Melamed watched as a CME staffer with a bullhorn waded into the S&P futures pit and read a brief statement that closed trading. Six minutes later, the Dow made its low for the day, 1616.21. Even this pitiful number was artificially high due to trading halts, but the Dow was now down 122.53 points, or 7.0 percent, for the day. It was down 980.07 points, or 37.7 percent, for the month, and 1106.21 points, or 40.6 percent, from the August high reached just fifty-six days earlier. Troublingly, closing the S&P futures pit didn't seem to help stocks in New York, because between noon and 1:00 P.M., another 161 issues were halted.

After calling Melamed in Chicago, Phelan stayed on the phone, spreading the word that he had a fallback plan, but if the selling pressure got much worse, the NYSE would have to close. He called Corrigan at the New York Federal Reserve and Ruder at the SEC. He called White House Chief of Staff Howard Baker, who told Phelan, "You're at the helm. Do whatever you have to do. You have our full support." But Baker wasn't taking any chances, and he instructed the White House counsel to draft the document that would allow President Reagan to force closure of the exchange.

At 12:30 P.M., officials from the NYSE trading floor again pressed Phelan with the specialists' appeals that he close the exchange. Phelan didn't give in, but he did tell the officials to check with him in thirty minutes. Phelan knew the market could fall again, that it "was off 100 points and looked like it had potential to drop another 200 or 300. It looked like it would go again; it would be faster and heavier than the day before because there would be panic in the system." Phelan also must have known the specialists were past their financial limits, and now the big securities firms who'd been in favor of staying open on Monday no matter what happened were calling the SEC and asking them to pressure the exchange into closing. But Phelan thought that an exchange-wide closure was the last possible step. As J. P. Morgan had recognized, Phelan knew that closing the exchange would highlight the severity of the problem. "The strain on the country . . . would be taken as an extremely bad sign," he said. "If we close it, we would never open it."

Many stocks were halted, and the S&P futures pit in Chicago was closed, so it would be easy to assume that any outlet for selling pressure would be inundated, but at 12:38 P.M. an obscure stock index futures contract turned out to be the market's lifeline. The Chicago Board of Trade (CBOT) was the largest futures exchange in the world, located five blocks southeast of the CME at the foot of Chicago's LaSalle Street canyon. The rivalry between the two Chicago exchanges was fierce, and when the CME started trading futures on the S&P 500, the CBOT launched an effort to trade futures on the Dow Jones Industrial Average. When the family that controlled the Dow Jones empire balked at licensing the Dow for a futures contract, the CBOT instead launched the Major Market Index (MMI) futures, based on an index of twenty blue-chip stocks very similar to the Dow. By 1987, the MMI, as it had come to be known, had lost the fight for institutional investor attention to the S&P 500, but the MMI futures were still a creditable if not quite dazzling presence on the CBOT floor. Now it became the site of the stock market's salvation. As traders waited to hear that the NYSE had finally closed, MMI futures experienced what the *Wall Street Journal* would call "the most powerful rally in its history." With so many markets and individual stocks closed, the MMI futures were thinly traded, with almost no liquidity, so when aggressive buyers bid for 808 contracts worth just $60 million, the MMI surged. By 12:40 P.M., just two minutes after the buying commenced, it had driven the MMI futures to a premium over the value of the basket of stocks making up the index.

Just as traders were seeing or hearing of the stunning rally in the MMI, buy orders started to dribble into the NYSE. Some of the orders were from corporations tentatively buying back their own stock. The investment banks hadn't been just wringing their hands, watching the Dow crater. They had been calling corporate clients and suggesting that they buy back their own stock at the steep discounts to where the stock was trading just two months before. A single investment bank, First Boston, called two hundred corporate clients and recommended immediate buybacks. Even Howard Baker, the White House chief of staff, who earlier in the day had instructed White House counsel to draft the documents that would forcibly close the NYSE, called corporate CEOs and circuitously asked them to buy back stock.

Financial firms were overrepresented in the buybacks—they can't really recommend clients execute buybacks if they're not willing to do so themselves—and Shearson Lehman Brothers, Citicorp, and Merrill Lynch executed buybacks of their own stock. Companies like Allegis and USX, which were takeover targets just a week ago, were also overrepresented. They were trading at even bigger discounts than the average stock thanks to Representative Dan Rostenkowski's Ways and Means Committee and the attack on potential acquirers. At its low on Tuesday, Allegis was trading at a 46.9 percent discount to its closing price just before the tax deal was announced on Wednesday. USX was trading at a 43.8 percent discount, while both Gillette and Dayton Hudson had been cut by more than half.

At 12:40 P.M. the buying had the MMI trading at a giant premium to the basket. When it was at a discount, the weakness was transmitted to the stock market. Now the index arbs were selling the MMI futures and entering orders to buy stocks. If someone was trying to save the market by manipulating it higher, they picked the right time and the right vehicle in the MMI. Made up of just twenty stocks, each an absolute blue chip, it spoke for the broad market. And there was another strange reversal: the rush of buy orders for blue-chips and takeover names overwhelmed the shares available for sale on the NYSE; at 12:43 P.M. the specialist for USX halted the stock due to a buy imbalance.

Between 12:30 P.M. and 1:05 P.M., the Dow gained more than 120 points as specialists took advantage of the S&P 500 pit closure and the inability of portfolio insurers to use DOT, as well as the small dribble of buy orders coming in and reopening their stocks. With this turn, it became obvious the NYSE would remain open, and Phelan called Leo Melamed in Chicago with the news. The CME reopened the S&P futures pit at 1:04 P.M., and the rally was strong there, too. The reopening price was 213, 16.4 percent above the going price when the contract had been halted. It was still trading at a discount to the basket, but the tenor of trading was substantially better in both New York and Chicago.

As more buyback orders hit New York, the stocks that hadn't reopened would do so soon. Merck reopened at 1:15 P.M.; IBM reopened eleven minutes later. USX reopened after its halt for a buy imbalance at 2:00 P.M., and the specialists learned their lesson and reopened at reasonable, sustainable price levels. Merck reopened lower than the previous day's close. IBM reopened unchanged from yesterday's close, and USX reopened up just 63 cents. The discount in the S&P futures and the reopening of most stocks gave committed sellers a chance, and the rally tailed off a bit—the Dow lost 80 points of the 120 it had gained between 12:30 P.M. and 1:05 P.M.—but it never again threatened to hit the 1616.21 low from earlier that day.

Just after 2:00 P.M. the rally strengthened. In the next ninety minutes, the Dow gained another 170 points. It was now at 1,919, more than 200 points and more than 12 percent above its low that morning. Although the Dow gave back 80 points in the final thirty minutes of the day, it was seen for what it was, position squaring by short-term traders. It was not enough to extinguish the emerging optimism. The Dow closed on Tuesday with a gain of 102.27, the biggest point gain ever to date, a gain of 5.9 percent on NYSE volume of 608 million shares, even greater volume than had traded on Monday.

The frenetic rally in the MMI futures that afternoon established the floor for the market. Many, including an investigator for the Senate Finance Committee and numerous journalists, among them some from the *Wall Street Journal*, would wonder if the closure of the S&P 500 futures pit and the subsequent buying in the MMI contract was a premeditated manipulation by someone trying to save the market. But it was the surge of buyback orders—on Monday and Tuesday, American corporations would announce a total of $6.2 billion of share buybacks—hitting the NYSE trading floor Tuesday afternoon that extended the recovery long enough so that it could be believed.

The 1987 crash was over. Portfolio insurance had been disgraced, and the House Ways and Means Committee would walk back its plans to kill takeovers. The week after the crash, committee chairman Rostenkowski suggested that the anti-takeover tax provisions might be changed, and he reinforced his remarks the next day, October 29, when he said he would agree to a "reasonable compromise" on the issue.

October 19, 1987, remains the worst day the American stock market has ever had. The year's symmetry was startling, since 1987 had started with the longest winning streak the American stock market had ever known. But the stock market would recover, and a new all-time high was made in August 1989, one day short of exactly two years since the previous high. The 1987 crash tempered the greed of the "Me Decade." But the market would crash again.

MELTDOWN

2008

M arion Sandler went to business meetings with her husband and sat knitting quietly. She made him sweaters, which he wore to work, presumably to meetings where she was knitting him other sweaters. Herb Sandler was a Columbia University-trained attorney and co-CEO of a California-based savings and loan, the grandiosely named World Savings, whose nearly exclusive business was savings accounts and home loans for middle-income buyers.

Herb's co-CEO was his sweater-knitting wife. Despite Marion's homebody persona, she was a Phi Beta Kappa graduate of Wellesley, with an MBA from New York University. She was the second female professional to work on Wall Street and the first woman to work at the firm of Dominick & Dominick in any capacity other than secretary. While there, most of her time was taken with analyzing publicly traded savings and loans for investment clients. In 1961, she moved to Oppenheimer & Company, where she continued to focus on savings and loans.

The Sandlers met on a Hamptons, Long Island, beach in 1960.

They were both living in New York. Herb was doing legal work for the sort of savings and loans Marion spent her days dissecting. As they fell in love, they realized they shared a disdain for the way most savings and loans did business. So, in 1963, just after marrying, they moved to California to see if they couldn't do better. They got some seed money from Marion's brother and spent $3.8 million to acquire a small savings and loan in gritty and inexpensive Oakland. When they bought it, Golden West Savings had two offices, twenty-six employees, and just $34 million in deposits.

The Sandlers were no longer backseat drivers, and they put what they'd learned in New York to use. First, they fixated on costs, not only the cost imposed by mortgages that went bad but the cost of running their Golden West branches. They initially refused to offer checking accounts because of the expense. They knew what time of day and what day of the week depositors showed up, so they put part-time workers on those shifts rather than have full-time employees during the entire business day. They refused to install automated teller machines because they couldn't justify the cost. The business press referred to the entire organization as "penny pinching" because branch managers billed headquarters when visiting executives made phone calls on branch lines. Through that discipline, Marion and Herb built a successful if smallish business, until they merged with World Savings in 1975, keeping the World Savings brand although the corporate entity retained the Golden West name.

The early 1980s were a difficult time for many savings and loans like Golden West. Their business involved borrowing money from depositors overnight and lending it to homebuyers for thirty years. The mismatch in timing was enormous and dangerous. Since deposits could leave at any moment—and would if the savings and loan down the street offered a higher rate of interest—there was always the risk that the interest rate a savings and loan had to pay to attract and keep deposits would become higher than the rate being paid on the mortgages it had already written.

The obvious solution was for a mortgage to have an interest rate that adjusted to reflect the current cost of money, but, prior to 1981, adjustable-rate mortgages were illegal; in 1971 and 1974 consumer advocates had fought against authorizing them because of worry about "payment shock," an abrupt increase in a mortgage's monthly payment caused by an increase in interest rates and the long wait between resets in the payment due. When interest rates rose dramatically in the late 1970s, many savings and loans had to pay more in interest than they were collecting, driving many into bankruptcy. Congress had little choice but to make adjustable-rate mortgages, known as ARMs, legal in 1981. Federal banking regulators, charged with ensuring the soundness of banks, actively encouraged savings and loans to offer ARMs because they nearly eliminated interest rate risk.

Marion and Herb Sandler didn't invent the adjustable-rate mortgage, but they were responsible for a notable change when they added their own twist. The "Pick-a-Payment" adjustable-rate mortgage let a homeowner select one of four payment amounts each month. The lowest allowable payment didn't even cover the interest due that month; another payment option covered just the interest due; a third included the interest as well as enough principal to pay off the mortgage in thirty years; and the largest payment paid all the interest and enough principal to retire the mortgage in fifteen years. It became known as an "option ARM," and since the interest rate on a Golden West Pick-a-Payment option ARM mortgage reset every month, there was no "payment shock." Doing away with the payment shock allowed Golden West to lower its default risk. These were not what would come to be called subprime loans.

Nearly every loan the Sandlers made was accompanied by a

down payment of at least 15 percent, and their average down payment was nearly 30 percent. And although Golden West was notoriously cheap, they spent money in areas they thought necessary. For example, Golden West hated using independent real estate appraisers despite the lower cost, because they felt these appraisers couldn't be trusted, so most homes were appraised by a Golden West employee.

But the key to Golden West's profitability was the Pick-a-Payment feature, because it let them charge about one percentage point more in interest than traditional fixed-rate mortgage competitors. By spending less and charging more, Golden West Savings earned a lucrative spread of about three percentage points on their loans. Even when it later became popular for banks and savings and loans to sell off mortgages to be bundled into mortgage-backed securities, Golden West remained a rarity, a "portfolio lender," a firm that kept the loans it made, bearing the risk of default in order to enjoy the profit.

Marion Sandler was no Madame Defarge, knitting quietly while the revolution decayed into anarchy. Rather, the Sandlers had a sensible product that borrowers demanded and that they could sell at a premium because of the flexibility it offered. The Sandlers' creation of the option ARM was a little like man's discovery of fire. It warmed him and cooked his food until others took it, and similar financial innovations, and used them to burn down the economy.

If the mortgage business had a drawback, it was scale. Bankers made loans to neighbors and people they knew. A lender like Golden West was dependent on a borrower walking into a branch, which restricted them to a geographic area. Also, eventually a savings and loan would saturate its market. But at that point, a savings and loan would have a big portfolio of mortgages that paid regular interest. This meant a portfolio of mortgages was very similar to a bond; a portfolio of mortgages would sustain the occasional foreclosure, but if the bankers were reasonably careful, those losses would be small, and the mortgages would pay an attractive interest rate.

The higher yield and the bondlike nature of a portfolio of mortgages eventually attracted the notice of institutional investors such as pension funds. While pension funds and other institutional investors flush with cash might have wanted to buy a portfolio of mortgages, that would have been enormously unwieldy, leaving the pension fund responsible for collecting monthly payments, making property tax and insurance payments, and tending to defaults and foreclosures.

Then, in 1970, the Government National Mortgage Association, known as Ginnie Mae, created the first mortgage-backed security, essentially a pool of mortgages owned jointly by many investors. Everyone who owned a chunk of the pool owned a chunk that was identical to every other chunk. Some fiduciaries, such as pension funds, couldn't invest like that; they had charters that demanded investments be very high quality, higher than a simple pool of mortgages with default risk. So, in 1983, another government-sponsored entity, the Federal Home Loan Mortgage Corporation, known as Freddie Mac, assembled a pool of mortgages and then split it up. But this time they split it into risk levels rather than identical chunks.

The individual mortgages weren't assigned to any particular risk level (the risk levels became known as tranches, from the French word for "slice"). The first tranche to be paid was the least risky and offered the lowest interest rate. The last to be paid was obviously the riskiest and therefore offered the highest return. Investors who needed more safety could now invest in the mortgage market through these safest tranches—and they did, because even though they were extremely safe, they paid more in interest than Treasury bonds. In 1983, before Freddie Mac first tranched a pool of mortgages into layers of risk, American pension plans had no money invested in the mortgage market, even though they had more than half a trillion dollars in assets. Just three years later, they held mortgage-backed securities worth $30 billion, about 5 percent of their assets.

Now a mortgage lender no longer had to stash every mortgage in its vault for thirty years. Instead it could sell them to be bundled into mortgage-backed securities that would then be sliced into tranches, with the tranches again sold to investors. It appeared to be an interesting solution, but with this selling and tranching and selling again, the link between the borrower and the ultimate lender—the investor who owned the tranche—was slowly being destroyed.

Just after 9:00 P.M. on Thursday, March 23, 1989, a ship eased from Alaska's Alyeska Pipeline Terminal and headed for Long Beach, California. Nearly a thousand feet long, the *Valdez* was one of the newest tankers in Exxon's fleet and carried more than 50 million gallons of North Slope crude oil in its eleven cargo tanks.

After leaving Alyeska and sailing west through Valdez Arm, the *Valdez* turned southwest and entered its assigned tanker traffic separation lane; to avoid collisions, tankers entering and leaving Valdez followed separation lanes through the navigable portion of Prince William Sound. At 11:25 P.M., the *Valdez* captain informed the onshore traffic center that he preferred to maintain speed of 12 knots rather than slow as he moved through the icebergs that had been reported. To avoid the ice, he requested clearance to cross the half-mile-wide separation zone that serves like the grassy median on a highway so that he could move into the lane for oncoming tankers. After checking that there was no inbound traffic, controllers agreed. What the traffic center didn't know was that the captain had steered the *Valdez* onto a southerly heading, across the separation zone, across the inbound lane he was supposed to stay in, and beyond the inbound lane's eastern boundary. That meant that at 11:47 P.M. the *Valdez* was two dangerous miles from the center of—and was now beyond—the navigable channel through the sound. A few minutes later, Exxon's *Valdez* ran aground on Bligh Reef, at the northern boundary of Prince William Sound. The rocky bottom of the sound tore open eight of the *Valdez*'s eleven cargo tanks, each of which extended the entire length of the ship.

More than 10.5 million gallons of crude oil poured from the *Valdez* to congeal in the icy water before it floated off, eventually coating fifteen hundred miles of Alaskan shoreline. The *Exxon Valdez* spill was an ecological disaster, but the financial contraption created in response to Exxon's liability would result in a different kind of damage nineteen years later.

Florida's Boca Raton Resort and Club is a pink-stuccoed Moorish giant built in the grand style of the 1920s and draws wealthy vacationers and groups of businesspeople on expense accounts. In 1994, J.P. Morgan & Company's "swaps team" assembled there for an "off-site" brainstorming weekend. A swap is a particular type of derivative in which two parties agree to exchange cash flows from two separate but related assets. The J.P. Morgan team included the traders and salespeople who would help clients execute swaps in order to hedge away a particular risk. The goal of the weekend was to engineer new financial products the team could peddle in the cutthroat world of investment banking. The weekend had its share of debauchery—at least one nose was broken, one jet-ski was destroyed and billed to an unsuspecting colleague's room, and a lot of people ended up in the pool fully clothed—but the assembled bankers also came up with a good idea.

Exxon had just borrowed $4.8 billion from J.P. Morgan & Company in anticipation of paying a $5 billion fine for the *Exxon Valdez* debacle, which left all that congealed crude oil on all that formerly pristine Alaskan coastline.

Morgan wasn't particularly worried about Exxon defaulting on the loan; the oil company remained a solid credit risk. Even so, a bank like Morgan was required to sequester capital to cover the small but real risk of default. In the case of Exxon's $4.8 billion loan, Morgan had to set aside an additional $384 million in reserves— money that would be sitting idle, not earning a nickel, instead of being lent out to others who would have been charged 7 percent interest, about $26.9 million a year. Reserving such an enormous sum of money to cover an unlikely default made extending the loan less profitable for Morgan.

As they brainstormed in Boca Raton, the Morgan swaps team realized they needed someone who could ensure that Exxon's loan would be satisfied, like a cosigner for hire, who would dramatically reduce the risk and allow Morgan to put those sequestered reserves to better use. If the price was right, this insurance would cost less, maybe much less, than what Morgan could make loaning those reserves back out.

Blythe Masters has become a legend on Wall Street for coming up with the idea of paying a third party with deep pockets an up-front fee to bear the risk of Exxon defaulting. Masters was just twenty-five years old. She had been born in the English county of Oxfordshire, sixty miles west of London, and attended a school dripping with British tradition, the elite King's School Canterbury, which, having been founded in A.D. 597, was considered to be the world's oldest school. From there, Masters went to Cambridge, where she graduated with a degree in economics. She joined J.P. Morgan & Company in 1991. Lean, fair-complexioned, an accomplished equestrian, and blessed with a perfect "BBC voice," she was thought of as quintessentially British, despite a modest upbringing and voracious ambition.

Masters recognized how the Exxon loan guarantee deal should work and which of her clients might be willing to bear the risk in exchange for payment. The client was the European Bank for

Reconstruction and Development (EBRD). Anxious to put its money to work, the EBRD was happy to be paid to shoulder the small likelihood that Exxon would default on its loan, which in the banking world was known as a credit default. Morgan would pay EBRD cash in exchange for the latter's promise to pay off Exxon's loan if it defaulted. Morgan called it a credit default swap.

The Exxon/EBRD credit default swap was a revelation, in that it separated the risk inherent in J.P. Morgan's loan from the loan itself. Yet as ingenious as this bifurcation was, it was also insidious, because, like the Sandlers' option ARM, others would seize on the concept and pervert it.

By 1997, it seemed that every bank had caught on and had begun peddling its own version of the credit default swap. That's when Blythe Masters and the J.P. Morgan swaps team decided to extend the concept. Morgan identified 307 commercial loans it had on its books, totaling $9.7 billion. These loans were eating up more than three-quarters of a billion dollars in reserves, money that was sitting idle in a vault. Morgan bankers wondered if they could buy credit default swap protection for the entire portfolio of loans.

Unlike the Exxon loan, the diversification offered by 307 loans made to 307 different borrowers should reduce the likelihood of a crippling loss. However, that diversification created problems of its own; it seemed impossible for an insurer to do satisfactory due diligence on each of the 307 debtors.

As the Morgan team was casting about for solutions to the issues inherent in the concept, they realized that the third-party rating agencies—Moody's, Standard & Poor's, and lesser-known Fitch—were already doing due diligence on the 307 debtors. The rating agencies' business was to measure the financial health of companies and generate a simple score of their creditworthiness, a score that anyone could understand.

These ratings solved the due diligence problem. Correlation was a thornier one. If the 307 borrowers were all alike, then the

basket of loans would be riskier than if they were different and
their financial results and abilities to repay their loans were uncor-
related.

Moody's agreed to issue a credit rating on Morgan's basket of
loans, which were now being treated as a single legal entity and
were saddled with the unfortunate name of BISTRO, an acronym
for Broad Index Secured Trust Offering. Actually, Moody's issued
several ratings on BISTRO because, in another advance, Morgan
broke the basket into tranches, just as bankers had been doing
with mortgage-backed securities since that first Freddie Mac deal
in 1983.

Moody's gave their highest rating to two-thirds of the tranches,
the ones bearing the least risk (rating agencies use slightly different
terminology for each rating level; Moody's highest rating of Aaa
corresponded to the industry standard AAA used by both Standard & Poor's and Fitch, which is used here for all rating agencies'
highest rating for consistency). These were the BISTRO portions
considered to be as safe as any financial vehicle in the world. With
this stamp of approval, Morgan was able to turn to an insurance
company—after all, a credit default swap is just insurance—and
buy protection on the AAA-rated sections, for just two one-
hundredths of a cent per insured dollar per year. Morgan still had
to reserve a small amount of money, but for less than $1.3 million
a year, Morgan had freed $512 million from the tyranny of being
locked away, earning no money for the bank.

The stock market crash of 2008 was marked by the creation
of a raft of arcane and amazingly opaque financial contraptions
such as option ARM mortgages, credit default swaps, and tranched
mortgage-backed securities. These inventions were logical, and
they had social value because they solved specific problems, but
they also created new ones. How safe was an option ARM mortgage if a borrower consistently made the lowest possible monthly
payment? How could someone insuring J.P. Morgan & Com-

pany against loss with a credit default swap really understand the inherent risk in the loans? How could the buyer of a tranche of a mortgage-backed security really know what sort of mortgages the bond contained and how careful the original lender had been in extending the loans? How was that buyer to gauge the correlation between the loans or mortgages? These financial contraptions introduced opacity, an inability to see to the core of each deal, and these vehicles would grow to an immense size. There were more to come that would serve no more social purpose than a roll of the dice or the turn of a playing card. They came into existence only because they could be sold and those sales provided investment bankers with their annual bonuses.

The two presidents responsible for the boom in subprime mortgages were born just forty-four days apart, but they could not have been born into more different circumstances.

When Bill Clinton's mother, Virginia, brought him home from Julia Chester Hospital, she was bringing him to her parents' house. A modest place on Hervey Street in Hope, Arkansas, it was built in the American foursquare style, and though Virginia had moved there with her parents in 1938, when she was fifteen years old, the family hadn't been able to purchase it until the year her son was born.

Forty-six years later, President Bill Clinton was facing a problem. Every administration for more than sixty years had encouraged homeownership. Herbert Hoover described the owner-occupied home as "a more wholesome, healthful, and happy atmosphere in which to raise children." Lyndon Johnson said, "The man who owns a home has something to be proud of and reason to protect and preserve it." Ronald Reagan touted homeownership because it "supplies stability and rootedness."

Clinton's administration was committed to this long-held belief that homeownership is a good thing, but during the 1980s home-

ownership had declined slightly as the decade's astonishing affluence bypassed some. Although the decline was small, from 65.8
percent in 1980 to 64.1 percent in 1991, just before Clinton was
elected, those who had been left out—low-income families with
children, and younger Americans—were falling behind in homeownership.

So, in August 1995, the Clinton administration launched the
National Homeownership Strategy, an initiative to help eight million American families buy their own homes over the next six
years to boost homeownership to a new record of 67.5 percent of
families. The rationales Clinton's administration cited ranged from
the financial benefits of investing in owner-occupied real estate to
some that sounded like they'd come from a 1970s California-based
self-actualization cult, including increased "self-esteem" and "life
satisfaction."

Clinton recognized that the vast majority of families that could
afford a home already owned one, so his administration's goal
became making "financing more available, affordable, and flexible," including increasing "the availability of alternative financing
products" while reducing "down payment requirements and interest
costs." Many of these borrowers had bad or incomplete credit histories. Lower down payment requirements led to down payments
that were below the traditional "prime" standards. Making financing "more flexible" reduced the reams of income and employment
documentation required. With his creation of the National Homeownership Strategy, Bill Clinton put his stamp of approval on the
subprime mortgage in the same way that regulators in the 1980s had
encouraged adjustable-rate mortgages.

The Clinton administration would ultimately extend the Federal Housing Administration's support for mortgages to those who
put down as little as 3 percent. Later it would get even easier to buy
a home.

*   *   *

Like Tolstoy's happy families, prime, or "conforming," mortgages are nearly all identical. Subprime mortgages are subprime for any one of many reasons, although prior to the 1980s all subprime mortgages had one thing in common: they were illegal.

The freedom to charge the higher interest rates and fees required to offset the default risk of subprime mortgages didn't exist until the Depository Institutions Deregulation Act of 1980, which pre-empted interest rate caps set by the states. Then the Alternative Mortgage Transaction Parity Act, passed in 1982, allowed for nontraditional terms like negative amortization (a monthly loan payment that didn't cover the interest due, so that the mortgage balance was always increasing—Golden West's Pick-a-Payment loan had legally skirted these regulations), adjustable-rate mortgages, and balloon payments. When the 1986 Tax Reform Act ended the deductibility of consumer interest payments, leaving mortgages as the only tax-advantaged loan available and driving a wave of cash-out refinancings, subprime lending was coming into its own.

A mortgage could fall to a subprime level for one of three major reasons: poor borrower credit history, a small down payment relative to the amount of the loan, and a lack of borrower documentation such as income or employment verification. Although adjustable interest rates don't necessarily make a loan subprime, the majority of subprime loans were adjustable.

Subprime lending started relatively slowly; of mortgage loans made in 1994, subprime loans totaled just $35 billion, less than 5 percent of the total. The next year, Bill Clinton launched his National Homeownership Strategy, and by 1996 that number reached $70 billion, having doubled in just two years. The number of subprime mortgage loans made that year was 9.5 percent of the total mortgage market.

Those who supported subprime mortgages as a policy tool believed they would help the underdog; they were even seen as a solution to a history of discrimination in home lending, including redlining, the practice of refusing to write mortgages on homes in certain neighborhoods—the term comes from the time when financial institutions would literally draw a red line on a map around a neighborhood they wouldn't lend in. The affected neighborhoods usually contained a preponderance of people of color.

Predictably, with the home market opened to more buyers, home prices started climbing. During the five years prior to Clinton's initiative, home prices had increased by a total of 5.6 percent. During the two years subsequent to Clinton's announcement, they climbed nearly as much again, and by the time Clinton left office, they'd climbed another 28.3 percent, as subprime lending reached $160 billion.

Just before Bill Clinton left office, the swaps team at J.P. Morgan & Company received an unusual request. One of their clients, Bayern Landesbank, the Bavarian State Bank, wanted Morgan to help them extend the innovations that had begun in Boca Raton five years earlier by structuring a BISTRO-style deal on a different package of loans. Instead of a portfolio of commercial loans, Bayern Landesbank had $14 billion worth of American home mortgages it wanted to insure.

Even though mortgage portfolios had been tranched for more than a decade, no one had ever written credit default swaps on the tranches, largely because the hurdles were so challenging.

When J.P. Morgan first packaged BISTRO, it was fully transparent; everyone knew the companies with loans in the basket, as well as the amount of those loans. Participants had access to the rating agency reports, and, more important, the world knew exactly how these companies had performed through multiple business cycles. There was an abundance of data.

But mortgage-backed securities were entirely different. First, these mortgages were purposefully stripped of identifying personal data. The buyer of a mortgage-backed security had to trust the lender and "securitizer" that the mortgages in the portfolio were really of the quality they promised. Even if there was more specific data about each mortgage, it wouldn't provide any longer-term understanding of how mortgages in general had performed through business cycles. Home prices nationwide hadn't fallen since the Great Depression, but across regions, they sometimes fell as a group. They'd famously collapsed in Texas after oil prices fell by 75 percent in the 1980s. They'd fallen in California and Florida. But even this data was anecdotal.

This lack of concrete data was problematic, because it was hard to know how any drop in value would correlate with that of other mortgages. Morgan had all that data for the BISTRO loans. Nobody had it for home prices and mortgages.

J.P. Morgan eventually did the deal with Bayern Landesbank, extrapolating data from Texas in the late 1980s to the entire United States in an attempt to gauge the impact of a 1930s-style decline in housing prices. But nobody was comfortable with it. Less than a year later, Morgan did another deal, this time a credit default swap on just $10 billion worth of mortgages. That was the last mortgage-backed security credit default swap deal Morgan would do for years. In the same way that in 1907 it was impossible to know what stocks were worth, ninety-two years later the Morgan staff thought it was impossible to know what a basket of mortgages was really worth. Not everyone would be as disciplined.

In 1911 Cornelius Vander Starr dropped out of the University of California, Berkeley, and opened an ice cream stand and soda fountain in the Northern California city of Fort Bragg. After clearing a $1,000 profit, Starr sold out, and in 1914 he moved south to San Francisco, where he got a job selling automobile insurance to passing motorists.

Starr joined the U.S. Army in 1918 but didn't deploy to Europe before the war ended. Intent on seeing the wider world, Starr took a job with the Pacific Mail Steamship Company in Japan. Starr's new supervisor had the infuriating habit of buzzing for Starr, rather than calling for him across the tiny office. Starr threatened to quit if the buzzing continued; his boss quickly buzzed, and Starr just as quickly resigned.

Wanting to stay in Asia, Starr moved to Shanghai, where he eventually managed agencies that sold policies for a number of American insurers. Starr realized that if he had superior information and diversified his risks, he could underwrite the policies himself, bearing the risk but keeping all the premium. In 1919, Starr founded what would become American International Group, and he became known for covering unusual risks. He would eventually insure a baseball team against a rainout—the sort of "weather derivatives" that would become popular ninety years later—as well as a ship owned by an Eastern European company that was ferrying refugees from Eastern Russia to Europe. During World War II, Starr would put his information-gathering abilities to work for the U.S. Office of Strategic Services, the forerunner of today's CIA, by creating a unit that extracted useful strategic data through analysis of insurance documents.

In 1968, Starr tapped Maurice R. "Hank" Greenberg as CEO of American International Group, now better known as AIG. The son of a candy-store owner who died when Hank was five years old, Greenberg used a fake birth certificate to enter the army when he was seventeen. Greenberg landed on Omaha Beach on D-Day and received a commission before his unit became one of the first to liberate the Dachau extermination camp. After also serving in Korea, Greenberg talked himself into a job with New York's Continental Casualty Insurance Company by berating the personnel director for being "rude."

In 1987, Greenberg had been CEO for nineteen years, driving AIG's growth as it became the largest insurance company in the world. AIG was so large, Greenberg had taken to pointing out that

AIG never had to swim against the tide because "we are the tide." Even more important to Greenberg, AIG was one of the safest companies of any sort, enjoying a rare AAA credit rating.

For Greenberg, the problem with being the tide was the difficulty of consistently delivering the 15 percent annual earnings growth that he set as a goal. So when an opportunity arose to emulate Wall Street, and grab some of the profits bankers were generating, without the overhead of a fully fledged investment banking operation, Greenberg jumped at it.

Howard Sosin started his finance career in a place that had once been foreign but was becoming common—academia. He worked at the pure-science behemoth Bell Labs before leaving for a finance job at Drexel Burnham Lambert. Once at Drexel, Sosin gathered a team of Ph.D.s and they put advanced math to work in trading one stream of interest rate payments against another, a trade called an interest rate swap. But Sosin, who worked in New York, the center of finance, was orbiting too far from Drexel's center of gravity, Michael Milken's trading desk in Beverly Hills. And since Sosin wasn't in the junk bond part of Drexel's business, he might as well have been in another universe.

Unless you were on Milken's team, Drexel was not the place to be. Nor was it the place to be if your trading strategies required a lot of capital—and trading interest rate swaps required substantial capital—because Drexel had a crappy credit rating. That poor rating meant Sosin and his team had to pay more in interest to finance their positions, because it cost Drexel more to get the capital for them. Some people wouldn't trade with Sosin at all because of the risk.

Companies with AAA credit are rare, but Sosin walked past the headquarters of one nearly every day. AIG was based on the east side of New York's Financial District, just steps from Drexel's own headquarters. Once introduced to Greenberg, Sosin struck an enormously lucrative deal in January 1987. He, and the twelve

Drexel traders he would bring with him, would get 38 percent of the profits they generated for the company they had started calling AIG Financial Products (and soon shortened to AIG FP). Also, in a stunning bit of negotiation, they'd get paid on their unrealized profits, even if those profits were years away from becoming actual cash. But most important to Sosin and his group, at AIG Financial Products they'd be free to trade, and create, the sort of innovative interest rate swaps they'd been unable to do at Drexel, either because of the culture or capital constraints. When thinking about the freedom of working at a firm with a AAA credit rating, Sosin would daydream out loud, "Imagine what we could do." For Greenberg, the arrangement would be a way to monetize his AAA credit rating. Sosin and his rocket scientists would enter a trade only if they fully understood the risks and were able to hedge those risks away. The firm even set up a "murder board" to analyze all transactions at the end of each day, looking for weaknesses in their understanding or pricing anomalies they didn't recognize, or examining the effectiveness of their hedges. Sosin wasn't relying on a trader's instinct: "We're not going to do trades that we can't correctly model, value, provide hedges for and account for." They were trying to make trades that others couldn't and then offset all the risks involved. As one mathematician who joined Sosin later explained, "This was not a company that involved speculating."

Despite being housed in a windowless storage room and initially having to sit in chairs intended for kindergartners due to a screwup with their rental furniture, Sosin's team made $3 million on their first deal and cleared $60 million during their first six months. AIG FP continued to churn out reliable profits for years, but eventually Greenberg and Sosin butted heads and by 1993 Sosin was out of the firm. His replacement was Tom Savage, a mathematics Ph.D. who'd also started at Drexel, where he'd used his love of numbers to create computer programs to analyze a particular type of mortgage-backed security. Savage was a math geek's math geek, but he was also Greenberg's man in a way that Sosin never was. Greenberg warned Savage that if "you guys up at FP [AIG FP had relocated its offices to Connecticut] ever do anything to my AAA rating, I'm coming after you with a pitchfork." Under Savage, FP's profits grew from $140 million in 1995 to $323 million in 1998.

When AIG FP considered writing credit default swaps in 1998, potentially insuring the owner of corporate debt against the potential of the borrower defaulting, it was a departure for the company. First, credit default swaps insure against an outcome that is extraordinarily unlikely; AIG FP believed the odds of having to pay out even a single dollar on their first deals was just 0.15 percent, about 1 in 667. The models said the likelihood of a larger, catastrophic payout was orders of magnitude smaller. Tom Savage would say, "The models suggested that the risk was so remote that the fees received were almost free money." This was because credit default swaps lurk in the realm of "tail risk," the risk of events so improbable that they exist only on the extremes, or "tails," of the bell-shaped curve that is a plot of all the potential outcomes. The remoteness of the risk in writing credit default swaps led to a second departure for AIG FP: they wouldn't be able to hedge away the risk.

These credit default swap deals were small compared to the other risks AIG FP was taking on, so when Hank Greenberg signed off, AIG FP started writing credit default swaps. The first was the J.P. Morgan BISTRO deal. AIG FP insured that the highest-rated tranches wouldn't become worthless.

Joe Cassano was among the original dozen who went with Howard Sosin from Drexel to start AIG FP. Cassano had a degree from Brooklyn College but didn't have the quantitative horsepower of some of the others. After Sosin's departure, Cassano moved from the back office, where he led the group that processed and accounted for AIG FP's trades, and became chief financial officer. In 1994, Tom Savage put Cassano in charge of the division that found new markets and products AIG FP could trade. Cassano was an odd choice. The business AIG FP already did was astonishingly complex. Any new markets or products would be even more so. Then, in the wake of September 11, 2001, Tom Savage retired to Florida and Hank Greenberg put Joe Cassano in charge of AIG FP.

When Cassano took over AIG FP in early 2002, it had 225 employees and generated $1 billion a year in profit. It had expanded its credit default swap business, and under Cassano AIG FP became everyone's first call for credit default swaps on mortgage-backed securities, even as J.P. Morgan, its partner in the BISTRO deal, pulled back from the business because they couldn't model the risk.

Mortgage-backed securities barely existed before 1983, but just twenty years later there were $5.4 trillion worth outstanding. In those twenty years, the mortgage-backed security market had become nearly half the size of the U.S. stock market, which had started in the 1700s.

One reason mortgage-backed securities became so popular had to do with a quirk in banking regulation. A bank that made home loans had to reserve a substantial amount of money, but that changed with the creation of tranched mortgage-backed securities. As the U.S. Financial Crisis Inquiry Report would show, a bank that held $100 in mortgages had to reserve $5 in capital. But the mere act of pooling those same mortgages, tranching them, having the tranches rated by one of the rating agencies, and then buying all the tranches meant the bank would have to reserve about $4.10 (the precise amount would depend on the ratings for each tranche), a reduction of 18 percent. If the tranches were all rated AAA or AA, the reserve requirement would be just $1.60.

There was another reason the issuance of new mortgage-backed securities grew: a frantic search for yield on the part of investors around the world. As 2000 ended, the federal funds rate—the Fed-controlled interest rate at which commercial banks lend to each other overnight—stood at 6.5 percent. By the end of 2003, it had dropped to 1 percent. The United States wasn't alone in experiencing a precipitous drop in interest rates—the one-year interest rate in China had been nearly cut in half between 1998 and 2003, just as China was seeking investment opportunities abroad.

The bursting of the Internet bubble in 2000 threatened to push the American economy into recession, so in 2001 the Fed pushed down rates to head one off. The Fed began cutting dramatically in January and continued to do so until the federal funds rate reached a temporary bottom of 1.75 percent one year later, its lowest level in forty years, consistent with the unwinding of the tech bubble and 9/11's sucker punch.

Alan Greenspan, one of the heroes of the crash of 1987, was still guiding the Federal Reserve in 2001, and he was the engineer of this drop in interest rates. He was now seventy-five years old.

Greenspan had been raised by his divorced mother in his grandparents' one-bedroom apartment in New York. Showing a precocious ability with numbers, nine-year-old Alan found and devoured a book his father, Herbert, an occasional economic analyst, had written about the economic policies of Franklin Roosevelt. In the inscription, Herbert had expressed the wish that Alan would follow his father's path as an economist, but Greenspan originally began at the Juilliard School with the hope of becoming a clarinetist. He quickly changed course, enrolling at New York University, where he could put his facility with numbers to use by studying economics. He graduated from NYU in 1948 and began work on his Ph.D. at Columbia but left before graduating. He eventually received his Ph.D. in economics from NYU in 1977, warning in his dissertation that a decrease "in prices of existing homes would pull down the prices of new homes to the level of construction costs or below, inducing a sharp contraction in building." Twenty-four years before he embarked on the string of interest rate decreases that would launch a manic search for yield and drive investors to mortgage-backed securities, Greenspan warned, "There is no perpetual motion machine which generates an ever-rising path for the prices of homes."

A friend Greenspan met through his first wife became an even larger influence on his economic outlook than his father. Ayn Rand was an acquaintance of Greenspan's first wife, and though the marriage lasted less than a year, Greenspan became close to Rand, internalizing her objectivist philosophy and beliefs on capitalism. According to the *New York Times*, Rand even urged Greenspan to deliver a series of lectures in the early 1960s titled "Economics of a Free Society," in which he condemned "one of the historic disasters in American history, the creation of the Federal Reserve System."

As the stock market fell in 2001, Greenspan started looking for a stable sector of the American economy that might pick up the slack. In congressional testimony in November 2002, just as he started pushing rates even lower than the 1.75 percent federal funds rate he'd put in place nine months earlier, Greenspan said he hoped the housing market would come to the rescue. He pointed out that the Fed's short-term interest rates were at their lowest since the 1950s, and "mortgage markets have also been a powerful stabilizing force over the past two years of economic distress by facilitating the extraction of some of the equity that homeowners had built up." Unfortunately, much of that equity was being extracted by subprime mortgage sharks, not homeowners.

In the late 1920s, investors weren't satisfied with the low interest rates available from banks that could get cheap money from the Federal Reserve. Those investors in search of higher returns instead financed stock market speculation, inflating that decade's bubble. In the 2000s, it was foreign money being invested in mortgage-backed securities, but the flood of cash would lead to a similar surge in housing prices.

In 2000, when the short-term federal funds rate was 5.5 percent and the yield on ten-year Treasury notes was 6.6 percent, total foreign ownership of mortgage-backed securities was $350 billion. Four years later interest rates around the world had collapsed; the short-term federal funds rate was 1 percent, and the yield on ten-year Treasury notes was just 4.4 percent. After the bursting of the tech bubble and then the attacks of 9/11, the Fed should have pushed rates low to keep the economy from slipping into recession. But Greenspan kept them too low for too long, just as Benjamin Strong had done eighty years earlier.

This decline in rates made mortgage-backed securities attractive. When ten-year Treasury notes were paying 4.4 percent annually, mortgage-backed securities were paying nearly 6 percent, an enormous difference. Salespeople from investment banks were knocking on doors, selling these higher-yielding securities, and investors, particularly foreign investors, were snapping them up. Between 2000 and 2003, Japan increased its holdings of U.S. mortgage-backed securities by two and a half times, while China tripled theirs.

Foreigners weren't the only ones turning to mortgage-backed securities as the Fed drove short-term interest rates to the lowest levels in decades. American institutional investors, such as pension funds—who hadn't even been able to buy mortgage-backed securities two decades before—as well as endowments and hedge funds, bellied up to the trough to get as much of the tranched, rated, higher-yielding stuff they could. Between 2000 and 2003, outstanding mortgage-backed securities would more than double, and by 2006 the amount had tripled to $7.7 trillion.

Finally, voracious demand for investments that paid above-average returns created what one observer called an "irresistible profit opportunity" for those investment banks that were in the business of buying the avalanche of mortgages being written, and packaging them and selling the resulting mortgage-backed securities. It seemed that any mortgage-backed security they could create they were able to sell, just as businessmen had sold investment trusts in the 1920s.

Historically low interest rates had another impact: they turned the Dow Jones Industrial Average from three consecutive years of losses, the longest stretch since the four years of losses ended in 1932. In 2003, the Dow gained 25.3 percent, its twenty-second-best year ever.

Even when Greenspan had the opportunity to return post–tech bubble and 9/11 interest rates to a more normal relationship with inflation, he demurred. As one economist explained, "During the period from 2003 to 2006, the fed funds rate was well below what experience during the previous two decades of good economic . . . performance . . . would have predicted. Policy rule guidelines showed this clearly."

Why didn't Greenspan raise interest rates when having a federal funds rate below 2 percent was no longer appropriate? Likely he was waiting for inflation to spike, and by his measure inflation remained tame. In 2003 it rose by just 2.3 percent, and in 2004 it rose by just 2.7 percent. What Greenspan missed was housing inflation; during those years, housing prices climbed by 9.8 percent and 13.7 percent, respectively, even though the annual average had been just 5.1 percent since the beginning of the 1980s. Greenspan was looking for inflation in all the wrong places.

Unlike Bill Clinton, George W. Bush was born into privilege, in New Haven, Connecticut, where his father was a student at Yale. He spent most summers at his family's compound on Walker's Point, Maine, a regal promontory on the state's seashore named for his grandmother's family.

Bush's administration would make the ultimate advance over Clinton's 3 percent down initiative. On January 19, 2004, Department of Housing and Urban Development commissioner John

Weicher, speaking at a housing industry event in Las Vegas, announced that HUD was proposing to offer a "zero down payment mortgage." Bush hoped this initiative would create an additional 5.5 million minority homeowners during the next six years. Weicher explained that HUD hoped to "remove the greatest barrier facing first-time homebuyers—the lack of funds for a down payment on a mortgage." Unfortunately, many of these first-time homebuyers also lacked the funds to make the monthly payments. As a result, Las Vegas, the site of Weicher's announcement, would be devastated by foreclosures before Bush's second term was up.

As demand for higher-yielding mortgage-backed securities ballooned, so did demand on the part of securitizers for home mortgages, the raw material for those securities. Beginning in the early 2000s, even the language changed. The firm that issued a mortgage to a homebuyer was no longer a "lender" but an "originator," because as quickly as they created the mortgage, they sold it to one of the investment banks that combined it with thousands of other mortgages to be pureed in the banking apparatus until out came tranches that could be sold to sophisticated investors around the world.

The demand for mortgages became so acute that one originator started selling mortgages "in advance," months before they were even made. Inevitably, the demand for mortgages led originators to lower their standards.

Countrywide Financial was started in 1968 by Angelo Mozilo and David Loeb. It had originally operated much like Golden West, as a sober lender with rock-solid underwriting standards. For decades Countrywide demanded 20 percent down and the sort of credit history a borrower could be proud of, and by 1993 it was the largest mortgage lender in the country. But Angelo Mozilo had a chip on his shoulder. His father had been a butcher in the Bronx who'd died of a heart attack at fifty-six. At the age of fourteen—the age of James Hill and E. H. Harriman when they quit school for good—Mozilo went to work for a small local mortgage company while finishing high school. By the time he'd started at Fordham University, he had a complete understanding of the mortgage business. When their employer was bought out, it was time for Mozilo and Loeb to start Countrywide.

Mozilo was acutely aware that as far as the elite of New York finance was concerned, he came from the wrong side of the tracks and lacked the right pedigree. Once he had become a force in the mortgage business, he seemed to go out of his way to comment on the foibles of the big banks whenever they got themselves in trouble. Regardless, Mozilo constantly drove himself to outperform these same banks, and as competition heated up among the originators in the 2000s, Countrywide gradually lowered its standards rather than be left behind.

By 2004, Countrywide Financial Corporation was still the country's biggest mortgage originator, in part because Countrywide now prided itself on a strategy that David Sambol, Countrywide's president and chief operating officer, would later describe as "originating what was [mortgages that were] salable in the secondary market," by which he meant the investment banks that were buying mortgages and creating mortgage-backed securities. The new Countrywide sold 87 percent of the mortgages it originated. Quantity took on a quality of its own.

By early 2005, Countrywide was known to write loans for 95 percent of a home's value, and for borrowers with credit scores of just 620, below the 33rd percentile. That year, 68 percent of the option ARM mortgages written by Countrywide and competitor Washington Mutual required little or no documentation, such as work or income history, from borrowers.

The entire fiction that quality mattered was summed up by the acronym IBGYBG, which stood for "I'll be gone, you'll be gone."

It was short for, *We will get paid when the mortgage or tranche goes out the door, and by the time the ultimate lender realizes there's a problem, we'll be gone.*

It wasn't long before outright fraud began. Reports made by banks of suspicious criminal activity related to mortgage lending grew twentyfold between 1996 and 2005.

Why didn't someone do something? Because the only organization with the authority to create and enforce regulations for lenders and mortgages was Alan Greenspan's Federal Reserve, and the Federal Reserve had ignited the demand for mortgage-backed securities, which led to the dubious mortgages required to populate them.

The Truth in Lending Act of 1968 made the Fed responsible for creating and maintaining reasonable mortgage lending standards and for protecting borrowers against harmful lending practices. In 1994 that responsibility was expanded when Congress passed, and Bill Clinton signed, the Home Ownership and Equity Protection Act (HOEPA).

HOEPA specifically called on the Fed to "prohibit acts or practices in connection with [mortgage lending] that the Fed finds to be unfair, deceptive or designed to evade the provisions" of the Truth in Lending laws. For example, HOEPA specifically prohibited lenders from making loans based solely on the value of the property, "without regard to the consumers' repayment ability, including the consumers' current and expected income, current obligations, and employment." Too often, a lender granted a mortgage for a refinancing knowing the borrower couldn't afford to make the monthly payment but confident the equity in the property would cover any loss when the lender foreclosed. This provision of HOEPA was intended to prevent the lender from benefiting from loans that stripped the equity from a home. But Greenspan refused to take the steps to enforce the regulation. It took two years just to schedule the first set of public hearings on HOEPA, and in

January 1998, the Fed publicly affirmed its tradition of "not routinely conducting consumer compliance examinations in nonbank subsidiaries [mortgage lenders] of bank holding companies."

Robert Gnaizda and John Gamboa, the cofounders of the Greenlining Institute, an advocacy group for homeownership for lower-income Americans, repeatedly begged Greenspan to take action to satisfy the Fed's legally mandated role to regulate mortgage issues. In 2001, Edward Gramlich, a Federal Reserve governor, privately warned Greenspan that the Fed should dispatch bank examiners into the mortgage origination arms of the nationally chartered banks to uncover the worst abuses and stop them. Susan Bies, another Federal Reserve governor, went on the record in 2006 with her warnings, and Sheila Bair, who in 2006 became chairman of the Federal Deposit Insurance Corporation (FDIC), the governmental organization that insured bank deposits, had been warning about subprime mortgages since Gramlich alerted her to the danger. But Greenspan was against the idea of the Fed getting involved, and nothing ever happened.

Instead, Greenspan thought banks would self-regulate, for their own good, in some sort of Ayn Randian exercise. He believed "[t]he self-interest of market participants generates private market regulation. Thus, the real question is not whether a market should be regulated. Rather, the real question is whether government intervention strengthens or weakens private regulation." Unfortunately, the rapacious grasping of investment bankers anxious to get every possible dollar each quarter, no matter what might befall the company three years later, would thwart the "private market regulation" Greenspan was relying on. Bair called sensible mortgage regulation, specifically that envisioned by HOEPA, the "one bullet" that could have prevented the financial crisis if the Fed had used its authority to create mortgage lending standards "across the board for everybody, bank and nonbank."

Ben Bernanke, Alan Greenspan's successor as chairman of the

Federal Reserve, would say that the Fed's failure to establish and enforce reasonable regulation for the mortgage market was "the most severe failure of the Fed in this particular episode." The Financial Crisis Inquiry Commission, created to investigate the causes of the financial crisis, was the most damning in the conclusion to its report, issued in 2011: "The sentries were not at their posts, in no small part due to the widely accepted faith in the self-correcting nature of the markets and the ability of financial institutions to effectively police themselves. More than thirty years of deregulation and reliance on self-regulation by financial institutions, championed by former Federal Reserve Chairman Alan Greenspan and others . . . had stripped away key safeguards, which could have helped avoid catastrophe."

The link between the borrower and the ultimate lender, whoever owned the mortgage-backed security, had been destroyed; they were too far removed from each other, with mortgage brokers and investment banks getting between them. Without that link there was no reason to self-regulate. Given that so many mortgages were now sold to securitizers, a mortgage banker would see "self-regulating" as both oxymoronic and a really good way to deny him- or herself money.

It was Hank Greenberg, not AIG FP, who cost his company its beloved AAA credit rating. In March 2005, Greenberg, who had been CEO of AIG for thirty-seven years, lost the support of his board of directors when New York's attorney general charged that AIG had artificially inflated its reserves. Rather than drag AIG into battle with both the SEC and the state of New York, Greenberg resigned on March 14, and the next day Fitch reduced AIG's credit rating to AA. The credit rating wasn't merely a scorecard or a measure of the interest rate AIG FP would have to pay to finance its trading positions. It had a more immediate effect.

The dependability of AIG's AAA rating put them in position to write the credit default swaps that were designed to reduce credit risk. After all, it doesn't make sense to buy protection from someone who is likely to go bankrupt themselves. The contracts had been written so that if AIG itself became a bigger credit risk, and if its credit rating fell, it would be forced to pay collateral to those who had already bought protection. So the Fitch credit downgrade on March 15, 2005, required AIG FP to immediately pay $1.1 billion in collateral to those who had bought the protection. This was the beginning of the end for AIG. The amount of collateral due was so large because AIG FP's credit default swaps business had exploded since that first small deal with J.P. Morgan & Company in 1998.

AIG FP had a huge blind spot—they thought they had become Wall Street's "go-to" provider of credit default swaps on a range of new securities that contained mortgages because of their AAA credit rating as well as their familiarity with the products. But in truth, they weren't nearly as familiar with these products as they should have been, and they didn't understand what they were insuring.

In the autumn of 2005, Joseph Cassano asked Eugene Park to take over AIG FP's credit default swap business; Alan Frost, who had been in charge, had sold so many credit default swaps he was getting a promotion. But Park was hearing rumors that the general quality of the mortgages being securitized and insured had declined as more mortgages were being written.

Another reason the volume of mortgage-backed securities being created ballooned was that everyone thought they had finally solved the correlation problem that had dogged J.P. Morgan & Company. The man who seemed to solve the problem was David Li.

Li was born in 1963 in a remote town in China. He earned a master's degree in economics from Nankai University in Tianjin. He moved to Canada to get a master's degree in actuarial science and then a Ph.D. in statistics from Ontario's University of Waterloo before joining Morgan.

Many had tried to solve the correlation problem. The idea that one mortgage's performance correlates to the performance of the mortgage on the home next door is comfortably logical. Maybe the homes are in a one-company town, and that company lays everyone off. Maybe a homeowner stops maintaining a house that's in foreclosure, pushing a neighborhood that's already on the brink over the edge into decay. But calculating this correlation is enormously difficult, and subjective measures of correlation like "somewhat" or "just a little" are not enough when a mathematician is trying to price a credit default swap on a mortgage-backed security. Traditionally, the only way to calculate correlation was to crunch mountains of historical data to see how things had worked in the past. But there was little historical data on how mortgages and mortgage-backed securities had performed, and there was no data at all on how they had correlated to each other when housing prices were falling nationwide.

David Li had two insights into the problem. First, he didn't need historical data to tell him what would likely happen to mortgage values in the future because he had credit default swap prices that told him what the market thought was going to happen. Li substituted real credit default swap prices for historical data and relied on markets being the most accurate predictor of the future outcome. Second, he looked to his work in actuarial science, where it is well understood that when a spouse dies, the surviving spouse has a substantially greater likelihood of dying within two years than would otherwise be expected.

Li published his paper describing what came to be called a "Gaussian copula" in the academic *Journal of Fixed Income* in March 2000. *Gaussian* describes the shape of the normal bell-shaped curve; a copula is simply the device that links two or more distributions together. For mathematicians, Li's Gaussian copula was an elegant solution to an intractable problem, and Wall Street embraced it as the solution to the problem of correlation in mortgage securities, since Li's copula reduced all the variables describing correlation in a pool of mortgages to a single value. It was a lot like asking a student what they thought of one of Shakespeare's plays and getting nothing but a number between one and ten as a response.

Investment banks around the world started using the Gaussian copula to price and trade a menagerie of products. By 2005, it had become so central to mortgage bond trading that bankers began quoting prices for mortgage derivatives based not on their yield or safety but on the Gaussian copula measure of their correlation to each other. The rating agencies, inundated by securitizers who wanted them to rate mortgage-backed securities and the collateralized debt obligations that washed the stink off the worst tranches, seized on Li's Gaussian copula as the solution to their most vexing problem. When Moody's instituted the Gaussian copula model in June 2005, all the other agencies came on board, too.

But like the Black-Scholes model that Leland and Rubinstein had used in 1979 to create portfolio insurance, Li's Gaussian copula was too elegant. It wrung out too much complexity from the question of how correlated the mortgages in a mortgage-backed security were to each other. One problem was that credit default swaps on mortgages had existed only during a period of constantly rising home prices, so they underestimated the risk of those prices falling. And the model made assumptions, again like Black-Scholes, that escaped most users. Soon after Moody's and other rating agencies began to use Li's model, he told the Wall Street Journal, "Very few people understand the essence of the model." But the world of mortgage-backed securities had convinced itself that the Gaussian copula model allowed them to understand all the risks in mortgage securities, even though Li warned, "The most dangerous part is when people believe everything coming out of it." Over the next two years, the amount of mortgage-backed securities that had been created and sold would grow to $8.5 trillion.

It's unlikely a single dollar's worth of mortgage-backed securities could have been sold by the banks if they hadn't been abetted by the rating agencies. Between 2002 and 2007, the three rating agencies—Standard & Poor's, Moody's, and Fitch—pumped out ratings on more than $3 trillion worth of subprime mortgage-backed securities, mortgages that were purposefully stripped of identifying information, making it impossible to verify the care taken by the original mortgage broker and issuer.

Prior to 2000, the rating agencies were the referees of the bond world. They weren't the stars of the show and were expected to do their analysis and "call them as they see them." Then, on October 4, 2000, Moody's was spun off from Dun & Bradstreet in an IPO. Moody's was now publicly owned, with all the pressures to produce profits that entailed. Moody's may have been the referee, but if it got picked to call more games it stood to make more money.

For the rating agencies, including Standard & Poor's, which was privately owned, and the much smaller Fitch, which had to compete with Moody's for contracts to rate mortgage-backed securities, the sales focus changed from who would do the better job to something that was driven by profit. In 2000, Moody's market share for rating mortgage-backed securities was 43 percent. In 2001, its first full year as a publicly held corporation, its market share was 78 percent. An executive at one competitor described the change: "Then Moody's went public. Everybody was looking to pick up every deal that they could."

The point of differentiation was the ultimate rating, with a higher rating better for every group except the market at large. Moody's replaced some mortgage-backed securities analysts in an effort to make themselves more palatable to the banks giving out ratings business and asked the banks which analysts were troublesome, meaning tougher when the ratings came out. One academic study says that in rating corporate bonds, Moody's was tougher than Standard & Poor's before going public and more lenient after going public.

It's easy to understand why the rating agencies were sharpening their elbows when trying to win the business of rating mortgage-backed securities: it was extremely lucrative. Fees to rate a mortgage-backed security averaged 7 cents for each $100 worth of mortgage bonds. A mortgage-backed security worth $500 million, which was a common size, would pay the rating agency $350,000 for a rating. The easiest way to get that business was to have a reputation for being easy. One Standard & Poor's managing director said the result was a "market-share war where [rating] criteria were relaxed."

The fig leaf for the agencies was the "model," a ratings methodology filled with mathematical equations, market data, and assumptions that was intended to be objective but which still offered plenty of subjectivity. The models were incredibly complex mathematically, and with the advent of the Gaussian copula, the rating agencies thought they understood correlation, one of the most difficult facets of rating a pool of mortgages. It was easy to stand behind the false belief that complex and sophisticated meant accurate.

Regardless, the agencies began competing for business using their models as another point of differentiation. In August 2004, Moody's released a new model that would generally produce more desirable AAA tranches from a mortgage-backed security or get more mortgages into the AAA tranches and fewer into the lower-rated tranches. Faced with what another Standard & Poor's executive called the "threat of losing deals," S&P had released its own revised, more lenient model by the end of the next month. The first Standard & Poor's executive later said, "I knew it was wrong at the time. It was either that or skip the business."

Not everyone at S&P was so reticent. In one email exchange an employee warned that a mortgage-backed security was "ridiculous." The emailed reply: "We rate every deal . . . it could be structured by cows and we would rate it."

The business continued until the mortgage market crashed. According to Bloomberg, Moody's announced AAA ratings on more than $12 billion of pools of the worst tranches of mortgage-backed securities during the last week of August 2007, and every one was downgraded within six months. If Moody's got paid 7 cents for each $100 worth of mortgages, they received $8.4 million.

Joseph Stiglitz is a Nobel Prize–winning economist. In an interview with Bloomberg, Stiglitz made it plain where much of the blame for the crash of 2008 lies: "I view the rating agencies as one of the key culprits . . . the banks could not have done what they did without the complicity of the rating agencies."

As Eugene Park considered the promotion that would put him in charge of AIG FP's credit default swap business, he wondered if there was another, more troubling reason why AIG FP had become the "go-to" when it came to insuring mortgage derivatives. Park ran a little experiment and dug through a mortgage-backed security to get to the individual mortgages. He wanted to see how many qualified as prime and subprime. He asked his colleagues to predict what percentage of the mortgages they thought would be subprime. The consensus was about 10 percent. His investigation revealed that it was 85 percent. But this shouldn't have been surprising, because Wall Street had turned $508 billion in subprime mortgages into securities that year, up from just $56 billion five years earlier. And as the demand for mortgages had outpaced supply, underwriters of mortgage-backed securities had been populating them with whatever they could get and then paying AIG FP to insure them against loss. AIG FP had been the sucker at the table.

AIG FP had priced the protection they sold with the belief

that only a small percentage of each mortgage-backed security was crap, but actually nearly all of each one was. When AIG complained to the investment bank that had assembled the mortgage-backed securities, the bank didn't understand the concern because, they said, housing prices were going up. AIG FP had failed to understand one of its own core tenets: this was trading, and there were risks involved. It was a stunning collapse in management.

Late in 2005, AIG FP decided to stop writing credit default swaps on new mortgage-backed securities; they finally decided they shouldn't trade risks they didn't understand and couldn't measure. But AIG FP had already insured $80 billion worth of mortgage-backed securities through credit default swaps, and these securities were made up of the very worst mortgages. Inexplicably, rather than offset their existing risk, AIG FP decided to let it ride. This was the missed opportunity for AIG. The loss of their AAA credit rating made the credit default swap business less attractive because their cost of capital was now higher—the lower cost of capital AIG's AAA rating offered was the primary reason Sosin had approached AIG in the first place. With the initial downgrade they'd been forced to post $1.1 billion in collateral. If their credit rating declined further, they'd have to post more collateral by sending cash to whoever had bought the credit default swaps, because AIG itself was seen as a riskier counterparty. If housing prices started to decline and some of the mortgage-backed securities absorbed defaults, the losses would be enormous. But they still thought the premiums they collected for selling credit default swap insurance was free money.

Every other modern stock market crash has been fueled by a new financial contraption that was poorly understood and that metastasized at the worst moment. The 2008 stock market crash was fueled by a half-dozen such contraptions. Adjustable-rate mortgages eliminated interest rate risk for the lender by teasing the borrower with a low rate for the first few years that could go much higher later, a potential shock that many mortgage originators were not explaining and many buyers didn't understand. The Pick-a-Payment scheme allowed too many borrowers to pay less than a full monthly mortgage payment, money that was likely spent elsewhere when it might have been building equity in a home. Mortgage-backed securities made sense because institutions could own a bundle of mortgages, but when the bundle became a dumping ground for securitizers, underwriting discipline disappeared. Credit default swaps may have provided a bank with a way to reserve less money against bad loans, but when credit default swaps were applied to mortgage-backed securities, insurers were fooled by consistent increases in housing prices that made the credit default swaps seem less risky than they really were.

The final contraptions were an effort to get rid of the worst part of the mortgage-backed securities. Like so much industrial waste, nobody wanted to buy the riskiest tranches once a pool of mortgages had been split up. So bankers turned to alchemy to spin these undesirable tranches back into gold. They did this by buying and combining the worst tranches of several mortgage-backed securities into a new security of their own, with the safest tranche of this new security getting paid first until it had been repaid completely, at which point the payments would go to the next-safest tranche, and so on until every mortgage had been repaid or defaulted.

The vessel for this alchemy was the collateralized debt obligation, or CDO, which promised that the diversification effect was so powerful that if enough crappy tranches were combined with other crappy tranches, the result would deserve a AAA rating.

And in a final insult to common sense, "synthetic" CDOs were created. The synthetic CDO didn't own anything. It assumed it owned certain tranches without actually buying them. It was merely a way to speculate on the performance of the tranches without actually acquiring them.

Each of the half dozen contraptions was seen as the solution to a problem. The enormous growth in generic mortgage-backed securities was the response to the Federal Reserve forcing interest rates too low for too long. Unfortunately, the problem that spurred creation of the other contraptions was often nothing more than an investment bank's need to find something to sell, and the more difficult to understand the better.

Alan Greenspan finally relented. After leaving the federal funds rate at a historically low 1 percent for one year and five days, and below 1.5 percent for a total of nineteen months, he began raising rates on June 30, 2004. The Fed, likely realizing they'd gotten it wrong, began an unprecedented series of rate increases, notable not for the amount of each increase but for the fact that they raised rates by 0.25 percentage points at each of seventeen consecutive meetings from June 2004 to June 2006, reaching a rate of 5.25 percent on June 29, 2006. Rising interest rates hurt stocks. The Dow gained just 3.1 percent in 2004 and lost 0.6 percent in 2005.

The housing market didn't yet know it was dead, but housing prices peaked in April 2006, just after the fifteenth rate increase by the Fed.

Housing prices had been fooling everybody, climbing reliably since the 1970s with small reversals seen only when the economy was in a recession like the one in the early 1980s and again in the early 1990s. But beginning in 1995, the appreciation accelerated, even managing to increase during the brief recession of 2001, when house prices rose 4.8 percent from March to November.

With forty years in the mortgage business, Angelo Mozilo, who'd lowered Countrywide's mortgage standards dramatically and shoveled billions of dollars' worth of mortgages into the maw of the securitizers, saw the problems looming. The same month home prices reached their absolute peak, HSBC, the investment bank that had purchased Countrywide mortgages to be bundled into mortgage-backed securities, forced Countrywide to take them back, complaining that the mortgages Countrywide delivered were of lower quality than had been promised. In response, Mozilo sent an internal email pointing out that Countrywide had originated mortgages "through our channels with disregard for process [and] compliance with guidelines" and that he had "personally observed a serious lack of compliance within our origination system as it relates to documentation and generally a deterioration in the quality of loans originated." Four days later he issued a warning about a particularly profitable Countrywide mortgage product: "In all my years in the business, I have never seen a more toxic [product]. . . . With real estate values coming down"—they would peak that month—"the product will become increasingly worse."

The first clue that underwriting standards had been ridiculously lax was seen in defaults in subprime loans. Early defaults had always been a problem for subprime lenders; too often borrowers had stretched themselves so thin to get into a house that even the simplest unexpected expense of homeownership would lead to a default. In 2004, 11.2 percent of all subprime mortgages were defaulting in the first twelve months. In 2005, it jumped to 16.2 percent while it actually declined slightly for prime mortgages. But in 2006, both figures jumped, with 23.8 percent of subprime mortgages defaulting in the first twelve months, more than double the number of just two years before. Many new homeowners were so strapped they never even bothered to move in.

And in the worst possible news, subprime delinquencies were spiking just as subprime mortgages became a larger portion of the total mortgage market. In 2003, subprime had still been less than 10 percent of the total mortgage origination market. In 2004 it more than doubled its share, and in 2005 it reached 22.7 percent.

Like the investors and traders who watched it, the Dow Jones Industrial Average didn't realize the end was in sight. The Dow ended April 2006, the month when housing prices peaked and

Angelo Mozilo warned of "toxic" mortgages, at 11367.14, already up 6.1 percent for the year.

The housing market was where the real growth appeared to be. Every one of the eighteen largest monthly increases in housing prices since 1979 took place in 2004 and 2005, and thirty-two of the thirty-four largest monthly increases took place between 2002 and the end of 2005, during the time when Alan Greenspan was lowering rates aggressively (or leaving them too low for too long). Between 2002 and 2005, housing prices nationwide increased by at least 9.6 percent, with increases of more than 13 percent in the last two years of the rally.

The crash would spread to the stock market, but mortgage derivatives had become so central to Wall Street that it all had to start with booming housing prices.

Less than five months after home prices peaked, New Century Financial was running out of cash. New Century was founded in Orange County, California, in 1995—when Bill Clinton was launching his initiative to make "financing more available, affordable, and flexible"—by three mortgage industry veterans intent on taking advantage of the opportunities of subprime lending. By 2000, New Century had written $4.2 billion in mortgages; four years later, it originated ten times that amount and ranked twelfth on *Fortune* magazine's list of "100 Fastest Growing Companies." In 2005, New Century originated $56.1 billion in mortgages, and in 2006 it was the country's second-biggest subprime mortgage originator.

But at the same time that New Century was reaching second place in subprime originations, mortgage defaults were beginning to rise, and it was being forced to buy back billions' worth of subprime mortgages. On August 16, 2006, Patti Dodge, New Century's chief financial officer, alerted Brad Morrice, New Century's CEO, that the forced buybacks were taking a toll. "We started the quarter with $400 million in liquidity, and we are down to less than $50 million," she said. The forced buybacks didn't improve. By December "almost 17 percent of [New Century's] loans were going into default within the first three months after origination," according to the Financial Crisis Inquiry Commission. New Century was toast. The company would file for bankruptcy on April 2, 2007.

Although Wall Street was aware of New Century's problems, it took a crisis at HSBC to warn the wider world. During the first week of February 2007, the British bank announced that its bad debt expense for 2006 was more than $10.5 billion, about 20 percent above expectations due to losses in its mortgage portfolio. HSBC had been aggressive about maintaining the quality of the mortgages it bought and securitized. After all, HSBC had made Countrywide repurchase inferior mortgages in April 2006, and that led Angelo Mozilo to issue a warning about shoddy practices and mortgage products that were "poison." But even so, HSBC was getting hammered by delinquencies.

The bankers selling mortgage derivatives should have recognized the danger but they got suckered, too. Back in October 2003, Bear Stearns, the smallest of the U.S. investment banks, launched the High Grade Structured Credit Strategies Fund, a hedge fund that would buy mortgage-backed securities. On August 1, 2006, just after home prices peaked, Bear Stearns launched another version of its mortgage derivative hedge fund. But they described this one as "enhanced," meaning it would borrow $9 for each $1 investors put into the fund. Bear raised a total of $600 million initially, $40 million of which came from the company itself and its executives. By the end of 2006, this enhanced hedge fund had $9.4 billion in assets but only $936 million in real capital. A loss of less than 10 percent would wipe out the investors, and since $5.3 billion of those assets were in the worst tranches from mortgage-backed securities, the Bear hedge funds were riding the ragged edge of the home price rally.

Less than eleven months after the launch of Bear's "enhanced" hedge fund for mortgage derivatives, it was in trouble. On June 11, 2007, Bear announced that the "enhanced" fund had lost 6.7 percent in April and was down 23 percent for a year. On June 16, the *Wall Street Journal* reported that the two funds were "on the brink." Other investment banks that had lent money to the Bear hedge funds had had enough; no banker ever gets fired for pulling the plug too quickly, and Merrill Lynch was about to do just that. On Friday, June 15, Merrill Lynch, fearing that the Bear hedge funds wouldn't be able to make a $400 million payment to cover losses, seized assets from the funds and began auctioning them off. In an effort to salvage the funds, Bear Stearns agreed on June 22 to commit $3.2 billion of its own money. It was an impressive show of confidence in an asset class (mortgage derivatives) that had been in the news lately for all the wrong reasons.

It's understandable how Bear Stearns might have thought these actions would work, but by this point the mortgage market was too far gone, and the rating agencies, Standard & Poor's and Moody's, agreed. On July 10, 2007, both agencies announced that they were reviewing the ratings of hundreds of mortgage-backed securities, with plans to downgrade them significantly. S&P put 612 bonds worth a total of $12 billion on review. Moody's followed suit almost immediately, preparing to downgrade 399 mortgage-backed securities issued in 2006. This blow from the main rating agencies made official what market watchers had felt for months: the mortgage-backed securities market was dead, killed by greed and stupidity. On July 17, Bear Stearns told investors in its first mortgage hedge fund that they had lost 91 percent of their money. They were the lucky ones. The investors in the "enhanced" fund, which had been in business for less than twelve months, were completely wiped out.

* * *

The stock market, meanwhile, was still reaching all-time highs. The Dow had gained 16.3 percent in 2006 as the Fed stopped raising interest rates. On July 12, 2007, two days after the rating agencies signaled that massive downgrades of subprime mortgage bonds were coming, the Dow Jones Industrial Average gained 283.86 points, or 2.1 percent, in the best point gain it had had since 2002, to close at an all-time high of 13861.73. With this new high, the Dow had gained 25.9 percent over the past twelve months. On July 19, the Dow closed above 14,000 for the first time.

AIG FP had stopped writing credit default swaps on mortgage-backed securities in 2005 when Eugene Park demonstrated that they had already insured anywhere from $60 billion to $80 billion of crap without realizing it. The collateral call that resulted from AIG's downgrade to AA and forced them to pay $1.1 billion to the owners of the credit default swaps AIG had sold had been a jolt. But the downgrade of AIG's credit rating wasn't the only possible trigger for a collateral call. When AIG FP wrote the credit default swaps, it seemed nearly impossible to imagine losing even one dollar on them, so they had agreed to post additional collateral if one of three things happened: AIG itself was downgraded, which had already happened; the tranches it had insured were downgraded; or the value of the tranches deteriorated.

In July 2007, one week after the Dow closed above 14,000 for the first time ever, the unraveling in the mortgage market began to accelerate. On July 27, Goldman Sachs, one of the biggest buyers of AIG FP credit default swaps on subprime mortgages, informed AIG FP that $20 billion of mortgage securities AIG FP had insured had dropped in value by 9 percent. Goldman demanded, per the terms of their contracts, that AIG FP send that amount, $1.8 billion, to Goldman. One AIG FP executive called it "a fucking number that's well bigger than we ever planned for." AIG FP refused to pay, saying that the mortgages would ultimately be good, so no collateral was due. But the contracts were explicit. The ultimate value of the mortgages was irrelevant: the current market value was what mattered.

Goldman had expected AIG FP to protest the amount of the call, and everyone saw Goldman's number as the first step in a negotiation. AIG FP countered that Goldman was artificially lowering their estimate of the mortgages' value so they could demand collateral, like a buyer starting with a lowball bid in order to pull down the price.

On August 2, Goldman gave just a little, lowering its demand to $1.2 billion. Finally, on August 10, the two sides agreed that AIG FP would pay a collateral call of $450 million. Both sides considered it a victory, but it was most significant that AIG FP had been forced to make a collateral payment because the value of at least some of the $60 billion in mortgages they'd insured had declined in value.

Goldman had almost certainly lowballed their values, but while the two firms were quietly haggling over the amount of collateral AIG would post, the problems at Bear Stearns mortgage-related hedge funds were boiling over.

On August 1, the two Bear Stearns hedge funds filed for bankruptcy. The subprime mortgages they'd bought, using borrowed money, had fallen in value so much they'd eaten up the little cash that had been invested. On August 5, 2007, Bear's copresident and co-chief operating officer resigned, and Alan Schwartz took over as the sole president. One of his first responsibilities was sending a letter to Bear's clients assuring them the bank was on solid financial footing, despite the $3.2 billion Bear had spent trying to salvage the hedge funds. The odd nature of the investment banking business is that, like commercial banks that take customer deposits, they essentially rely on borrowing money every day to remain in business. If lenders—or depositors, in the case of a commercial bank or one of 1907's trust companies—start to wonder about the safety of their money, they pull it.

On the same day that Bear Stearns was telling the world it was going to be okay, investors decided the stock market was going to be okay as well. On August 6 the Dow gained 286.87 points, about 2.2 percent, in the biggest point and percentage gain in more than four years. But the stock market had begun to display a disconcerting volatility. It had moved by more than 100 points five days in a row and on seven of the previous eight days, including back-to-back losses of 311.50 on July 26 and 208.10 on July 27.

Sophisticated players like AIG FP and Goldman Sachs could have legitimate differences of opinion about the value of mortgage-backed securities—even if they were clearly worth less than they had been. The lack of transparency in the mortgage market meant that most investors might have missed much of the turmoil, particularly because the stock market seemed to be doing okay; the Dow's close at 13468.78 on August 6 was just 3.8 percent below its all-time high, made that summer. But even the most optimistic were about to get a shock.

On August 9, BNP Paribas, the mammoth French bank, announced that it was freezing withdrawals from an investment fund it managed. That fund had $2.2 billion invested in mortgage-backed securities, and this action served as an announcement that the problems in American subprime mortgages were being felt all over the world. Distressingly, the problem wasn't just that the value of the mortgages in the funds had collapsed, but that the market for these mortgages was frozen. No one knew what the mortgages were worth.

On August 23, 2007, Lehman Brothers was starting to feel the heat. Lehman was the fourth of the big five investment banks (the five were Goldman Sachs, Morgan Stanley, Merrill Lynch, Lehman, and Bear Stearns, in order of decreasing size), and it had developed a sizable niche in bond trading. Lehman had been particularly aggressive in building its mortgage-backed securities business. In 2005 and 2006, it had bought more than $50 billion in subprime mortgages and packaged them into mortgage-backed securities. In 2006, Lehman was the biggest underwriter of subprime mortgage-backed securities, with a little more than 10 percent of the market (the business was split between the five domestic investment banks, a number of domestic commercial banks, and all the big international banks). In 2006, Lehman generated approximately $500 million in revenue through mortgage securitization, about 2.8 percent of its total. This was a huge business at Lehman, and an important one for a bank that didn't have a big business in stocks.

Lehman had established itself in subprime mortgages by scraping the bottom of the barrel earlier than other banks. In 1995 they began financing First Alliance, a subprime mortgage originator headquartered in Irvine, California. The *Wall Street Journal* would later report that the Lehman vice president sent to analyze First Alliance called it a financial "sweat shop" and said its business was "high pressure sales for people who are in a weak state," and that employees deposit their "ethics at the door." Regardless, Lehman gave First Alliance a $100 million line of credit to finance its origination of subprime mortgages that Lehman would then buy.

Seven years later, subprime mortgages were popular and common, but on August 22, 2007, Lehman was forced to shutter BNC Mortgage, a subprime originator Lehman had acquired in 2004 and which had originated $14 billion of subprime mortgages in 2006, because too many subprime borrowers were defaulting within the first twelve months and securitizers were refusing to buy new mortgages.

At the end of August, the government officially got involved when the new chairman of the Federal Reserve, Ben Bernanke, said that "the adjustable-rate subprime mortgages originated in late 2005 and 2006 have performed the worst, in part because of slippage in underwriting standards. . . . With many of these borrowers facing their first interest rate resets in coming quarters . . . delinquencies among this class of mortgages are likely to rise further."

AIG FP knew more collateral calls were coming on their credit default swaps, but they probably felt they'd dodged the worst of it when they quit writing insurance in 2005. AIG stock had closed 2006 at $71.66 a share, while Lehman had closed just below $80. As August ended, AIG was at $66.00 and Lehman was at $54.72, even though the Dow was higher by 7.2 percent for the year. Bernanke further warned speculators that the Fed wouldn't rescue them, but then he seemed to contradict himself when he admitted that if market volatility threatened economic growth, the Fed would cut interest rates.

AIG FP may have been proud that they'd stopped insuring subprime mortgages, but they still had about $60 billion worth of them on their books, and on September 11, Goldman Sachs demanded another $1.5 billion in collateral, saying the value of the subprime mortgages it had insured through AIG FP had fallen by that much more. And this time Goldman wasn't alone, because the French bank Société Générale demanded $40 million through its own contracts with AIG FP. AIG FP again questioned the prices Goldman was quoting, insisting that they were too low.

One week after Goldman sprang its latest collateral call on AIG FP, the Fed let the world know it had noticed the pressure building and cut the federal funds rate by 0.5 percent, to 4.75 percent. This was great news for the stock market, and the Dow gained 335.97, to close at 13739.39. And though the Dow wasn't back above 14,000, it was once again up more than 10 percent for the year.

On October 1, 2007, the Dow closed at 14087.55, its thirty-third new high for the year, and was now up 13.0 percent. The Dow pushed higher despite Bear Stearns announcing two weeks earlier that its quarterly income had fallen by 68 percent, and the

Swiss bank UBS announcing just the day before that it was taking a $3.4 billion loss on a variety of bonds, including those tied to subprime mortgages. On October 5, Merrill Lynch announced its own mea culpa, a write-down of $5.5 billion. The total amount written off by the banks operating in the subprime space now exceeded $20 billion. That would be a fraction of the final number.

Strangely, on the day Merrill Lynch announced its write-down, its stock gained $1.89, about 2.5 percent, because, as one reporter put it, the write-down "reflected investors' relief that Merrill is trying to put the problems behind it." The Dow gained 91.69 to close at 14066.01, just 1.5 percent from its all-time high. Two days later the Dow gained 120.80 to close at 14164.53, another new high for a stock market that was now up 13.7 percent for 2007. This was the top. Home prices had peaked more than a year earlier, and the stock market had finally gotten the message. From this point, the bad news from the banks—all of which focused on mortgages—would overwhelm any good news.

One week later Citigroup announced a 57 percent drop in quarterly profit, due in part to a write-down of $1.6 billion on mortgages that were waiting to be packaged and sold as mortgage-backed securities.

The next week Merrill Lynch announced a quarterly loss of $2.2 billion due to a write-down of $7.9 billion, which was $2.4 billion more than the company had predicted.

This was the tipping point for the stock market. That the stock market had continued to rally in the face of so much turmoil in mortgage-backed securities is shocking. Two Bear Stearns hedge funds had gone bankrupt. Several banks had been forced to halt withdrawals from funds invested in subprime mortgages. Until now the only crash had been in the value of subprime mortgages. That was about to change.

Now the questions focused on how Merrill could have gotten it so wrong. Were the subprime markets deteriorating so quickly that

Merrill's loss ballooned by 44 percent in just three weeks, or was management the problem? Had they just now come to terms with the size of the problem? On October 15, Bernanke was asked about subprime mortgages at the Economic Club of New York. He said, "I'd like to know what those damn things are worth." With Merrill's news, it seemed everyone was wondering the same thing.

Goldman Sachs thought they knew, and on November 2, they upped their total demand for collateral from AIG to $2.8 billion. AIG FP continued to push back, admitting that the securities they had insured had fallen in value but not by the nearly catastrophic amount Goldman was claiming. The debate would continue for three weeks.

As this haggling continued, and as everyone on Wall Street, including the chairman of the Federal Reserve, was asking what subprime mortgages were worth, AIG announced its third-quarter results, claiming a quarterly profit of $3.1 billion and oddly taking a write-down of just $149 million on the value of mortgage-backed securities, despite having insured $64 billion of CDOs, many of which were on subprime mortgages, and having a drumbeat of collateral calls that claimed those mortgages had plummeted in value.

Banks were stumbling toward the end of the year, but AIG FP was still telling the world that everything would be okay. At an investors' meeting on Wednesday, December 5, 2007, AIG CEO Martin Sullivan tried to reassure investors by pointing out that AIG's sheer size meant the company had "the ability to hold devalued investments to recovery." Sullivan was using the argument AIG FP had made to Goldman, that the mortgages they had bought or insured would ultimately be good and that AIG had the wherewithal to wait until the value of the mortgages recovered. Not realizing that the bankers at AIG FP didn't really understand what they had insured, later at the December 5 investors' meeting Sullivan said, "This business is carefully underwritten and structured. . . . We believe the probability that it will sustain an economic loss is close to zero." At the same meeting Joseph Cassano went further, saying, "It is very difficult to see how there can be any losses in these portfolios."

The Dow ended 2007 at 13264.82, up 6.4 percent for the year. But it was now also 6.4 percent below its high point, reached that October. Another $650 billion of subprime mortgages, 23.5 percent of all mortgages, had been originated in 2007.

As the year ended, Goldman Sachs was still hounding AIG FP for collateral, and they weren't alone. Goldman wanted $2.1 billion, and other banks wanted a combined $600 million to compensate for the decline in value of the various mortgage derivatives they held.

The total amount of U.S. mortgage-related securities outstanding at the end of the year was $9.4 trillion. A product that hadn't existed twenty-five years earlier was now half the size of the entire U.S. stock market.

The year 2008 started badly for the stock market, and then it got worse. On January 2, the Dow lost 220.86 points, or 1.7 percent. It gained back a bit the next day, but there was never a day in 2008 when the Dow closed in positive territory for the year.

On January 11, Bank of America agreed to acquire Countrywide, the formerly sober lender that had gone nuts in an effort first to maintain, and then to build, market share. Bank of America was going to give Countrywide shareholders Bank of America stock worth $3.8 billion for a company that had been worth six times that just one year earlier.

AIG and Goldman could bicker about the value of the mortgage derivatives that AIG FP had insured, but the market had its own referee: AIG's auditors, PricewaterhouseCoopers. The problem was now too big for the auditors to ignore, but still Joseph Cassano tried to convince them that the problem stemmed from a volatility that had elevated the prices of the credit default swaps beyond where the underlying mortgage-backed securities indicated they should be. By his reckoning, AIG should take a writedown of $1.2 billion. PricewaterhouseCoopers was dubious about Cassano's math, and they were the experts on how these products should be priced for financial disclosure. The auditors said the preliminary number should instead be $5 billion. But worse than the number, PricewaterhouseCoopers declared that AIG had a "material weakness in its internal control over financial reporting and oversight relating to the fair value of the AIG FP . . . credit default swap portfolio." Saying that a company had a "material weakness" was the auditor's version of the nuclear option.

Goldman had never believed AIG FP's prices, and now AIG's auditors had told the world they didn't, either. The news caused AIG stock to drop more than 6 percent. When AIG reported its fiscal year-end results on February 28, the write-down wasn't Cassano's $1.2 billion, and it wasn't PricewaterhouseCoopers's initial estimate of $5 billion. It was $11.5 billion. AIG stock had ended 2006 at $71.66 and had ended 2007 at $58.30. It ended February 2008 at $46.86, having lost 14.8 percent for the month and 19.6 percent for the year to date. During the same two-month period, the Dow had lost 7.5 percent.

On Alan Schwartz's first day as Bear Stearns' sole president in August 2007, he was forced to send a letter to the bank's best customers assuring them Bear was financially stable following the failure of its two mortgage-focused hedge funds. Bear survived 2007 but did not make it to the end of the first quarter of 2008. During the second week in March, rumors were percolating that Bear was running out of cash and overnight lenders were pulling back. Bear stock lost 11.1 percent Monday, March 10. On Wednesday, March 12, Schwartz appeared on CNBC and told reporter David Faber he didn't know of anyone refusing to do business with Bear.

When investment banks die, it happens quickly. The morning after Schwartz's appearance on CNBC, Bear's outside legal counsel told an official at the Treasury Department that the firm was having liquidity problems.

By Friday, Bear was dead. Admitting that the company's "liquidity position in the last twenty-four hours had significantly deteriorated," the company sought a bailout from J.P. Morgan, with backing from the Federal Reserve.

A year before, Bear Stearns stock had reached record highs. On March 12, 2008, just after Schwartz had gone on TV, Bear stock closed at $61.58. By Monday, March 17, 2008, J.P. Morgan had agreed to expand the deal announced on Friday and buy all of Bear Stearns for $2 a share, representing a loss of 96.8 percent since Wednesday. J.P. Morgan later had to increase the purchase price to $10 a share to keep other bidders from picking off the best parts of Bear, but the final number was still a stunning collapse for a firm that had been founded in 1923. The Dow lost 194.65 points on Friday to close at 11951.09, a loss of 1.6 percent for the day and 9.9 percent for the year to date.

With Bear gone, eyes turned to the weakest of the remaining investment banks, Lehman Brothers. Lehman was even older than Bear Stearns, having been founded as a general merchandise store and cotton trading firm in antebellum Alabama.

On June 9, 2008, Lehman announced a quarterly loss of $2.8 billion. Lehman had moved up the date of the announcement to stop the rumors that were circulating that it was experiencing the sort of trouble that had torpedoed Bear Stearns. Their report didn't help. Lehman had ended 2007 at $65.41. It ended February 2008 at $51.00. On June 9 it closed at $29.70.

Before the 1930s a subprime mortgage would have been laughable. The few mortgages available then were short-term loans that were due in ten years or less and demanded a 50 percent down payment.

It's little surprise that in 1920 just 45 percent of American families owned their own home. The Great Depression didn't make owning a home any easier, and 20 to 25 percent of mortgages were in default by 1933.

In 1938, President Franklin Roosevelt pushed through legislation to create the Federal National Mortgage Association, known as Fannie Mae, to buy home mortgages from lenders and thereby spur homeownership by putting the resources of the federal government to work and making certain no buyer was ever denied a mortgage simply because capital wasn't available. In 1968, Fannie became a for-profit company owned by shareholders. Fannie's brother, the Federal Home Loan Mortgage Corporation, known as Freddie Mac, was founded in 1970 as a counterweight to Fannie, with the specific charter of buying mortgages from lenders to help them manage interest rate risk, rather than Fannie's goal of simply deploying government capital to help Americans buy homes.

From the moment they were each founded—both through acts of Congress—Fannie and Freddie, which came to be known collectively as "government-sponsored enterprises" (GSEs), held an odd place in American finance. Five of the eighteen members of each company's board of directors were appointed by the president of the United States, even though they were privately owned.

The GSEs made money in two ways. First, they bought mortgages from originators and held them in their portfolio, earning the "spread," the difference between the interest rate the portfolio of mortgages paid and the very low interest rate they had to pay to attract the capital they'd use to buy the mortgages. Alan Greenspan called this spread "a big fat gap," and it was enormously lucrative. The second way Fannie and Freddie made money was by guaranteeing mortgages they would bundle into mortgage-backed securities, which they then sold to investors.

By the 2000s, these GSEs had grown into monsters; in 2000, Fannie alone bought mortgages worth $154 billion, and its portfolio had a total of $607 billion. Freddie owned mortgages worth $386 billion. The two had guaranteed another $1 trillion worth of mortgages. This was also the first year that Fannie and Freddie started buying subprime mortgages.

In 2008, both companies found themselves in the worst businesses possible, guaranteeing mortgages or buying them and keeping them for their own account. Yet Fannie and Freddie remained enormously important to the economy because, as Secretary of the Treasury Henry Paulson would point out that September, they owned or guaranteed about half of all the mortgage debt in the country, and they were two of the largest creditors in the world, with outstanding debt of $1.7 trillion.

Because of all this borrowing, Fannie and Freddie were astonishingly leveraged. The investment trusts that had collapsed in 1929 were leveraged with eight dollars of debt for each dollar of invested capital. Before Bear Stearns collapsed, it had thirty dollars of debt for each dollar of invested capital. Fannie and Freddie in 2008 had seventy-five dollars of debt for each dollar of invested capital, leaving no room for error.

On Monday, July 7, Lehman Brothers—a firm that knew a little about capital shortfalls due to a decline in the value of a mortgage portfolio—released a research note questioning the basic soundness of Fannie and Freddie. Lehman suggested both organizations could need as much as $75 billion in additional capital to stay afloat. Fannie's stock lost 16.2 percent in value—it was now down 60.6 percent for the year—and Freddie lost 17.9 percent and was now down 65 percent for the year. That same day, the Dow lost just a bit to close at 11231.96, but it was now down 15.3 percent for the year. Lehman lost 10 percent (it had lost 11.3 percent the previous Monday) and was now worse off than either Fannie or Freddie, with a loss of 68.6 percent for the year.

Things got worse by the end of the week. On Friday, July 11, Fannie lost 22.3 percent, and Freddie lost 3.1 percent after having lost more than 20 percent on both Wednesday and Thursday. Wall Street had watched bank after bank take a hit to earnings because of write-downs in the value of mortgages they owned. Nobody owned more mortgages than Fannie and Freddie.

Treasury secretary Paulson had gone to Congress earlier that summer to ask for the power to help Fannie and Freddie, if help was needed. Paulson had been purposefully vague about what he was requesting because he didn't want to quantify the size of the potential problem, knowing that doing so could make things worse. Instead he asked for a "bazooka," explaining to Congress, "If you've got a bazooka, and people know you've got it, you may not have to take it out."

During the weekend of September 7, Paulson used his bazooka. Under Paulson's direction, the Federal Housing Finance Agency found that Fannie and Freddie's capital was deficient. FHFA would take control of these GSEs, placing them in "conservatorship," a sort of "bankruptcy lite" that would maintain their current legal form and avoid any impact on their trillions of dollars of outstanding debt. To eliminate the capital shortfall, the government would contribute $100 billion in additional capital to Fannie and to Freddie. This money gave regulators complete access to Fannie and Freddie's books, and they learned they had combined losses of more than $5 billion for the year to date.

Shareholders of Fannie and Freddie were wiped out. Fannie's stock fell another 89.6 percent on Monday, September 8, while Freddie lost 82.7 percent. They were both down more than 97 percent since the beginning of the year. Wall Street has an amazing ability to recognize where the stress is being transmitted, so Lehman lost 13.6 percent on September 8 and was now down 78.6 percent for the year. But the broad-market Dow loved hearing that the government was rescuing Fannie and Freddie, and it gained 2.6 percent for the day.

* * *

Attention immediately turned to Lehman, the weakest of the invest-ment banks and the boldest in the mortgage business. Lehman had spent the year looking fitfully for a buyer or a strategic partner to inject substantial capital. Bank of America was the most likely buyer, but the previous autumn, their CEO, Ken Lewis, had seen his own bank post a $527 million trading loss on interest rate products. Lewis said at the time, "I've had all of the fun I can stand in investment banking at the moment." Lewis had also looked at acquiring Lehman before and had always decided it wouldn't make sense for BofA. Henry Paulson, after the Fannie and Freddie con-servatorship, was pushing Lewis to take another look, pointing out that Lehman would be cheaper now. Lewis said, "This would be a big bite for us." Another potential buyer was the British bank Bar-clays, which was looking for a U.S. investment bank.

Then, on September 9 news broke that Lehman's only other potential savior, the Korea Development Bank, had ended negotia-tions to take a minority ownership stake in Lehman. This was the end. As Paulson later wrote, "Wall Street smelled a corpse." That day Lehman stock lost 43.7 percent and closed at $7.90 a share. The next day, Lehman hosted a conference call to preannounce its results from the previous quarter. The news was horrible. Lehman had lost $3.9 billion due to a write-down of $5.6 billion on real estate investments, including mortgages. With the release of this news, Lehman stock lost another 8.5 percent, and it had now lost more than 50 percent of its value in a week that was only two days old. That put it down 88.9 percent for the year.

Paulson decided it was time to draw a line in the sand. He had always said he hated the idea of government bailouts, and though he'd agreed to some government assistance to get J.P. Morgan to buy Bear Stearns, now on September 11, 2008, Paulson told the thirty to forty people from the Securities and Exchange Com-mission, Treasury Department, and Federal Reserve assembled on a conference call that there would be no public money to bail out Lehman. He also instructed his spokesperson to reiterate to reporters there would be no government participation in any rescue of Lehman. His only hope was to get to the weekend and find someone to buy Lehman before the markets opened on Monday morning. The Dow closed on Thursday at 11433.71, down 13.8 percent for the year.

The next day, Friday, September 12, Paulson pulled a page from history and, like the man J. P. Morgan did 101 years earlier, assembled the heads of the biggest U.S. banks in a room at the New York Fed's fortresslike downtown headquarters on Maiden Lane. Flanked by Tim Geithner, president of the New York Fed, and Chris Cox, chairman of the SEC, Paulson told the assembled bankers that the economy was nearing calamity and it was their responsibility to dig deep into their pockets and come up with the capital to save a competitor. These men, the heads of J.P. Morgan & Company, Goldman Sachs, Citigroup, Morgan Stanley, Merrill Lynch, and Credit Suisse, were supposed to find a way to "ring fence" the bad Lehman assets, segregate them, and unburden Lehman so it could be sold. Their deadline was Sunday evening; they had about forty-eight hours.

They had so little time because the market knew that either Lehman would be bought for pennies on the dollar in a Bear Stearns–type deal or it would declare bankruptcy late Sunday night. Those were now the company's only options. Lehman stock had closed at $3.78 on Friday, down another 10.6 percent for the day and down 76.7 percent for the week. The Dow had lost only 1.8 percent during the week because investors assumed Lehman would be sold. The expected fire sale would be a disaster for Lehman shareholders, but the bankruptcy of an American investment bank, connected to nearly every meaningful financial firm in the world, was still unthinkable.

On Saturday morning, Bank of America's leadership met with Paulson to explain what they'd discovered during their due diligence of Lehman's books. To buy Lehman, BofA would need to shed at least $65 billion of toxic Lehman assets. Although the number was huge, that wasn't the end of the questionable assets, which included another $50 billion of questionable commercial mortgages, commercial real estate, and residential mortgages. Total losses on all those assets would be at least $30 billion. At the end of August, Lehman had said the company had equity—the amount of money left after assets had been reduced by liabilities—of $28.4 billion. Taking $30 billion in losses would wipe out that equity. Lehman was therefore insolvent.

Since that weekend, staffers at the New York Federal Reserve have revealed that they did their own analysis of Lehman that week and concluded instead that Lehman's assets met, or exceeded, its liabilities, meaning the company was solvent, although just barely. But in the chaos, the senior leadership at the Fed, including Chairman Bernanke and New York Fed president Geithner, never saw this analysis. More than a year earlier, French bank BNP had halted withdrawals from an investment fund because it was "impossible to value certain assets fairly." BofA might have been right with its valuation. The New York Federal Reserve might have been right. But at a moment like this, value is in the eye of the beholder, and what mattered most was that questions about Lehman's solvency meant the government couldn't help even if it wanted to. Using its "unusual and exigent circumstances" clause, the Federal Reserve could lend to Lehman as long as the loan was secured and the Fed was reasonably sure it would be repaid. But if Lehman was insolvent, a loan to the firm could not meet that test.

On Sunday morning, September 14, 2008, Bank of America's interest in Lehman had evaporated, but the assembled banking CEOs had fashioned a plan to commit a combined $30 billion to plug the hole in Lehman as long as Barclays, the only potential buyer remaining, agreed to the acquisition. This was an amazing display of financial power as well as staggeringly enlightened self-interest by these bankers, because the money they were committing would vanish the moment it was thrown into the Lehman hole. But it would fill that hole and get Lehman's worst assets off its balance sheet, allowing the acquisition by Barclays. Men running banking firms known for their brazen greed were acting eminently selfless. Unfortunately, the British didn't want Barclays, one of their country's biggest and most important banks, to buy Lehman and drag America's financial problems to their island nation. In a late-morning call on Sunday, September 14, Alistair Darling, chancellor of the Exchequer, told Henry Paulson that Barclays would not be buying Lehman, saying, "We have real concerns as to whether it [Lehman] is adequately capitalized." When Paulson told the group of CEOs about Darling's phone call, he said succinctly, "The British screwed us."

Bank of America wouldn't buy Lehman without help, and the turmoil had delivered up a more interesting target. Before the weekend was out, BofA would acquire Merrill Lynch and its "thundering herd" of twelve thousand stockbrokers.

Barclays wouldn't buy Lehman even with help. Bankruptcy was now the only option. Lehman filed its petition with the U.S. Bankruptcy Court for the Southern District of New York at 1:45 A.M. on Monday, September 15. The petition included a section made up of 260 pages, each with three columns, filled with the list of Lehman's creditors.

The Dow lost 504.48, or 4.4 percent, that day. The Treasury Department and Federal Reserve had allowed a U.S. investment bank to plunge into the financial riot that is a giant, messy bankruptcy.

On that Saturday, Paulson had learned that an even larger problem was coming. On Monday evening, AIG would have its credit rating downgraded again, spurring $14.5 billion in new collateral calls. Meeting them would leave AIG without any cash in less than two weeks.

The $79 billion in exposure to mortgage derivatives was the proximate cause of AIG's collapse, but it was just a symptom of systemic risk-taking across the entire company that can only be described as beyond reckless. AIG's realized loss in 2008 would be $52.7 billion, with an unrealized loss of $28.6 billion still sitting on the books. Joseph Cassano had been forced to retire in March, but in addition to more than $300 million he'd been paid over the course of his career at AIG, Cassano was given a $1-million-a-month consulting contract as part of his retirement.

Late on Tuesday, September 16, the Federal Reserve announced that it would bail out AIG by extending an $85 billion loan secured by the stock of the regulated insurance subsidiaries AIG owned. Paulson, who had refused to discuss a government bailout of Lehman, later wrote that AIG had to be bailed out because "[m]ore than almost any financial firm I could think of, AIG was entwined in every part of the global system, touching businesses and consumers alike in many different and critical ways."

AIG was different from Lehman in another critical way. Unlike Lehman, AIG's problem was that its assets easily outweighed its liabilities, but the assets were illiquid, particularly because so many were mortgage-backed securities that had some value (even if no one knew what that value was). As its price for the bailout, the Fed would own 79.9 percent of AIG and receive interest on the loans it was making; the interest rate was so high it had to be seen as punitive. As news of the government bailout broke, AIG lost 60.1 percent. With the Fed demanding the lion's share of the company, the little that AIG shareholders had left was wiped out as the stock price fell another 21.2 percent on Tuesday, and 45.3 percent of what remained on Wednesday, the first trading day after the government takeover news. AIG was down 96.5 percent for the year.

News of government intervention to save AIG panicked the broader stock market, and the Dow, which had already lost 504.48 on Monday, when the Lehman bankruptcy broke, lost another 449.36 points on Wednesday, to close at just 10609.66. It was now down more than 20 percent for the year and 8.1 percent for the month. Americans were so afraid of putting money into anything but the safest investment vehicle in the world, short-term U.S. Treasury bills, that they were happy to pay more for those Treasuries than they'd be worth at maturity. They were guaranteed to lose a small amount of money, but they were happy knowing they wouldn't lose it all.

Paulson figured that if the problem was the banks' ownership of toxic assets, then the solution was to buy them from the banks. On Thursday, September 18, his team put together the rudimentary outline of a plan for the government to buy anywhere between $500 billion and $1 trillion worth of toxic assets. When this news broke—and at this point, it was barely even a concept—the Dow, which had been down more than 150 points, rallied to close at 11019.69, a gain of 3.9 percent. But Paulson realized the Treasury and the Fed had done all they could do with the powers they had. The power to buy toxic assets would have to come from Congress.

At midnight on Friday, September 19, the Treasury Department sent its proposed legislation, the Troubled Asset Relief Program, which came to be known as TARP, to Congress. It was only three pages and asked for $700 billion to buy mortgages and mortgage-backed securities using market mechanisms to select and price the assets, with the actual execution of the plan at the discretion of the Treasury. The biggest pocketbook in the world, the U.S. government, was being asked to take ownership of the worst financial detritus, and the stock market reacted favorably. The Dow gained 3.9 percent on Thursday and another 3.3 percent on Friday. It was still down 14.1 percent for the year, but it was down only 1.3 percent for the month.

Since TARP had to pass Congress, it inevitably became political. Democrats were against it because it failed to give relief to homeowners struggling to pay their mortgages. Republicans hated anything that seemed like a government bailout of Wall Street. When it came to the floor of the House of Representatives on September 29, TARP failed by a vote of 228–205. As the votes rolled in and defeat became obvious, the Dow lost 777.68 points, just less than 7 percent, to close at 10365.45. It was the biggest point loss the Dow had ever sustained. It was now at its lowest point since October 2005 and was down 21.9 percent for 2008.

Even legislators who had resolutely voted "no" were horrified by the stock market reaction, and congressional leadership immediately started hearing from members who were hearing from constituents. They decided to vote again, but this time they would start in the Senate. On Wednesday, October 1, just two days after TARP failed in the House, it passed the Senate comfortably by a vote of 74–25. Unfortunately, this hadn't been a matter of the Senate doing the right thing. The TARP legislation had begun as a lean, three-page stiletto pointed at the heart of what Henry Paulson thought was the problem. But the Senate version had been larded with an additional 397 pages of unrelated tax proposals, including a ten-year deal worth more than $150 billion to cut the alternative minimum tax, provide companies with tax credits for research and development expenses, and change how health insurers were required to pay for mental health coverage.

And in a final irony, it would allow plaintiffs who had won a monetary award from Exxon for the *Exxon Valdez* oil spill nineteen years earlier to average receipt of those awards over several years for tax purposes, reducing their tax liability. This new TARP passed the House two days later by a vote of 263–171. President George W. Bush signed it the next day. The Treasury and the Fed now had to figure out how to price and buy billions of dollars' worth of mortgage securities.

The market may have pushed legislators to vote for TARP, and the same market would vote against Henry Paulson's plan to buy toxic assets. On the day TARP became law, October 3, 2008, the Dow lost 157.46 points to close at 10325.38, its lowest point of the year. The Dow was now down 7.3 percent for the week and 21.9 percent for the year. And as the market realized it would take months to figure out a mechanism for buying the toxic assets, implement it, and actually ease the burden of the banks, the crash picked up speed.

At the beginning of September, the Dow was down 13 percent for the year, certainly disappointing but nowhere near qualifying as a crash. It was just 18.5 percent below its all-time high, meaning it didn't even qualify as a "bear" market. Why did the stock market initially prove so resilient? Likely because Wall Street thought the Federal Reserve and Treasury Department would do everything necessary to prevent a crash and subsequent depression. But when the Fed was unable to save Lehman, investors placed their faith in TARP. When TARP's original plan to buy toxic assets proved unworkable, investors decided the government couldn't save them. It was time to sell.

On Monday, October 6, the Dow lost another 369.88 points to close at 9955.50, its first close below 10,000 in nearly four years. On Tuesday it lost another 508.39 points, and on Wednesday, October 8, it lost 189.00 when Henry Paulson admitted in a statement that it would take "several weeks" before the first assets would actually be purchased. On Thursday it lost 678.92 points, the second-worst point loss ever to that point, surpassed only by the 777.68 loss of ten days before.

Friday, October 10, was bewilderingly volatile: the Dow lost 680 points in the first five minutes of trading to trade as low as 7882.51, down 23.7 percent for the week and 40.6 percent for the year. Then it rebounded more than 600 points during the next hour, fell again, and then gained 850 points to get to 8,890 with thirty minutes remaining in the trading day, only to lose 439 points during those thirty minutes. The Dow closed at 8451.19 with a loss of 127.99 for the day. The week's loss ended up being 18.2 percent, the worst week since 1933.

If Paulson wasn't able to buy toxic assets fast enough to relieve the volatility, he'd go straight to the source. On Sunday, October 12, the CEOs of the nine most important American financial institutions were summoned to a meeting for Monday. Henry Paulson personally made the calls, telling the CEOs to show up, but he didn't tell them the topic or agenda.

When Paulson's meeting convened at 3:00 P.M. the next day, the bankers learned that his plan was harsh in its simplicity. The Treasury would use TARP funds to make direct investments in each of the nine banks represented, including Citigroup, J.P. Morgan, Bank of America, Merrill Lynch, Wells Fargo, Goldman Sachs, Morgan Stanley, and smaller banks State Street and Bank of New York Mellon, which were critical parts of the financial infrastructure that processes electronic payments and settles stock and bond trades. The total investment would be $125 billion. Paulson also did not give the banks a choice. He would later say he assured the banks, "We're making you an offer." Dick Kovacevich, CEO of Wells Fargo, one of the soundest banks, said he would refuse the capital because he didn't need it. According to Kovacevich, Paulson's "offer" became a threat. In a later interview, Kovacevich said that when he refused, Paulson looked at Ben Bernanke and warned Kovacevich that if Wells Fargo refused the capital, Wells's primary regulator, Bernanke's Federal Reserve, would declare Wells's capital as insufficient to continue operations. All nine banks, including Wells Fargo, took the capital.

Although the meeting didn't officially end until after the market had closed, the news was out, and the Dow enjoyed its biggest one-day point rally ever, climbing 936.42 points, or 11.1 percent, to close at 9387.61 on the thirteenth. But the worst wasn't over. The Dow lost 733.08 on October 15, its second-worst point loss ever. It lost 514.45 one week later, then lost 312.30 on Friday, October 24, and 203.18 when trading resumed on Monday. When the Dow closed on October 31, it was at 9325.01. It had lost 14.1 percent for the month and was down 29.7 percent for the year, having been down as much as 38.4 percent. Only two months during the postwar era have been worse. TARP was supposed to solve the problem, but by demonstrating the government's impotence, it seemed to have only added to the volatility.

On October 23, Alan Greenspan responded to those who blamed him for keeping interest rates too low for too long and failing in his role as the only regulator with authority to rein in the worst of the mortgage abuses. Testifying before the House Committee on Oversight and Government Reform, Greenspan called the crisis a "once-in-a-lifetime credit tsunami" and expressed his disappointment that the policies of "I'll be gone, you'll be gone" had overtaken his hopes that bankers would regulate themselves and refuse a quick profit for the larger good. Greenspan said that those who "believed lending institutions would do a good job of protecting their shareholders are in a state of shocked disbelief."

On November 12, 2008, Henry Paulson had to admit to the media that the government would not be buying any toxic assets. No one had solved how to buy the toxic mortgage securities. Congressional criticism was damning, with complaints that TARP was a giant bait-and-switch. But the plan to buy toxic assets had been logical even if time pressures meant it wasn't as well thought out as it had appeared to be when the legislation passed. Paulson's news caused the Dow to lose 411.30 points, to close at 8282.66. It was now down 37.6 percent for the year.

One week later, on November 19, the consequences of TARP's failure to buy troubled assets became obvious when Citigroup announced that it was forced to return $17.4 billion worth of toxic assets—just the sort of assets TARP had been created to buy—to its own books from a related entity. This news came two days after Citi announced that it would lay off 53,000 employees. Citi also said it would not complete the announced sale of $80 billion worth of other assets. Wall Street immediately imagined the worst: Citi either couldn't find a buyer for the assets or couldn't afford the hit they'd take if they sold the assets at depressed prices. The Dow lost 427.47 that day and another 444.99 the next day, November 20, to close at just 7552.29. The Dow was now down 43.1 percent for the year, making it worse than every year except 1931. Pessimists pointed out it was just the middle of November.

The Dow had now given back all the gains made since March 12, 2003. The S&P 500 was even worse off, closing at 752.44, its lowest level since April 1997.

On December 5, the Department of Labor released data about November's change in payrolls. The U.S. economy had lost 553,000 jobs in November and had lost a total of 1.9 million jobs so far in 2008, a number that would eventually surpass 2 million for the year.

When 2008 came to an end, the Dow was at 8776.39, down 33.8 percent for the year. There was never a single day when it closed higher for the year. It lost ground during nine months, including the last four of the year. Two months, June and October, showed losses of more than 10 percent. It ended up being the third-worst year the Dow has ever had, better than only 1931 and 1907.

But the bottom wasn't in yet. That finally came for the Dow on March 9, 2009, when it closed at 6547.05, 53.8 percent below the all-time high made in 2007. Finally, on that day, it seemed that things were improving when Citigroup announced after the close of trading that it was profitable during January and February. The Dow gained 379.44, or 5.8 percent, on March 10. Citigroup gained 38 percent that day.

The crash of 2008 had extended into 2009, but the causes went back more than a decade to a time when homeownership became a political football, and shortsighted measures of inflation led the Federal Reserve to think that a policy of leaving interest rates near zero wouldn't later generate problems. But the biggest failure was the abject refusal to craft and implement sensible regulation on mortgages and mortgage lenders because of a misplaced trust that short-term greed could be stifled.

Given what we now know about the excesses in the mortgage market, we shouldn't be surprised that the stock market crashed by more than 50 percent. In truth, we had it coming. What is astonishing is that the housing market, and the market for mortgage-backed securities, peaked more than a year before the stress was really transmitted to the stock market. The Bear Stearns hedge funds went bankrupt more than two months before the Dow set a new all-time high in October 2007. It was also two months after Countrywide drastically cut earnings expectations and two months after AIG FP got the first collateral calls for the credit default swaps it had written.

One reason was that the housing market is tough to gauge; how often does someone buy or sell a house? The market for esoteric mortgage-backed securities, and particularly for the second-generation securities that combined tranches of tranches, is absolutely opaque to even sophisticated investors, despite the magnitude of the market they're based on.

But when investors realized TARP wasn't the precisely calibrated solution they'd hoped for, there was no one left to save them from themselves.

FLASH CRASH
2010

Her husband was supposed to pick her up from work in fifty-two minutes. Angeliki Papathanasopoulou was pregnant with her first child, and she and Christos had an appointment to learn their baby's sex. But just before she was scheduled to leave, fifty hooded rioters yelling, "Fuck them, burn it, burn the rich," smashed the front windows of the bank she worked in, the Marfin Egnatia Bank on Stadiou Street in central Athens, and poured gasoline on the floors.

Unlike so many other Greek professionals, Angeliki and Christos were part of a new generation of Greeks who were returning home after being educated abroad. For decades Greeks had sought educations elsewhere and then bloomed where they'd been planted, far away from the stagnant Greek economy, with its old-fashioned financial system and low pay. Even though Angeliki and Christos had vastly better career alternatives on the western edges of Europe, they had returned in 2004 because prospects back home were finally improving. A good job in Greece allowed for a great lifestyle there, and getting a good job was becoming even more likely after Greece joined other European countries that were replacing domestic currencies with the pan-European euro. And as the centennial Olympics were approaching in Athens, Greece was for once being paid flattering international attention. But in 2010, as Angeliki and Christos were preparing to welcome their baby, nearly one-tenth of all Greeks with college degrees were living and working elsewhere.

As a child, Angeliki had been typically Greek, enjoying family outings to beaches in rustic Greek seaside towns, studying ballet, and even cutting her hair like Jackie Onassis. She and Christos met as nineteen-year-old mathematics students at the University of Athens. After graduating she and Christos moved to the United Kingdom, where she received a master's in actuarial science and he received a master's in finance and banking. On returning she accepted a job as a financial analyst, which required her to spend twelve-hour days laboriously crunching numbers, and for which she took home $1,300 a month after taxes.

Athens's Vyronas neighborhood is haphazard with the sort of narrow streets and blocks of small apartments favored by newly minted graduates drawn to big cities around the world. Angeliki and Christos bought an apartment there less than three miles from her work and got on with getting married and making their life together.

On her wedding day, she told her mother she felt like a princess. A wedding photo shows a radiant bride with long dark hair and a joyous smile obviously passed down from her mother, who stands beside her while her father displays the slightly goofy grin common to fathers of brides everywhere.

After the rioters poured gasoline on the bank's floors, they threw in one of the fifty Molotov cocktails they bragged about having, and soon the three-story building was filled with thick, greasy, gray-black smoke. Trapped by the fumes, Angeliki called Christos and told him the bank was on fire and she was dying. Her body was eventually found splayed across the desk in her top-floor office. Firefighters also discovered the bodies of two colleagues, Vivi Zoulia and Nondas Tsakalis.

Protests were a way of life in Greece. Occasionally Athens's collective outbursts turned violent as anarchists and the few remaining communists protested what they saw as their government's domination by others.

On May 5, 2010, the radicals were venting their anger at a debt crisis of the country's own making but which had been enabled by the sort of unlikable foreign bankers who had too often appeared on the scene, trying to collect what was owed, whenever the Greek nation found itself in financial distress. The rest of the country agreed with the marchers on this point, even if they disagreed with the protesters' violent methods.

Rioters had started that day in front of the Parliament building on Syntagma Square. At the tomb of Greece's Unknown Soldier, the mob faced the tomb's guards, the Greek army's elite Evzones unit, with their ceremonial pleated tunics, white leggings, pom-pommed shoes, and guard huts the color of the Mediterranean. Despite all their clockwork marching for tourists and modern weaponry, the guards were chased from their posts by the rioters, and the tomb was left defenseless. Emboldened, the mob moved northwest around the square and up Stadiou Street to Sina Street, where, for some reason, they firebombed the Attikon Cinema, home to the annual Athens Film Festival, and, accompanied by the hateful chanting, Marfin Bank, where Angeliki, Vivi, and Nondas would die.

On the day the three died, Americans were starting to share only the tiniest bit of concern. While the Dow lost 2 percent on May 4 and 0.5 percent on May 5, it had redeemed itself after the worst of 2008 and the first months of 2009. From the low of 6547.05 made on March 9, 2009, the Dow had rallied eleven of the next thirteen months and closed at 10868.12 on May 5, 2010, a gain of 66 percent in less than fourteen full months. Only one of those two losing months saw a pullback of more than 1 percent, while there were monthly gains of 8.6 percent and 7.3 percent.

The Dow had only endured one close below 10,000 during the year, on February 8, as the banks most vulnerable to the bubbling problems in Europe got hit.

The S&P 500 had done even better than the Dow. It was up 72.3 percent from its March 2009 low. However, there was still much to worry about. It seemed that the problems that the American economy was putting behind it were just now being addressed in Europe. Many were calling for Greece to simply leave the eurozone and reintroduce the drachma. And while the Greeks were rioting, it seemed they were most distressed by the fact that the ones making the decisions once again lived elsewhere in Europe.

The Greeks had a history of being dominated by others, which seemed to fuel their habit of protesting. Even the terms of their 1830 independence from the Turkish Empire were dictated by third parties in London. For example, the Greeks were forced to name a monarch, because that's what London understood. The result was a Bavarian with the decidedly un-Greek name of Otto becoming king of Greece.

Once free of the Turks, Greece saddled itself with what were called "independence loans," massively unfair arrangements to help the new country get on its feet but which charged huge fees and usurious interest payments that were paid up front to the bankers in London. Barely more than half of the money Greece was obligated to repay had made it to Athens.

Even if the Greeks wanted to repay these debts, they were unable to, and that led them into more than fifty years of external control of their national finances. Finally in 1878, their creditors in London agreed to accept a small discount on the principal due while forgiving the extortionate fees and unpaid interest, in exchange for Greece agreeing to set aside specific revenues from state businesses and customs duties for debt repayment. Greece had effectively agreed to sell its future revenues for current debt relief, a tactic it would turn to again in a more secretive fashion 122 years later, starting a string of events that would include the deaths of Angeliki and her colleagues and temporarily throw the United States stock market into chaos.

But in 1893, Greece defaulted again, and an ill-conceived attempt to annex Crete from Turkey led to reparations and subjugation to an international control commission, once again surrendering the entire country's financial sovereignty.

By the end of World War I, Greece had accumulated mammoth debts. It repudiated them in 1932, the fifth default of the country's sovereign debt in barely one hundred years, in what had become a comic habit.

The period following World War II saw the first bud of real prosperity, as the Marshall Plan poured $350 million into an economy slowly making the shift from agriculture to industry, but the opportunity was lost as Greece became a fulcrum for the battle between democracy and the communists to the west, north, and east. Although Greece eventually settled into Western Europe's camp, it would always be restive there; Athens is 650 miles east of Trieste, where the Iron Curtain began its run to the north, and communist countries such as Albania, Yugoslavia, and Bulgaria distanced Greece physically from the rest of Europe. Greece formed a democratic government, but communist and anarchist sympathies were constantly seeping across the border.

Europe had been cleaved in 1945, but the collapse of communism in the 1980s spurred Europeans to suture the wound and reunite. As the rest of Europe began to coalesce around economic union in 1992, Greece could only watch from the southeasternmost corner of the continent that got its very name from the ancient Greek word *eurys*. Throughout its independence, Greece had faced excruciatingly bad luck coupled with strategic missteps and the poor decision making common to any addict—in this case, a society addicted to foreign borrowing. Even the ebullient 1980s were horrible for Greece; while the rest of the world was flourishing, it again abused its newfound economic sovereignty by devaluing the drachma twice, in 1983 and in 1985. The result was a spiral of unsustainable inflation that led to unsustainable wage growth.

The end of World War II had seen the creation of two Germanys, yet West Germany had become the gravitational center of the European economy, giving it greater incentive than most to pursue economic amalgamation. The reintegration of the two Germanys would be a massive undertaking and spawned concerns across that stretch of Europe that had twice been overrun before the country's military was neutered then split. Helmut Kohl, the German chancellor, advanced the cause of European economic integration, in essence creating an economic suicide pact with the rest of Europe. If a reunited and belligerent Germany returned to its old ways, the economic impact on a Germany so intricately tied to the rest of Europe would be catastrophic.

The first formal step toward European integration was taken on February 7, 1992, when twelve members of the European Council, the combined heads of state that define the general political direction of the European Union, signed the Maastricht Treaty, mutually binding themselves to criteria that each would have to meet as the first step toward economic integration and a common currency. The five criteria represented common sense drafted with lawyerly precision: long-term interest rates that were no more than two percentage points above the rate in the three EU countries with the lowest interest rate over the previous year; inflation of no more than one and a half percentage points above the average rate of the three EU members with the lowest inflation rate over the previous year; a national currency that had participated in the Exchange Rate Mechanism for two years (the Exchange Rate Mechanism was designed as a prelude to a common currency, with the goal of reducing volatility of national currencies); a national budget deficit equal to or less than 3 percent of gross domestic product (GDP); and national public debt equal to or less than 60 percent of GDP. The inflation rate, interest rate, annual government deficit, and total government debt criteria were daunting. For many candidates for the common currency, they would require going on a diet.

As the euro club started to form during the mid-1990s, Greece was nearly left out. Most of Europe that bordered the teal waters of the Mediterranean was in danger of being left out. The countries of the north expressed concern that their supposedly hot-blooded brothers to the south wouldn't be able to muster the fiscal discipline required for such a mutual undertaking. The stolid countries in the north feared chaining themselves economically to untrustworthy partners who might—in an orgy of stereotyping—lurch into deficit spending and cover up their divergence from the agreed-upon debt limits, pretending that they were sober and abstemious. Germany, with its Teutonic righteousness, specifically feared that someone in southern Europe, proud to be included in the elite club but intoxicated by the flush of deficit spending, would pretend to be upstanding while looking more duplicitous if a real accounting were to be done. While Germany and the rest of northern Europe didn't know who the culprit would be, they could name the likely suspects.

Many assumed Greece would be one of the offenders. In the early 1970s, Greece, still a largely backward, agrarian economy controlled by a military junta known as the "Regime of Colonels," had admirably low government debt of only 25 percent of GDP. By 1992, again democratic but just eighteen years removed from military rule and considering pledging itself to the Maastricht criteria, Greece already had outstanding government debt of nearly 100 percent of GDP, a fourfold increase during those eighteen years. What did they spend all that money on? With the election of Andreas Papandreou as prime minister in 1981, Greece loudly proclaimed itself a socialist state. It went from spending 10 percent of GDP on social programs to spending 25 percent of GDP as it was entering the eurozone. The minimum social pension benefit doubled. Citizens became eligible for that more generous pension as early as age fifty and were handsomely sent off to a robust retirement with 96 percent of the income they had earned while working. And retirement came sooner if one was leaving one of the 637 occupations considered to be "arduous and unhealthy in nature," a job so strenuous that one had to retire before reaching the normal retirement age of fifty. Jobs considered "arduous and unhealthy" and deserving of early retirement included trombonist, masseur, hairdresser, and baker.

When the European Council unanimously agreed in May 1998 on the eleven charter countries that would join the euro common currency in 1999, Greece was left out. With its inflation rate of 5.4 percent, a deficit of 6 percent of GDP, and long-term debt that nearly equaled GDP, it was far from meeting the Maastricht criteria.

Spain, Portugal, and Italy did make the cut, but Germany demanded that the price for inclusion was a "no-bailout clause," which expressly stated that neither the larger European Union nor its member governments would be liable for the sovereign debts of another member government. It was an unequivocal warning to borrowers and lenders that the European Union might be all for one, but it wasn't one (Germany) for all. There was a reason the interest rates demanded of different countries had always been different. For example, during much of the 1990s, Greece paid a full 10 percentage points more than Germany on sovereign borrowing.

The reason: each nation was a unique credit risk. Italy and Spain were riskier than Finland or Germany, and Germany was warning the world: sovereign lending wasn't without risk, and lending to some countries was riskier than lending to others, and would remain so. The European arms of the rating agencies that had been guilty of so much nonfeasance in rating U.S. mortgage-backed securities in the 2000s would completely ignore the warning.

Greece had been left out for good reason: its economy remained a mess. In 2000, Greek GDP was about $130 billion, while total sovereign debt was nearly $135 billion, worse than it had been in 1992, when the whole process began, and well above the 60 percent of GDP threshold of $78 billion. The problem wasn't going to get any better, because that year's budget deficit was above the 3 percent of GDP threshold.

The problem was closely related to the protests that came about because of distrust of government. The Greeks believed they had an ongoing duty to avoid paying taxes. While under the control of the Ottomans in the nineteenth century, tax evasion was seen as a patriotic responsibility. Unfortunately that attitude continued even when Greece began to govern itself. The result was a democracy that listed heavily toward socialism, with the Greek electorate demanding big government and lots of social programs and perks, while also seeing government waste and inefficiency as an excuse to cheat. And they cheated with gusto.

Greece has a higher percentage of self-employed than any other European country, but it's not due to any long and honorable history of entrepreneurship. Rather, the self-employed can cheat on their taxes more easily than those paid a salary that is disclosed to the government, with the appropriate taxes withheld from their paychecks. For example, newsstand owners could claim a default annual income of just 12,000 euros (about $11,340 in 2001) and be taken at their word. Mechanics would post two prices: one if no receipt was required, meaning no taxes would have to be paid, and a substantially higher price if a receipt was required and a paper trail was created.

The cheating percolated through the entire Greek economy. Doctors, lawyers, accountants, and those in financial services were some of the most egregious offenders. Approximately two-thirds of Greek physicians in private practice claimed annual incomes of less than 12,000 euros, the threshold below which income wasn't taxable. Those doctors employed by the national health system weren't left out, despite receiving a paycheck and having taxes withheld. More vigilant care could be bought from these doctors through *fakelaki*, Greek for "little envelope," which described how a tax-free cash bribe was often delivered.

How did people with so little reported income afford homes as mortgages became more popular among Greek buyers during the 1990s? Loan officers, recognizing that underreporting was rampant, started estimating applicants' real incomes and issuing loans based on those estimates. In the process the cheating became both sophisticated and institutionalized. Greek banks began to systematically adjust upward the income reported on a credit application based on occupation, using standardized tables to reflect the bank's best estimate of actual income. On average, banks assumed the actual income of a self-employed Greek taxpayer to be 92 percent higher than, or nearly double, the income the individual reported to the government and paid taxes on.

Rather than emulating the practice of American homebuyers in the 2000s, who fraudulently inflated their incomes to get home loans they could not afford, Greek borrowers fraudulently deflated their incomes yet got loans they could comfortably manage.

Greece also had a robust underground economy, and its government personnel were routine participants. Small bribes to local officials became so common that fees for everyday services became standard. Ironically, tax collectors had a reputation for being the greediest and easiest government employees to bribe. Again, the deal was widely understood: the taxpayer would pay a third of any additional tax assessed by the collector to the treasury, a third would be pocketed by the tax collector, and the taxpayer would get to keep the final third.

In many ways Greece wanted to join the countries using the common euro currency merely for prestige and to say it had an economy to be reckoned with after so much financial ignominy. But Greece was a relatively small economy that was geographically closer to much of Asia than to the financial centers of Europe, and with a GDP less than one-tenth that of Germany's or France's and about one-fifth that of Spain's. But the Greek government argued that it was larger than several of the founding members of the euro, including Finland and Ireland, and was immensely larger than charter member Luxembourg. The response: those countries were disciplined, they met the entry criteria, and each had something extra going for it.

Desperate to have its country taken seriously, the Greek government launched a storm of financial shenanigans that were intended to make it appear they were meeting the Maastricht criteria. To rein in inflation, the Greek government manipulated the basket of goods used to measure prices. In 2000, they decided that no one in Greece was spending any money on "gardens, plants, and flowers," despite an idyllic Mediterranean climate. Costs for services provided by state-owned utilities, such as electricity and water, were frozen or reduced; the cost for electricity in the inflation basket actually fell by 29 percent between 1997 and 2000, when Greece was trying to get into the euro zone. During the same period Greece was probably the only country in the civilized world that was reducing "sin" taxes, including those on alcohol and tobacco, and they did so in order to reduce the cost for the purposes of the inflation basket. The type of citrus fruit in the hypothetical basket was even changed from more expensive lemons to cheaper oranges. And pricey tomatoes were removed from the inflation basket even though no one was supposedly growing them at home.

But these statistical contortions were nothing compared to the outright frauds Greece perpetrated to get its budget deficit and national debt under the threshold for membership. The Greek national railroad was one of the biggest holes in the government's annual budget, but it was seen as untouchable by cost cutters. The national railroad had total annual revenue of 100 million euros, but its expenses—more than half of which were wages, because the railroad had more employees than passengers—were 700 million euros. The Greek finance minister pointed out that the government would save money by shutting down the railroad and paying passengers to travel by taxi.

The Greeks were masters at hiding these losses. To keep the 600-million-euro annual loss from showing up in the government deficit, the national railroad issued 600 million euros' worth of stock that the government would buy but could never sell. Instead of subsidizing a failure of a public service, they were executing a financial transaction by "buying stock" in a failed public service. And the whole thing avoided any impact on the federal budget.

In 2000, Greece again applied for admission to the euro zone. It submitted an economic progress report, and while its finances had initially missed the criteria by a huge margin, this time they were miraculously much improved. Greece reported that the budget deficit had now seemingly decreased three years in a row, temporarily satisfying the deficit criteria and serving as a dispensation for the debt-to-GDP criterion.

As far as anyone knew, Greece had satisfied the Maastricht criteria. It had achieved "economic convergence" with other eurozone economies—although just barely, and only on a probationary basis—and it was admitted to the eurozone on January 1,

2001. Although they were late and had just squeaked in, Greece had joined in time for the physical manifestation of the euro, the replacement of the German mark, French franc, Greek drachma, and all the other national currencies with euro coins and bills on January 1, 2002.

But if Greece hoped to remain in the euro zone, it still had to reduce its national debt to just 74 billion euros (60 percent of GDP), even though it had recently been 129 billion euros (more than 100 percent of GDP). To achieve this, the Greek government needed accomplices, and those accomplices sat in the first-class section as they jetted in from New York and London. Investment bankers came to the Greeks bearing gifts in the form of convoluted financial deals that were vastly more sophisticated than merely buying shares in the national railroad. These deals would have Greece sell off a vast range of future government revenues in exchange for immediate debt relief that echoed the country's past financial machinations.

Aeolos was one such deal, which sold, or securitized, future air traffic control and airport landing fees to Morgan Stanley and others at an unconscionable discount. But the lump sum received erased 355 million euros from the national debt.

Another deal similarly reduced the national debt by 650 million euros by selling, at an enormous discount, the future cash flow from Ariadne, the state-run lottery. At least five international banks, including Morgan Stanley and UBS, took a share of the proceeds of the labyrinthine deal that was ironically named for the woman who helped Theseus, one of the Greek heroes, find his way out of the Minotaur's labyrinth.

But the largest deal the bankers brought with them was Atlas Securitization, named after the Greek titan who was condemned to support the sky for eternity. In November 2000, the European Commission promised to give Greece billions of euros annually as part of a no-strings-attached fund that was intended to finance investment in the country's infrastructure, such as upgrading the transportation system from the mainland to the Greek islands and improving telecommunications in rural areas. Greece almost immediately called in private-sector investment bankers who agreed to give the government of Greece a lump sum of $2 billion, while the bankers would get the vastly more valuable stream of recurring annual payments. Greece had sold the gift it had been given by the European Commission less than one year after receiving it. Instead of using the money for public works, it took a lump sum and used that to pay down its debt, fooling the same group that had gifted the money in the first place.

Greece seemed to believe that financial shenanigans like Atlas Securitization could keep them in the euro currency just as the Greek god Atlas had supported the heavens. But the bankers, wanting to highlight why a country like Luxembourg could be a charter member of the eurozone and Greece could not, established Atlas as "a special purpose company located in the Grand Duchy of Luxembourg."

These deals didn't make economic sense, but their rationale was obvious—everyone was getting paid. Greece got money up front to reduce government debt. The banks structuring the deals got paid—one received $300 million in fees for a single 2001 deal—and the rating agencies that vouched for each deal got paid.

Despite the shell-game aspect of these transactions, none of them were secret. On October 8, 2001, the rating agency Moody's was happy to publicize its prospective credit rating for Atlas: the investments "are judged to be upper-medium grade and are subject to low credit risk." Moody's explained that the reasoning for its rating was that "the Hellenic Republic will cover any shortfall." Greece continued hiding its schemes in plain sight as Moody's upgraded the Atlas debt on November 11, 2002, explaining that the improved rating was "based upon the unconditional and irrevocable undertaking of the Hellenic Republic as the ultimate risk to Noteholders." Moody's had raised the long-term credit rating of the entire "Hellenic Republic" just the previous week, so any obligations, such as Atlas, that ultimately relied on the Greeks' trustworthiness should be upgraded as well.

As progress toward a common currency moved along, the difference between what Greece had to pay to borrow money and what Germany paid narrowed, and on the day the euro replaced the drachma, Greece was paying a long-term interest rate of just 5.3 percent, while the Germans weren't that much better off, paying 4.9 percent. Membership in the club and adoption of a stable currency supported by the European Central Bank, the common currency's version of the United States' Federal Reserve, had inspired confidence among lenders. What could be more stable than the European Central Bank, and weren't they making certain Greece was playing by the financial rules? Moody's must have thought so.

Safely initiated into the euro, Greece promptly went on a borrowing binge. Between 2000 and 2010, the country increased total government debt by 130 percent. It never had a year in which government debt declined.

Why didn't the other countries in the eurozone pound the table and demand that Greece clean up its act? Because once Greece ran out of financial swaps and securitizations that could at least make it appear to be within the guidelines, the government simply started lying. When questioned in March 2002, Greece grudgingly revised its debt level upward by several percentage points. When this new data was submitted, it was questioned again and revised upward again, but there was never any repercussion for the lying, and sanctions were never imposed. The duplicity was taking place on a staggering level, but the other eurozone countries couldn't afford to appear too pious. France and Italy had both relied on the same sort of dubious financial swaps to meet admission criteria, although Greece had done so on a scale so much greater as to make its perfidy fundamentally different.

*   *   *

Greece's Papandreou clan is a political dynasty matched by the American Kennedys and Bushes—if those American families had founded the very political parties with which they were identified. Georgios Papandreou was prime minister of Greece three different times representing the Democratic Socialist Party. His son Andreas was even further to the political left. Andreas admitted to being a Trotskyite in an era when that was sufficient grounds for prosecution. After being briefly incarcerated, Andreas decamped for the United States, where he became a citizen, served in the wartime U.S. Navy despite his father's prominence in the Greek government, and earned a Ph.D. in economics from Harvard. After teaching at the University of Minnesota and rising to head the economics department at Berkeley, where Leland and Rubinstein would later meet, he returned to Athens in 1959 and served as his father's economic adviser beginning in 1963. Andreas, the communist and American naval veteran, was elected to Parliament in his own right in 1964.

Greek politics had periods that were resolutely conservative before Andreas founded the Panhellenic Socialist Movement, known as PASOK, in 1974 as a liberal-to-socialist party. Just as Greece was emerging from military rule and citizens were desperate for a change to what they hoped would be a benevolent, nurturing government, Andreas found fertile ground for his paternal political point of view.

In the 1981 election PASOK won 48 percent of the popular vote and 172 of 300 seats in Parliament, a landslide in an election that saw the second-place party get just 36 percent of the vote and included seventeen different parties on the ballot.

Andreas and PASOK lost the election of 1989 in a blizzard of scandals both sexual and financial, but he returned as prime minister in 1993 before retiring in January 1996 because of ill health, leaving Costas Simitis as prime minister.

During the first week of 2004, after eleven years as prime minister, Simitis, who had led Greece through its inclusion in the eurozone and the financial work that had been required, was ready to go, too, despite being a youthful sixty-nine years old, with a horseshoe of mostly still-dark hair. Saying "a younger generation must now take charge," Simitis was clearly paving the way for George Papandreou, Andreas's oldest son and Georgios's grandson, to take over. Simitis announced new elections in January of 2004, confident that his party's ability to bring Greece into the eurozone fold and to bring the centennial Olympics to Athens, coupled with the younger Papandreou's 72 percent approval rating, would assure victory. But the enduring taint of his father's scandals and corruption, as well as the sense that PASOK had lost touch with its classic constituency of middle- and lower-income voters, led the conservative New Democracy party to a surprise victory with 165 of the 300 seats in Parliament. Kostas Karamanlis, nephew of the founder of New Democracy and thus scion of a different political dynasty, and his new government were sworn in on March 10, 2004.

Peter Doukas initially had little interest in serving in the new Karamanlis government. Doukas had become wealthy as a banker for Citigroup in New York before returning to Greece, and when Karamanlis pressed him, Doukas reluctantly agreed to serve as the new budget minister. Savvier than many, and realizing that PASOK had been in power long enough to grow used to its own way of doing business, Doukas asked his senior staff to level with him. He told them not to "worry about persecution or anything, just tell me the true story." What they told him was horrifying. The budget department estimated the deficit for 2004 would be 8.3 percent of GDP, while they were publicly reporting expectations of just 1.5 percent.

Doukas's immediate suggestion was to start cutting the budget, which was ridiculously out of balance and far from the eurozone mandate. But as the opening ceremonies of the centennial Olympics neared, Doukas's higher-ups told him to keep quiet in an effort to avoid alarming a population that might lurch into the ever-possible strikes or demonstrations that would guarantee Olympic venues wouldn't be finished in time. The Olympics were about to make the budget situation significantly worse. The games would cost the Greek government more than 8 billion euros, almost 5 percent of its GDP and seven times the cost of the 2000 Olympic Games. Security alone for the first post-9/11 Summer Olympics cost nearly 1 billion euros.

As the post-Olympics glow faded, the bills started coming due and the budget pressure mounted. On September 22, 2004, finance minister George Alogoskoufis announced that Greece had falsified its way into the eurozone. Alogoskoufis blamed his socialist predecessors for the "creative accounting" and noted that they'd been voted out that spring, saying, "The fiscal derailment is due to actions and omissions by the previous government, and we cannot hide behind our little finger anymore," invoking the folksy imagery of a butcher tipping the scales in his favor. Greece's 2000 budget deficit had actually been 4.1 percent of GDP, not the 2.0 percent the previous government had reported, and in 2000, total government debt had been 114 percent of GDP rather than the 102 percent reported. Alogoskoufis admitted that since 1997, when the clock started ticking on Greece's inclusion in the eurozone, the country had never managed to trim its deficit to the 3 percent of GDP limit.

The European Commission immediately responded that they would not revisit Greece's membership in the euro. Politically, Alogoskoufis's New Democracy party had a tailor-made fall guy in ex–prime minister Simitis, who'd run a party known for financial corruption. But despite European Commission assurances that Greece would remain in the eurozone, Alogoskoufis didn't make a clean breast of Greek financial crookedness while skewering PASOK for its history of salacious scandal seasoned with financial malfeasance. He also failed to promise no more subterfuge. Greece had wasted its opportunity to become legitimate.

Young people, who were experiencing a 25 percent unemployment rate, had had enough, and they began rioting in December 2007 as the entire world began to slip into financial trouble. At the same time, the government was finally trying to rein in spending while tax revenues—such as they were—collapsed. In February of that year, Greek citizens held a twenty-four-hour work stoppage, and a month later millions of Greeks again left their jobs to protest a pension reform plan aimed at controlling the ballooning costs that Parliament was voting on the next day. Chanting "The bill is a fraud," protesters aimed to paralyze the entire country. They continued to rail against social cuts while also demanding a doubling of the monthly minimum wage in a country suffering from stifling unemployment.

The riots crescendoed on December 6, 2008, when a fifteen-year-old student was killed by a policeman's ricochet, prompting protests that dissolved into what one newspaper called "a revolt of schoolchildren and students" who quickly began looting and setting fires. Soon the Athens police were running out of tear gas after a week in which they used more than 4,600 canisters. They had to send to Israel to replenish their supply.

In the face of this violence, joblessness, and a drop in government revenues, the Greek government did what it knew how to do: it started madly borrowing as much money as it could. In 2009 alone the Greek government borrowed $67 billion, more than twice what it had borrowed just the year before.

Meanwhile, the U.S.-based rating agencies were complicit in Greece's borrowing. Even though Greek government expenses increased by 87 percent from 2001 to 2007, revenues grew only 31 percent. Thanks in part to the rating agencies, Greece was paying an interest rate on all this borrowing that was just one-third of what it had been a decade earlier. One Moody's executive would later say of the eurozone countries, including Greece, "nobody was ever going to default" and "everything was safe." The co-head of Moody's sovereign debt rating group later said that Moody's believed the strongest eurozone countries, including Germany, would pull along the weakest. Moody's didn't even change its rating for Greece after the 2004 admission that the country had faked its eurozone admission data. Standard & Poor's lowered its rating, but only slightly.

Why were the rating agencies practicing what now seems to be willful blindness? For the same reason all those securitization deals were getting done in the United States: everyone was getting paid, and as the business of rating subprime mortgages tailed off, the ratings revenue from countries like Greece was even more important than before. The general director of Greece's Public Debt Management Agency from 2005 to 2010 was quoted as saying that Greece paid Moody's at least $330,000 each year, and as much as $540,000, to rate its debt despite cost pressures forcing sovereign analysts at the rating agencies to spend less time in each country they followed.

These favorable ratings, as well as its membership in the eurozone, allowed Greece to accumulate mountains of debt at interest rates substantially lower than it would have otherwise paid. The low rates also made the Greeks see borrowing money as less painful than raising and enforcing taxes or cutting services, both of which could lead to more rioting. The Greek governments of both parties spent the entire decade of the 2000s taking this easy way out.

Amid 2009's spasms of violence and scandals that rocked the New Democracy party, Greeks directed their ire at the incumbents, and New Democracy was trounced by PASOK in the time-honored ritual of throwing the bums out when times are bad.

PASOK resumed control when George Papandreou was sworn in as prime minister on October 6, 2009. Two weeks later, Papandreou returned the favor and announced that New Democracy had been cooking the books; the budget deficit that year would be above 10 percent, and even that was conservative. The final official estimate released just two weeks later was 12.7 percent, four times the Maastricht mandate. In the face of financial distress around the world, and feeling foolish at having been duped for so long, each of the three major rating agencies finally downgraded Greece's credit rating just when the country was trying to raise money to fill its budget gap.

The Greek situation reached a critical stage early in 2010 when basic calculations based on due dates for payment of interest and principal on Greek debt told the financial world there was no way Greece could pay all that was owed. Greece would default soon. A default on sovereign debt would be catastrophic not only for Greece but also for the eurozone and the other major industrialized countries. Recognizing this, European leaders gathered on February 10, 2010, to consider a rescue package, but the next day German chancellor Angela Merkel crushed any hopes for a solution.

The Germans had no appetite for a bailout of the Greeks. German voters, as well as many politicians, viewed a rescue package as nothing more than a reward for the sort of profligate spending they had predicted a decade before. One February 2010 poll found that 68 percent of Germans opposed any bailout.

One of the members of the German parliament's Finance Committee and a member of Merkel's coalition explained the problem by saying, "You don't help an alcoholic by putting a bottle of schnapps in front of him." Germany's largest newspaper ran headlines warning Germans "Fear for our money," and "Greeks want even more billions from us," likely a reference to the infrastructure improvement fund the Greeks had raided to hide their indebtedness.

There was also no assurance the Germans had the capacity to help. The country had been forced to inject 500 billion euros into its own banking and insurance sectors during the worst of 2008 and 2009. Merkel initially said that Germany had to focus on fixing its own problems. As Papandreou received parliamentary approval for sweeping austerity measures, and the Greeks promised to crack down on tax evasion, the Germans slowly came to realize that in order to save themselves, they might need to save Greece.

The rationale was simple: European interconnectedness was complete. Greece owed nearly $10 billion to banks in Portugal— starting in 2009 they'd borrowed from whoever would lend. Portugal was already in trouble, and it couldn't survive a Greek bankruptcy. Portugal also owed $86 billion to Spanish banks, and Spain had seen a housing bubble inflated by northern European buyers of vacation homes along the Costa del Sol burst. Its credit rating had been downgraded. And that was just three of the countries in the eurozone. Ireland was exposed to Germany and Great Britain, and wildly overleveraged Irish banks were collapsing. Germany was exposed to Spain to the tune of $235 billion, while France held another $220 billion of Spanish debt, as well as more than $500 billion of Italian debt, as investors around the world wondered if Italy was secretly guilty of the same sins as Greece, albeit on a much larger scale. Greece was a relatively minor economy, with less than 3 percent of the GDP of the broader eurozone, but the same couldn't be said of Spain and Italy, which were 11 percent and 18 percent of the total eurozone economy, respectively. Even though Greece was small, the fear was that it would pull all the other eurozone countries down with it in a cascade of failure.

Even if a default by Greece didn't pull down those other countries, the event would be calamitous. With $250 billion of debt outstanding in the spring of 2010, a default would be the largest such credit event in seventy-five years, surpassing Russia's default in the late 1990s by a factor of four, and Argentina's default a few years later by a factor of two and a half. And this was the best-case scenario for a Greek default. Contagion was the worst.

Sixteen billion of those 250 billion euros would mature in May 2010, and every single euro of it had to be paid the moment it was due or a default would occur. While the distinction seems merely technical, it had draconian implications for banks around the world. Billions of euros in loans and derivatives, including credit default swaps on Greek government debt and insurance contracts, had been written when everyone but the Germans believed that a default was an impossibility. With a default, Greece would not be able to borrow a single euro at any interest rate, and substantial portions of its remaining debt would immediately be due. Derivatives contracts and credit default swaps would require losers pay to winners immense sums they did not have. Greece would again be at the mercy of foreign bankers, but they could no longer hide in their small corner of Europe and go it alone. Too much of its economy relied on global trade and tourism. A default would push Greece into a financial dark age.

On April 23, 2010, Papandreou formally asked the European Commission and the International Monetary Fund for a bailout. Despite Greece's admission that it was insolvent, S&P still took four days to downgrade Greece's credit rating to junk.

The next day a simmering Greece boiled over on the news of the proposed terms of an ECB-led bailout, which called for austerity from the Greek citizens on a scale absolutely foreign to a country that commonly elected socialist governments and where communists were the third-most-popular political party. Tens of thousands took to the streets in what quickly morphed from a general strike to a wild, days-long melee. Protesters stormed the Acropolis, and the Communist Party of Greece urged the "Peoples of Europe" to "Rise Up" by hanging banners emblazoned with the old Soviet hammer and sickle on the Parthenon, a temple built 2,400 years earlier as a tribute to Athena. *Parthenon* means "virgin," and the temple was dedicated to Athena because of her honesty and refusal to engage in unscrupulous dealings. Given this, the Parthenon was a profoundly ironic site for a protest spawned by more than a decade of institutionalized dishonesty and unscrupulous dealings.

The resistance seemed to reach its climax on May 5, as the Greek Parliament prepared to vote on the bailout, when the black-hooded rioters burned the Marfin Egnatia Bank on Stadiou Street.

Parliament was scheduled to vote on May 6. The bailout package required sacrifices that many Greeks had never even contemplated. Their government would no longer be a fountain of social programs to slurp from when they were young, programs that were replaced by tax evasion when they were starting their careers, evasion that was followed by a generous government pension and retirement at a stage of life the rest of the world considered the start of middle age. The three deaths the previous day and the intensity of the continuing demonstrations focused the attention of the world—including the financial media—on Athens.

Investors in the United States also wondered what this contagion would mean for the American stock market, particularly if Greece erupted in more violence on the sixth. Since its close at 1217.28 on April 23, 2010, when it was up 9.2 percent for the year, the S&P 500 Index had fallen by 4.2 percent to 1165.87 on May 5, the day before the scheduled vote. When the stock market opened on May 6, the S&P was down less than two points, even though every TV on every trading floor was tuned to live coverage of the Athens rioting. Footage showed the smoking shell that had been the Marfin Egnatia Bank. With the release of Angeliki's name, as well as those of Vivi and Nondas, it became clear that this was no longer a normal Greek outburst; the country seemed to be coming apart.

Just before the vote on May 6, 2010, George Papandreou explained his country's situation tersely: "Today things are simple.

Either we vote and implement the deal, or we condemn Greece to bankruptcy." The vote was concluded at 7:05 P.M. in Athens, 1:05 P.M. in New York, and the plan was adopted by a margin of 172–121.

As this was occurring in Athens, the U.S. stock market was weakening, with the S&P futures at 1152.50, down nearly 1 percent for the day. But one money manager thought the fallout from the Greek vote would only get worse, and he decided to exit a huge portion of his stock market holdings. Tragically, he decided to bail out all at once and sparked the most violent stock market crash the United States has ever seen.

Even when trading was a purely manual affair, traders used algorithms. They had basic ideas, or rules of thumb, about what to do if, for instance, the Japanese yen rallied or the yield on the ten-year Treasury note fell, but this was always balanced by the discretion of the human being charged with physically executing trades. However, as markets became more computerized and the majority of trading was executed electronically, the list of algorithmic instructions, which had now been reduced to computer code, was increasingly complex. When a machine is doing the work, there are a breathtaking number of possible inputs and outcomes for the buying or selling of stocks or futures or options or nearly any financial instrument. Users of these trading algorithms believed they had an advantage over human traders because the logic and programming at the heart of the algorithm would automatically pump out orders at blistering speed. Profit opportunities that would have been too fleeting for a human could be harvested, while big orders that might have negatively impacted the market if executed by a human could be easily and automatically broken up into much smaller chunks, minimizing the impact they might have on the market. All of this meant that trading had become less about divining the market's direction and was now almost completely reduced to getting data as quickly as possible, processing it in a flash, deciding what to do (cancel existing orders, place new orders, bid for more at the current price, bid for less at the current price, etc.) as quickly as possible and faster than anyone else.

One asset manager at a smallish midwestern investment house wanted to hedge some of his exposure in case the U.S. stock market continued to fall. It was a reasonable course to take, consistent with the stereotypical midwestern traits of prudence and sobriety. Televisions that day showed rioters in Athens and the scorched hulk of Angeliki's bank. The midwestern manager turned to an algorithm for his hedging in an effort to reduce the impact his own selling would have on the price received. It didn't work.

An algorithm is a precisely defined set of rules. On May 6 the hedger's rules were meant to account for the amount of trading and to adjust the number of futures contracts sold accordingly. If volume went up, the programmers responsible for the algorithm assumed the market would be able to accommodate larger sell orders, or more of them. If volume went down, they would reduce the size or number of their sell orders. Their goal was to limit the impact of their own selling by having the market tell them the size of its appetite.

Waddell & Reed is a modestly sized asset manager based in a leafy suburb of Kansas City. Known for its Ivy brand of mutual funds, its most popular product in May 2010 was the Ivy Asset Strategy Fund, one of the new breed of "go anywhere" funds, in which managers can invest in stocks but can leave stocks for bonds or any other asset class when the managers think it's appropriate. It was also allowed to hedge using futures, something the managers had done from time to time. The Ivy Asset Strategy Fund had enjoyed superb growth, attracting $21 billion from investors since late 2005, and in May 2010 it accounted for more than one-third of all the money Waddell & Reed had under management.

As the Athens riots were intensifying, Waddell & Reed reached the same conclusion that was dawning on millions around the globe. The risk of Greece's troubles infecting Germany, Spain, and France, and specifically the banks in those countries, and of those troubles spilling over to the United States and the rest of the world, was much greater than anyone had thought just a month before. In April the managers at the Ivy Asset Strategy Fund had been overwhelmingly bullish, and the portfolio they had accumulated expressed that optimism for the stock market: 87 percent of its assets were invested in stocks, the first assets that would be hurt—and the hardest to be hit—if Greece's troubles began to spread.

Waddell & Reed decided to hedge its position in the stock market by selling futures on the S&P 500 index. These futures would gain in value if the market tumbled and would offset losses in their existing portfolio. These were the same futures that Leland, O'Brien, and Rubinstein had used to hedge with their portfolio insurance in 1987, but now the futures were traded via computer. By programming an algorithm, Waddell & Reed was able to do their hedging without any messy human intervention such as a trader refusing to sell the contracts he was supposed to.

This wasn't the first time Waddell & Reed had used an algorithm to sell S&P futures as a hedge. They would later say they had done it a dozen times in the previous three years, but in those cases the selling had always taken several hours to complete. As the Greek riots played out on televisions on trading floors around the world, the U.S. stock market was under pressure, and Waddell & Reed didn't have hours. After the austerity vote, the S&P futures had fallen another percentage point, to 1141.00. They were now down 2 percent for the day, and the decline was accelerating. Over the next fifteen minutes, the futures dropped another 1.1 percent, to 1128.50. With the market deteriorating quickly, Waddell & Reed wanted to hedge by selling S&P futures. The size of their fund meant they had to sell tens of thousands of futures contracts if the hedge was to have a meaningful impact on the fund's performance.

Plus the market was closing in just one hour and forty minutes. Adding to their urgency was the scheduled release the next morning of the most important economic data of the month: the change in nonfarm payrolls and the unemployment rate. This news had the potential to drive the market sharply lower.

Waddell & Reed turned to British investment bank Barclays to execute its hedges. Barclays would charge Waddell & Reed a fee for each contract it sold, but as was common among executing brokers, it would offer Waddell & Reed use of a customizable execution algorithm. Once Waddell & Reed tailored certain parameters, the algorithm would automatically execute the trades electronically while breaking them down into small chunks, with the goal of preventing Waddell & Reed's own selling from depressing the price it received. To do this, the algorithm would allow Waddell & Reed to determine not just how many contracts to sell but also how quickly to sell them; the slower the selling, the less adverse impact it would have but the more likely the price would fall before Waddell & Reed could get its hedge in place.

Waddell & Reed wanted to sell 75,000 futures contracts, together worth approximately $4.1 billion, before the market closed. This would be a massive undertaking. In the past, trades of this size had taken several hours to complete. So Barclays launched three different versions of the algorithm that ran in parallel.

Waddell & Reed could choose to have the algorithms take price into account and ease up if the price fell too much or if it sold too many contracts in a time period so short that the market couldn't fully absorb them. Instead, each of the three would focus on volume. The selling wouldn't slow or stop no matter how low the price fell or how quickly it dropped.

To get the selling done quickly, each version was supposed to simultaneously sell 25,000 contracts, and each would break down the day into minute-long periods. In each minute, each of the three versions would attempt to sell 3 percent of the total volume traded during the previous minute, for a total of 9 percent of the previous minute's volume in each subsequent minute. By using the previous minute's volume as their yardstick, Barclays and Waddell & Reed were hoping the market would describe its ability to absorb the selling. A lot of volume would suggest to the algorithm that the market was very liquid, and it could release more sell orders without having the market drop too much under its own weight. Relatively light volume would tell the algorithm the market couldn't handle much additional volume, and the algorithm would taper the number of contracts it attempted to sell.

Waddell & Reed wouldn't just cram the orders into the market, selling at whatever price someone was willing to pay. Rather, they would join the lowest price at which others were also willing to sell, often called the *offer* price since that's the price at which the seller is offering contracts for sale. But this made little difference. If the market lurched downward and Waddell & Reed joined those selling at the new, lower offer price, the market could never recover. Waddell & Reed was still putting the market under unmanageable strain through the sheer volume of its selling.

Waddell & Reed would later say they "believed that trades of the size we initiated normally are absorbed easily," but by having the algorithms essentially ignore price and time, they were able to move much more quickly and could sell substantial numbers of futures contracts before the previous selling was absorbed. And more important, just as LOR had learned twenty-three years earlier, a market's capacity to absorb selling disappears just when it's needed most.

When Barclays executed Waddell & Reed's first trades at 2:32 P.M. Eastern Time, less than ninety minutes after the austerity vote had been recorded in Athens, the S&P futures had fallen a bit more. They were at 1127.75, down 3.1 percent for the day.

Almost immediately the drop worsened, and volume in the S&P futures jumped. During the first minute when the Barclays/

Waddell & Reed algorithms were at work, 10,135 futures contracts traded. In the three hours between 11:00 A.M. and 2:00 P.M. an average of just 7,666 futures had traded each minute.

At the end of this first minute of selling, the S&P futures stood at 1126.50, down another 1.25 points. Barclays's algorithms would try to sell 912 futures contracts, worth about $51.4 million, during the second minute, and would continue trying to sell 9 percent of the previous minute's volume in each subsequent minute as volume started to increase. During the minute that started at 2:35:00, the algorithms would combine to try to sell another 2,065 futures contracts worth $116.1 million as the price fell to 1122.50, its lowest price of the day so far and 3.5 percent below where it had ended the day before. With total volume of 31,297 contracts in the 2:35 minute, Barclays would also queue orders to sell another 2,817 contracts worth $158.1 million during the next minute. During that next minute, the futures would drop to 1120.00, and Barclays would prepare to sell another 2,285 contracts worth $128 million.

At 2:39 P.M., just seven minutes after the selling started, volume had quadrupled to 42,855 contracts, and the price had fallen another 6 points to 1114.00, a loss of an additional 0.5 percent for a market that was now down exactly 50 points, or 4.3 percent for the day. During the next minute, the algorithms would try to sell another 3,857 contracts worth $214.8 million, even though the previous minutes' selling hadn't been fully absorbed.

Somewhere between the mix of parameters (including price and time) that had previously caused the algorithm to function smoothly and the single, volume-only parameter the three algorithms were using now, a feedback loop was created. Previously, with other parameters occasionally throttling the selling, buyers were able to digest the volume and offset their exposure using other vehicles, including exchange-traded funds (ETFs) on the S&P and other indexes—an innovation since 1987—or the generic basket of stocks making up the S&P, as index arbitrageurs had been doing for decades. Trading baskets of stock was now also purely electronic and instantaneous, with no human oversight. Other algorithms had been programmed by electronic arbs to buy the futures that Waddell & Reed was selling, and, if the whole trade could be done for a profit, sell an ETF or basket of stocks. As had happened in 1987, the arbs were buying the futures based on the prices they believed they could get for selling the ETFs or the individual stocks that made up the basket, and would then often enter orders to sell the stocks "at the market," meaning whatever price was immediately available with the belief that price would generate a profit. Normally the price for each stock is close to the last traded price, but, just as in 1987, the prices arbs thought they could get was an illusion.

Despite the efforts of the arbs, at 9 percent of the volume, Waddell & Reed's constant selling couldn't be neatly moved outside the closed world of futures. Rather, the proprietary traders buying and selling in the S&P futures were buying from Waddell & Reed and were building an inventory they didn't want. Or they were just immediately selling those same futures to other proprietary traders, artificially inflating the volume Waddell & Reed believed they could rely on. These traders didn't want to have any inventory; their goal was simply to provide liquidity for vanishingly brief periods of time by buying from aggressive sellers and selling to aggressive buyers while trying to pocket the spread between the price the market was willing to pay, the bid, and the price the market demanded to sell, the offer. There was no certainty these proprietary traders would make money. On the contrary, if their trading rules, as expressed by the algorithm they'd programmed, were flawed, or if the market acted in a way they didn't expect, the losses could be sickening.

As real liquidity—the ability to absorb and disperse the selling pressure to other venues and products—was decreasing, the Barclays/Waddell & Reed algorithms, which had been programmed to erroneously equate volume with liquidity to the exclusion of all else, thought liquidity was exploding.

In the next minute, at 2:40:00, 37,916 futures traded, and the price at the end of the minute was down another point to 1113.00. The S&P futures were down 4.4 percent for the day, and each minute's volume had nearly quadrupled in the eight minutes since the algorithms started selling. As real liquidity dwindled, the Barclays algorithms were telling themselves that liquidity had nearly quadrupled, and that prompted them to try to sell 3,412 futures contracts, worth $189.9 million, during the next minute. Proprietary traders and index arbs would buy many of them. The proprietary traders were stuck with them, while the arbs launched a flood of orders to sell the constituent stocks. But many of the index arb algorithms weren't any better than Waddell & Reed's unthinking algorithm. The index arbs were again sending orders to sell the constituent stocks at whatever price they would bring, believing they knew what that price would be and hoping they were right.

Two minutes later, during the minute that began at 2:42:00, 38,943 futures traded, and the price fell to 1107.00 as the algorithms prepared to sell another 3,505 contracts, worth $194 million, during the next minute. Barclays had taken the ebb out of the market. With its algorithm constantly selling in a self-reinforcing manner, liquidity was never able to regenerate.

The price of the S&P futures had been down 3.1 percent for the day when Waddell & Reed began its selling ten minutes earlier. Now the price was down another 1.8 percent and was below 1110.70, the level where it ended 2009. As recently as April 23, the day Greece formally asked for help, the S&P had been up 9.2 percent for the year. In the previous eight trading days, it had surrendered half that gain, but it had closed on May 5 still up 4.6 percent for the year. It had given back all that and more.

By 2:42:40, buy-side liquidity—the only liquidity that mattered at this moment—had collapsed to just 14 percent of the buy-side liquidity that the market had displayed earlier in the day.

As Waddell & Reed continued selling, the index arbs struggled to buy the futures and then to lay off their risk by selling the ETFs or individual stocks. Though this arbitrage helped steady the futures in the face of selling, it created a problem never seen before and only possible in a fully computerized, algorithm-driven market, with thousands of computers searching to make a profit.

Every time the price of the S&P futures changed, scores of ETFs were repriced. With each repricing, a computer message had to be sent to exchanges canceling existing orders, and each cancellation had to be confirmed by another computer message. New orders had to be placed via a third message, receipt of any new order had to be confirmed via a fourth message, and once the orders had been executed, those executions had to be reported to both parties, again via electronic messages sent and received in the background. The same was true of each of the stocks making up the S&P 500, every time the futures traded or the price changed. With every repricing of the stocks making up the S&P and the ETFs that included them, another blizzard of electronic messages canceling, confirming, replacing, and again confirming was launched. And then the message traffic increased exponentially as those repricings drove the repricing of the options on each of those ETFs and stocks. A single stock can easily have fifty different options trading, so instead of a single change in the price of the S&P futures leading to 500 repricings, it can easily lead to more than 25,000, each of which might foster several unique electronic messages, plus all the messages launched as a result of the repricing of the hundreds of ETFs and the thousands of options on those ETFs. And that is for a single trader. With thousands of traders around the world—more than 7,500 traders traded just the S&P futures during the hour starting at 2:00 P.M. on May 6—and many thousands more trading other instruments, each price change in the S&P futures leads to hundreds of thousands or millions of computer messages. The world already knew the limits to liquidity. It was about to learn that these trading systems had similar limits.

Not everyone was surprised to see a computerized algorithm run away with the market. For decades the original high-frequency traders worked at their craft while wearing neon-colored polyester jackets and orthotic shoes, screaming their bids and offers from the futures pits on the floor of one of the two Chicago futures exchanges. They would scribble on trading cards, recording the buys and sells they had executed with a nod or wave or shout, often selling before they even found time to record the preceding buy. At the end of the day, they would tally the thousands of contracts bought and sold and hope that some profit had been shaken out of the market.

As the futures world went electronic, the bellowing, sharp-elbowed pit trader gave way to the computer programmer. But computers can get things frustratingly wrong. In March 2010, about six weeks before Waddell & Reed unwittingly conspired to crash the stock market, electronic traders were being warned about getting it wrong.

Across Jackson Boulevard from the Chicago Board of Trade stands the pillared fortress that is the Federal Reserve Bank of Chicago. Armored cars enter and leave on the plainer north side of the bank building, but higher up, above the columned eastern facade fronting LaSalle Street, are the economists. It being Chicago, many of them focus on the futures markets and the dangers that were ignored as these futures markets went from trading volume dictated by the number of men (they were overwhelmingly male) who could squeeze into a futures pit to the speed and quantity of trading volume that is possible when an electron passes through a computer chip in the exchange's trade computer.

On March 25, 2010, these economists, a group often seen as pale, pasty, and too focused on the nuts and bolts of electronic trading, wrote a letter to the SEC warning that "the competitive quest for greater and greater speed must be balanced with appropriate risk controls so that a clearly erroneous trade does not destabilize markets by precipitating a cascade of other trades in response." Before the SEC had an opportunity to respond, everyone became worried about Greece.

Between 2:00 P.M. and 3:00 P.M. on May 6, an average of 81 individual trades took place each second in the S&P futures, the vast majority of them driven by algorithms. That was the average, but during several seconds more than 500 individual trades occurred, and during one particular second there were 889 individual trades, each leading to a storm of repricings that then prompted a chain reaction of electronic orders and messages. But the system didn't have an unlimited capacity.

Often Waddell & Reed's selling was taking place at several different prices in the span of a few milliseconds (a millisecond is a thousandth of a second). As the frequency of price changes increased, the number of messages to and from exchanges was increasing exponentially. While the fiber optic lines and microwave towers that banks and trading firms have installed are intended to transmit those messages at nearly the speed of light, and the computers around the world have been souped up to create orders or cancel them or launch a different blizzard of execution messages and orders if just one of a firm's orders actually gets executed, there is a limit to the amount of message traffic the system can sustain. All the trading, including Waddell & Reed's selling and all the other message traffic it spawned, pushed the market lower while pushing the system to that limit. The market was at quote saturation.

The futures were still trading even as the price was dropping, but the arbs' orders to sell the baskets of stocks were now backing up without being executed, due to delays in transmitting orders and confirming messages. In 1929, the system had similarly reached quote saturation when the stock ticker ran hours behind the market. On the worst days in October 1929, the ticker running behind could mean only one thing—stocks were falling again—and that delay was often enough to prompt investors to sell, even if they had no idea where the market was trading. In 2010, the ticker was again backed up because stocks were falling, and the volume of trading had overwhelmed the system's ability to keep up.

The New York Stock Exchange's NYSE Arca exchange claims that it was the first all-electronic exchange in the United States. It was the first exchange to experience problems on May 6, and it did so just five minutes after Waddell & Reed started selling.

Electronic exchanges constantly monitor each other, and if one exchange recognizes that another exchange is experiencing a glitch, the first exchange will request "self-help" for the exchange that is troubled. Self-help is essentially a warning to the rest of the financial world to stay away from the troubled exchange until the problem has been resolved. At 2:36:59, NASDAQ recognized that NYSE Arca was experiencing problems and declared self-help. Orders routed through NASDAQ would logically ignore NYSE Arca. For those routing away from NYSE Arca, liquidity had been reduced again.

Eleven minutes after Waddell & Reed started selling, in the minute ending at 2:43:00 P.M., the proprietary traders who had been working to provide liquidity to Waddell & Reed were reaching their breaking points. Some traders simply turned off their systems and stopped buying and selling. The remaining traders accumulated an inventory of futures contracts, something they didn't want to do because they hadn't been able to move the pressure to other markets. This inability was partly due to the intensity of Waddell & Reed's selling and partly because, as always happens, liquidity was drying up as the market became volatile, partly because of problems routing orders and partly because the system was overloaded and saturated and orders to sell stocks weren't getting through. The fail-safe systems for the remaining market makers did as they were programmed to do, again without human thought. Some exited their positions and joined those who had already dropped out, further shrinking liquidity. Others, having accumulated a position in the futures and unable to offset or unload it, simply sold the futures they owned at whatever price they could get. As they prepared to sell, they canceled any orders they had placed to buy at prices well below the current market price. Resting orders to buy the S&P futures at any price, no matter how low, were now evaporating to a fraction of what was normally seen, another reason some proprietary traders who'd built up unwanted positions decided to sell at whatever price they could get. Together they prepared to sell the 3,300 contracts, worth $181 million, that they had accumulated.

With their orders to buy at any price canceled, the few remaining high-frequency traders who owned the futures executed their orders to sell them. With so few buyers left, the trades were filled at many different prices, each lower than the one before it. Each lower price unleashed another blizzard of computerized messages canceling existing orders, confirming the cancellations, placing new orders reflecting the new prices, and confirming the new orders.

This selling of 3,300 futures contracts in a few milliseconds represented substantial volume, but it was actually taking place between the few proprietary trading firms still participating in what the SEC would later call a "hot potato" effect, with one firm selling to another, which instantly sold to another, which instantly sold to another, all in a few tiny slivers of a second, totally consuming any remaining liquidity. These few firms continued to trade because that was how they had been programmed. They may have believed that chaos meant opportunity, or their programmers may have never contemplated one hedger trying to cram so much selling into so few minutes.

Unfortunately, the Barclays algorithms running for Waddell & Reed didn't recognize the "hot potato" volume as a sign that the market had exhausted its capacity to absorb trading. Instead, Barclays and Waddell & Reed thought it was a sign of nearly unlimited liquidity. So they prepared to sell a nearly unlimited number of futures in the next minute.

Human traders standing in a pit have always understood that sometimes the best way to execute a giant order is to shut up. By quietly selling bits and pieces and then stopping for a few moments, the opposing humans don't know if the selling is finished, so they can't game the order. It's a bit like playing hard to get. But the Barclays algorithm, operating without any human input, never knew to shut up. It blindly continued selling 9 percent of the volume every minute. Instead of playing hard to get, it was more like the psycho stalker ex-boyfriend who won't go away.

As the next minute began, the New York Stock Exchange started having problems of its own. While NYSE Arca had been created as a purely electronic exchange, the parent NYSE had by now morphed into a largely electronic exchange, with computers in server rooms replacing many of the humans on the trading floor. At 2:42:46 P.M., NYSE's prices for some of the most important stocks in the world stopped making sense. The prices NYSE was reporting were higher than those on all the other exchanges. One analyst later suggested that NYSE trading messages were backing up, and price notifications were getting stuck in a computerized queue, waiting to go out but inexplicably delayed. The delays caused the prices to become stale and no longer representative of the current reality. When they were finally released, they reflected prices from some seconds or minutes prior when prices were much higher. As Waddell & Reed was preparing to sell that nearly infinite number of futures contracts in the mistaken impression that liquidity had increased, one of the most important sources of liquidity and *the* icon of American finance, the New York Stock Exchange, was experiencing debilitating problems.

In the minute beginning at 2:43:00, the one-minute volume for the S&P futures nearly doubled from the previous minute to 73,083 contracts as trading firms passed the hot potato from one to another to another, driving the price down each time. Waddell & Reed was fooled into thinking liquidity was again increasing. Firms launched another flurry of computerized messages into an already delayed and clogged system. During this minute, the price of the S&P futures fell another 8.25 points, or 0.7 percent, to 1098.75. It was now down 5.7 percent for the day as the Barclays algorithms queued up another 6,577 contracts, worth $361 million, in a market that couldn't handle a tiny fraction of that.

During the minute that began at 2:44:00, Waddell & Reed sold those 6,577 contracts, and all that selling drove the price down to 1082.00, a loss of 7.0 percent on the day and 1.5 percent in just the last minute. A total of 67,432 contracts traded during this minute.

During the minute that began at 2:45:00, traders feared for their financial lives, as those who still owned futures or who had sold what they'd accumulated but had since built up more inventory again prepared to get out of them at any price. Waddell & Reed prepared to sell another 6,069 (9 percent of the 67,432 contracts that had traded in the previous minute) futures contracts, worth $328.3 million. At 2:45:27, the S&P futures dropped 12.75 points, or 1.2 percent, in 500 milliseconds (one-half of one second) as the last of the proprietary traders liquidated the last 1,100 contracts they owned. The futures reached 1056.00, down 26 points or another 2.4 percent since the end of just the previous minute. The S&P futures had now lost 71.75 points, or 6.4 percent, since Waddell & Reed started selling thirteen minutes earlier. The S&P futures were now down 108 points, or 9.3 percent, for the day, and were more than 18 percent below their high for the year (which had been reached just nine trading days ago).

The futures had lost 1.7 percent in the last fifteen seconds and more than 5 percent in the last four and one-half minutes. With this final move to 1056.00, nearly all buyers had disappeared from the futures market. Even those market-maker algorithms not programmed to automatically shut down were finally being stopped manually by the humans in charge at their respective trading firms. At 2:45:28, traders were willing to buy fewer than 1,050 contracts at any price, all the way down to zero, or about one-sixth of what Waddell & Reed was planning to sell this minute and about one-seventh of what they would try to sell in the next minute. Buy-side market depth, the total number of contracts the market was willing to buy within a reasonable distance of the last traded price, fell to less than 1 percent of the depth the market had offered that morning. If Waddell & Reed had simply decided to sell 6,069 contracts in the same way the proprietary traders had been selling them, at the market, they could have literally driven the market down to zero, just as LOR's trader had feared driving the market down to zero in 1987. At this, the Chicago Mercantile Exchange, the exchange venue for the S&P futures, said enough was enough.

This was the bottom in the futures market, because the Chicago Mercantile Exchange wasn't about to let anyone undermine any market by selling it down to zero; 1056.00 would be the low for the day. Waddell & Reed had sold only about half of the 75,000 futures they wanted to sell, but they had sold nearly $2 billion worth in the span of twelve minutes by ignoring price and any of the other criteria available to them and by selling based only on volume.

At 2:45:28, the CME temporarily and automatically halted trading in the S&P futures in a process called "stop logic." The S&P futures stopped trading for five seconds out of fear that the minuscule buying interest would allow the glut of sell orders to drive "extreme market moves resulting from cascading . . . execution." It was really an opportunity for the market to catch its breath, and for potential buyers to recognize that the market was too low—that Waddell & Reed had sold it down too far—and that they should buy. During this five-second pause, the buy orders started to come in.

When trading resumed at 2:45:33, the first trade was transacted at 1056.75, three-quarters of a point above the halt level. By the end of that second it was at 1061.00, and by the end of the next second it was at 1064.75. Traders who wanted to buy the S&P at a giant discount to where it started the day, to where it was just fifteen minutes ago, gladly bought the rest of Waddell & Reed's futures contracts, and at slightly higher prices as the market rebounded. Traders recognized a bargain.

During the five-second stoppage in futures trading, the flow of electronic messages to and from the CME slowed dramatically. The orders from index arbs to the stock markets stopped. This drop in total message traffic zipping along fiber optic lines, leapfrogging from one microwave tower to the next and piling up in computers, allowed the orders that had been backing up in queues, waiting to get to their relevant exchange or back to the computer that had placed them, to be released. The futures had hit bottom for the day and were rebounding, but with the problems in communication, many of the orders to sell individual stocks and ETFs were just being received by their exchanges. The broad stock market had bottomed, but nobody thought to tell some of the most important stocks in that market.

At 2:42:46, NYSE prices for just 100 stocks were flawed. By 2:44:30, the problem had spread to about 250 NYSE stocks. Fifteen seconds later, the NYSE problem was much bigger, and 1,665 stocks had price delays averaging more than five seconds—an eternity, given how quickly prices were falling—and some delays lasted more than thirty seconds. NYSE data was now totally out of sync with data from the rest of the world, just as orders to sell individual stocks were released from their purgatory and were reaching markets.

Other firms were running algorithms that recognized the trouble some major exchanges were having. These algorithms were automatically rerouting orders from the troubled exchanges to smaller, secondary exchanges that don't normally do much trading. Often the rerouting was accomplished without the human traders understanding it was happening. These algorithms were intended to help the firm get the best price available by searching all the stock exchanges and routing to the exchange with the best price. But as more orders were pointed toward second-tier exchanges, even blue-chip stocks collapsed in price.

Procter & Gamble was founded on Halloween 1837 after a father encouraged two sons-in-law—one a candlemaker and the other an apprentice to a soapmaker—to go into business together. On May 6, 2010, it was a consumer goods colossus that sold $78 billion worth of candles and soap and thousands of other items each year. It had closed at $62.16 on May 5 and had survived the early selling on the sixth well. At 2:42 P.M., it was still trading near $62.00, down on the day but not by much, just as you'd expect for a consumer goods company that was seen as a bit of a safe haven during turmoil. After all, everyone was still likely to buy shampoo even if Greece defaulted. But the orders to sell Procter & Gamble shares that had been stuck in a queue were starting to get through, and the potential buyers, having seen the chaos in the S&P futures and recognizing that different exchanges were showing dramatically different prices for P&G, were shying away—often without human intervention—and canceling any orders to buy. By 2:44 Procter & Gamble was below $60.00 a share, but the decline was still consistent with the context of the rest of the market. Just 210 seconds later P&G was trading at $39.37, a 36.7 percent drop from the day before, and a decline of 36.5 percent during the previous four minutes, as the pent-up orders broke through. P&G share-holders had lost a combined $63 billion in those four minutes yet they were much better off than shareholders in the consulting company Accenture.

Accenture had split from the renowned accounting firm Arthur Andersen in 1989, and in 2010 it was a consulting giant. After going public in 2001, Accenture had been a relatively quiet earner. It closed at $42.17 a share on May 5, but on May 6, buying interest started to decline after 2:25 P.M., and orders to sell Accenture ate away at the remaining interest. At 2:30 Accenture was still trading at $41.00, a sizable drop of 2.8 percent but in keeping with the broader market. Soon the decline accelerated, until Accenture was trading below $39.00 at 2:47:30. Things got much worse thirteen seconds later, as sell orders broke out of their computerized queues. At 2:47:43 Accenture traded down from $38.05 to $32.62 when a sell order for 3,780 shares was routed through the hobbled NYSE Arca despite NASDAQ's self-help warning. The next trade was only 100 shares, but they traded at just $5.43 a share. As orders to sell were routed away from the major exchanges by those aware of the problems faced, they were sent to a tiny regional exchange many traders and brokers didn't even know existed. Nine seconds later another 100 Accenture shares traded at $4.04, followed by more orders pushing the price down to $1.84. At 2:47:53 100 shares traded for the laughably low price of $0.01, the lowest price the system could recognize. Other trades followed at the same one cent per share before Accenture stock found its footing and rallied.

As these ridiculously low prices hit the market, the Dow Jones Industrial Average continued lower despite the halt and recovery in the S&P futures. The Dow hit its lowest point of 9869.62, a loss of 998.50, or 9.2 percent, just a few seconds after 2:47, as P&G traded at $39.37 and Accenture headed to $0.01. The Dow was now down more than 1,000 points from that morning's high, as the linkages between exchanges that kept prices rational dissolved.

This echo from the drop in S&P futures would become known as the Flash Crash, as three million shares traded at prices more than 90 percent below where they'd closed the previous day. More than two hundred securities, including both stocks and ETFs, essentially lost 100 percent of their value at one point on May 6. Three hundred twenty-six different securities traded at prices that were at least 60 percent below their 2:40 price, including twelve of the constituents making up the S&P 500 and thirty making up the Russell 2000 index of small capitalization stocks.

By 2:52 the damage had been done and the markets were starting to recover as Waddell & Reed finished the last of its selling. They managed to sell the 75,000 contracts they wanted, but given how they had driven the market lower, they represented much less than the $4.1 billion they did originally. About half were sold after the market had bottomed and the futures were heading higher thanks to the influx of bargain hunters.

Over the span of twenty minutes, Waddell & Reed executed 6,438 trades, selling an average of just under twelve contracts per trade. Each of those trades fostered a raft of electronic messages; thus the impact of the selling wasn't just that it drove the market down but that it also increased the message traffic to unmanageable levels that saturated the communication systems and caused price updates and index arb sell orders to circulate in message queues for seconds and minutes. Those seconds and minutes are a lifetime in a business that spends millions of dollars to send orders between Chicago and New York by microwave because it's 5 milliseconds faster than fiber optic cable.

The S&P ended the day on May 6, 2010, down just 3.2 percent, but that closing level was 5.9 percent above its low for the day. The Dow Jones Industrial Average closed down 347.80 points, 3.2 percent, matching the performance of the S&P, but similarly the Dow closed 650.70 points, 6.6 percent, above its low. Waddell & Reed hadn't intended to stampede the market. They wanted to do right by their investors by hedging, but they had forgotten that markets don't provide liquidity just because you demand it. A better question is why Barclays launched an algorithm that could be weaponized.

One of the reasons stocks tend to outperform other asset classes is that you don't necessarily get instantaneous liquidity. Depending on how big a position and how volatile the market, there are times when you're stuck with the position you have, even if you'd give anything to be out of the market. But the market doesn't work like that. It can reward investors generously at the cost of sometimes being along for a ride they'd just as soon not take.

The astonishing element of the Flash Crash is that smart people, who should have known better, forgot that. In fact, the modern stock market crashes are all instances in which people, some smart, some not so much, forgot the lessons that the market teaches repeatedly. It generates an attractive return but with the risk of loss. It's most vulnerable when it's overextended. Liquidity dries up when it's most desired. New financial products might seem to solve an immediate problem, while creating a much larger one in the future when stressed.

Because of this, the crashes are similar despite spanning more than a century; they might not repeat themselves, but they rhyme. That's because at their heart, it's not about money or numbers or individual stocks but about fear and greed. There is almost always too much greed. There is rarely enough fear—not of a drop in stock prices, nor of keeping interest rates too low for too long and inflating a bubble. There's not enough fear of unsettling the market by changing the rules abruptly and capriciously or of refusing to institute sensible regulation simply because we don't agree with those who adopted the regulations. And there's not enough fear that the financial products and trading algorithms we use can behave in a way we don't envision.

The American stock market has allowed corporations to raise capital, and thereby create jobs, for more than two hundred years. It has supported lifestyles and funded retirements and educations for that same period and will continue to be the best vehicle for doing so. But it will crash again.

EPILOGUE

On the day Teddy Roosevelt became president, the Dow Jones Industrial Average closed at 67.25. On May 6, 2010, the day of the "Flash Crash," it closed at 10520.32, and now it has reached an all-time high above 20,000. So things change. But they also stay the same: the Panic of 1907 was fostered by lax regulation of a new financial contraption (the trust company), just as the meltdown of 2008 was fueled by lax regulation of new financial contraptions (the plethora of mortgage-backed securities being peddled by bankers).

Our financial system has made tremendous progress, but at what cost? Like almost all societal progress, the cost has been an astonishing increase in speed and complexity, which often come into conflict, with disturbing consequences. The Panic of 1907 unfolded over eighteen months, with simple and simplistic financial vehicles. The Flash Crash of 2010 unfolded over minutes, with computers and financial communication systems limited only by the physical properties of the electron and the finite speed of light. This will be our warning for the next crash. When speed and financial complexity take another leap it will be time to watch for the phenomena that attend each crash: a robust stock market rally that pushes stock prices beyond reason, a financial vehicle that will foster selling at the worst possible time, a catalyst that will start the selling, even a warning that may seem odd but will later seem oddly prescient.

Any history of the United States as seen through the lens of the stock market will have its share of numbers, but by viewing the broader trends that led to the modern crashes, we might be able to see the next one coming. That is because although everything has changed, much has stayed the same. In learning about this history we'll also learn about ourselves, because the broader trends include not just the financial and economic but the political and social.

The first vital change has been speed. Today, with a click of a mouse we send money around the world, but in 1906 it took weeks for gold to be loaded onto ships in London and sent over the horizon to San Francisco. In 1929, many were astonished that it was possible to trade stocks from a ship in the mid-Atlantic and get a confirmation in less than ten minutes. But Michael Meehan's shipboard brokerage offices can be seen as a step toward the electronic exchanges that brought about the Flash Crash and led to our always-connected world, where we check our smartphones at the dinner table and wonder in frustration why a colleague hasn't responded to the email we sent ten minutes ago. By 2010, money moved around the world in a tiny fraction of a second (it would take about 35 milliseconds, or 35 one-thousandths of a second, for a trader in San Francisco to execute a trade in London), and traders were willing to pay nearly any price if they could trade a tinier fraction of a second faster than their competition. That velocity had become so consequential our entire financial system assumed this speed would work in its favor and took it for granted. But when technological glitches developed on May 6, 2010, and trades or price quotations were delayed for just a few seconds on some important exchanges, algorithms ignored those troubled exchanges, which essentially ceased to exist, and orders were routed to second- and third-tier exchanges that couldn't accommodate that level of trading volume.

The consequences of speed for the stock market weren't just felt through the rate at which things happened. Speed also changed the natures of trading and investing themselves, just as it changed the nature of travel. In 1907, the Wright brothers had barely gotten off the ground, and although the first real passenger air travel began in 1929, it was augmented by rail for certain portions of the trip because planes weren't reliable. By 1987, airlines had been deregulated and air travel was common, while in 2008 and 2010 the technology of videoconferencing meant we often didn't have to travel at all. Similarly, finance today is no longer primarily about companies and the people who run them, as it was in 1907. In 1929 it was about individual speculation and the investment trusts that finally made it possible for Americans of modest means to invest. In 1987, mutual funds were common, and those funds could use futures on the stock market to express their managers' strategies. By 2008, the products being sold by investment banks had become the blindingly complex miasma of mortgage-based products. In 2010, it was about how quickly an electron moves through the silicon chip at the heart of an exchange's computer.

In many ways, speed became an end in itself because, like information, money, and brawn, speed could be put to work. Today's algorithmic traders strip their computer programs to the bare essentials. The nanoseconds that an additional thousand lines of computer code add to the time it takes to execute a trade and capture a fleeting opportunity for profit are weighed against the additional safety the logic in those lines contributes, and since speed captures profit it often trumps safety. A programmer creating trading algorithms is like a soldier preparing for battle, measuring the usefulness of each piece of gear against the burden of carrying it once he's jumped out of the helicopter. Often the highest-paid pro-grammers on Wall Street are the ones who can take a trading algo-rithm that has five million lines of computer code and reduce it to three million lines, saving a fraction of a second. The inflection point for speed was 1987, when the New York Stock Exchange's Designated Order Turnaround (DOT) system was supposed to facilitate the execution of large orders by routing them electroni-cally to the trading floor, where they were to be executed by human specialists. Speed mattered, but the discretion and skill that a human broker might bring to bear still had value. Now we seem to believe that humans just slow things down, and so we program our systems to minimize the potential intrusion of human interaction. We focus on the objective issues at work, like the finite speed of light limiting how quickly we can transact, rather than the subjec-tive issues, like whether we should do the transaction.

Speed also played a role in credit default swaps, which were extended and transmogrified because of the speed at which new financial contraptions are adopted by competitors. If the swaps team at J.P. Morgan & Company had been able to keep the credit default swap to themselves rather than having to fend off usurp-ers, it's unlikely AIG FP would have written $80 billion worth on mortgage-backed securities. Instead, credit default swaps infected the financial world, with the European Bank for Reconstruction and Development being patient zero and the American financial system eventually getting the disease. It's easy to understand how this happened, given that immense sums can be earned in invest-ment banking by the glib salesperson able to peddle credit default swaps or mortgage-backed securities or any other financial con-traption, many of dubious value, to the new titans making even more immense sums by running hedge funds.

The speed at which American financiers can accumulate wealth has also increased. The greatest American fortunes are still made by industrialists—even if the industries are no longer steel, railroads, and oil but instead are software and websites. But for the first time in our history, the fortunes made in finance are rivaling those of the industrialists. In his day, J. P. Morgan was so powerful he served as a de facto Federal Reserve. Yet, when he died in 1913, his net worth was about $80 million, less than $2 billion in today's money. John D. Rockefeller, who'd made his fortune in crude oil production and refining, expressed shock that everyone in America had heard of J. P. Morgan, yet "he wasn't even a rich man." But today's list of America's billionaire financiers is studded with names most have never heard of, and they sit on fortunes many times larger than anything Morgan ever imagined. Warren Buffett, likely the only financier many Americans can name, has a net worth of more than $70 billion, thirty-five times that of J. P. Morgan.

The other important change—one that is often exacerbated by speed—is the increasing complexity of the financial products that have been at the heart of the modern stock market crashes. The trust company of 1907 was so simple it would now be considered quaint. The investment trust of the 1920s was a straightforward concept even after practitioners added leverage and tried to mask the resulting dangers by hiding behind a roster of university professors with Ph.D.s, the more of them the better, who tried to convince investors that diversification and professional management could somehow overcome the inescapably double-edged sword of leverage. The fifty-eight-year span from 1929 to 1987 was enough time for complexity to percolate throughout the financial system, just as it did across society at large, particularly after World War II. It took two economists at the top of their field to create portfolio insurance by using math that was so sophisticated that even today most professional investors don't understand it, and only a tiny fraction of them can explain it. This was the midpoint in complexity.

The next wave of complexity began simply enough. Investors

wanted to own a portfolio of mortgages, but institutional investors weren't allowed to bear the risk of default. To solve that problem, complexity was injected, and mortgage-backed securities were sliced into tranches, and then those tranches were rated. This first step meant the portfolio of mortgages could be deconstructed and the pieces reconstructed into something new and tragically flawed, even though no one seemed to recognize the risks. These bastard products, when cobbled together from the leftover pieces of mortgage-backed securities, became agonizingly complex and were therefore poorly understood. The analogy to Frankenstein's monster seems too easy, until we remember this line, uttered by the monster to Frankenstein: "Remember that I am thy creature. I ought to be thy Adam; but I am rather the fallen angel."

When increasingly complex financial instruments clash with speed, safety is forfeited and the magnitude of the potential damage increases. The *Exxon Valdez* was a breathtakingly complex system of steel tanks, safety valves, electronic navigation aids, and radios that allowed the ship to communicate with the human controllers onshore. But that just meant a string of lapses, each one small in isolation, could lead to catastrophe. Similarly, no human broker would have executed Waddell & Reed's May 6, 2010, sell order in the manner Barclays's algorithm did. But a series of lapses, including a desire to execute the hedges in an unrealistically short time frame and removing the limits on how many contracts might be sold in any particular minute, coupled with the decrease in liquidity that occurred as traders and brokers around the world watched the aftermath of the rioting in Greece, led to the Flash Crash, as the problems and flaws compounded each other. The entire American system of two dozen stock and option exchanges had become overwhelmingly complex, with many different traders using multiple algorithms of their own design, many stripped of prudent safeguards. The trading algorithms favored speed over safety, and a string of small lapses, each survivable in isolation, led to a crash in stock prices.

One good change is that personal finance has been democratized. Although American presidents have often gone too far in trying to bring homeownership to the electorate, the traditional thirty-year mortgage has increased homeownership from less than 50 percent in 1900 to more than 65 percent today. Securitizing mortgages likely made more money available to borrowers. This supply of money drove down the interest rate paid by those borrowers.

Americans have also democratized the stock market. When Jack Morgan warned before the Panic of 1907 that individual investors were coming into the stock market, the change he was referring to was an increase from a minuscule portion of Americans to a very small portion of Americans. By 2010, nearly half of Americans owned individual stocks or mutual funds as a means of financing retirement or education. Although this might appear to make our economy more susceptible to the ill effects of a crash, it has likely made our economy more resilient. In the 1920s, the stock market became a parlor game enjoyed by millions, but the real damage was done in 1929 and the wallowing decade that followed because many were merely speculators, living and dying with every uptick and downtick in a stock's price, rather than investors in for the long term. In 1929, the result was that a few controlled so much of the country's wealth and manipulated the stock market for their selfish ends. But today we again run the risk of wealth becoming concentrated such that too many of us depend on the spending of just a few of us.

These periodic convulsions in the market are often followed by an increase in regulation, which adds to the complexity. In 1907 there was almost no regulation. The Federal Reserve System was created during the next decade, but even then its primary role was to manage the money supply and serve as the lender of last resort, not to regulate the securities markets.

In the 1920s, too many commercial banks had become active in investment banking, often taking enormous risks by underwriting common stock issuance or engaging in other facets of investment banking. Then, in 1933, the Glass-Steagall Act prohibited commercial banks from engaging in the investment business. It was passed as a response to the more than five thousand commercial banks that failed between 1930 and 1932, often because they'd put their depositors' money at risk in these investment banking activities. Glass-Steagall built a wall between commercial banks, which would get insurance to protect their depositors against loss, at the cost of being forced to abandon some lines of business.

In 1934, after the Crash of 1929, Congress created the Securities and Exchange Commission to govern nearly every relationship that had to do with money, trading, and investing. Public corporations had to register the securities they sold and make regular disclosures of their financial details. Exchanges were regulated, and so were the brokers who traded through them. Stock pools that baldly manipulated the prices of securities for personal gain were outlawed.

Slowly the most important element of Glass-Steagall—this wall between commercial banking, with its promise of deposit insurance, and investment banking, with the risk inherent in the capital markets—was eroded, and giant commercial banks that might help a client hedge foreign exchange risk wanted to be able to offer additional, similar services, just as J.P. Morgan & Company wanted to lend Exxon nearly $5 billion so that it had an advantage when it was time to offer other, more lucrative services. Believing there was value in what came to be known euphemistically as "cross-selling," regulators became more lenient, and banks became more adept at finding and exploiting loopholes. Complexity was increasing in an attempt not to create value but to circumvent regulation. When in

1999 Bill Clinton signed the Gramm-Leach-Bliley Act, commonly known as the Financial Modernization Act in another example of euphemizing, Glass-Steagall was effectively repealed with the introduction of the financial holding company. Commercial banks like Citigroup and J.P. Morgan & Company were free to engage in investment banking with the undeniable advantage of lower-cost deposits as their funding source, and the backstop of federal deposit insurance. This insurance meant depositors had no reason to fear losses up to the insurance limits; there would be no "run" by fearful depositors, as had occurred in 1907. Since commercial banks were insured, there was no reason for the world to lose faith in their ability to repay. It was the loss of faith in this ability to repay that had doomed both Bear Stearns and Lehman Brothers. This was a gigantic advantage for a commercial bank engaging in investment banking. As a result, commercial banks became some of the largest securitizers of mortgages. Before the repeal of Glass-Steagall, the commercial banks wouldn't even have been in the room in late 2008, when Henry Paulson was forced to distribute TARP bailouts, the largest of which went to commercial banks.

The modern stock market crashes share several phenomena: The stock market rallies robustly. Some new contraption causes problems. The government often intervenes at the wrong moment or fails to intervene when it should. As speed and complexity increase, the manifestations of these commonalities change slightly, but the phenomenon that is least changed is the presence of a catalyst that triggers the crash. Hopefully we'll recognize the event that might spark a crash when it occurs, and though we may not be able to describe the catalyst in advance, as Justice Potter Stewart said about obscenity, we might know it when we see it. The primary concern is that as our society becomes increasingly modern, it seems to take less time for each new catalyst to exert its influence on our stock market. Nearly eighteen months passed between the 1906 earthquake and the Panic of 1907. One month passed between Clarence Hatry's shenanigans becoming public and the Crash of 1929. A weekend passed between Iran's October 1987 attacks on U.S.-flagged tankers in the Persian Gulf and our military response and Black Monday of 1987. Just hours passed from the rioting and arson in Athens to the Flash Crash.

If the market is vulnerable because it has rallied strongly in the recent past and is now beyond a level that might generate a reasonable return, the catalyst will push the market toward chaos. If a poorly understood financial contraption then causes selling at the worst time, we'll get our next crash.

By comparing the phenomena common to every crash we can better understand America and how it continues to change. These phenomena are the consistent elements; they are the mile markers that allow us to measure our progress. It's by examining these consistent elements that we can recognize the increase in the rate of change and the mounting complexity of our financial world. Speed increases. Complexity increases. When speed and complexity collide, speed usually wins, and since the first casualty of our obsession with speed is safety, our stock market crashes.

ACKNOWLEDGMENTS

While the image of a solitary author working away is a popular one, I had a tremendous amount of help in completing this book. That said, any errors are mine.

Without David Fugate at Launch Books, this work simply would not exist. David knew exactly who the publishing-world audience should be and precisely how to reach them. He helped fine-tune the concept and the voice. He's been a great partner.

Without Henry Ferris at William Morrow this book would be much less than it is—less interesting and less readable. Having someone edit your work can be as uncomfortable an experience as having someone tell you your baby is ugly. But Henry was almost always right and I caught myself realizing it as I read his suggestions. He's been a great partner.

Emma LeGault was a tremendous help with research. She managed to find all of the old, esoteric information and articles I was searching for and always amazed me at how quickly she could turn around a random list into a pile of items to be read and digested.

Thank you to the Theodore Roosevelt Center at Dickinson

State University, which has a wonderfully rich archive of Roosevelt's speeches and letters and was a tremendous help in piecing together the private papers relevant to Roosevelt's public speeches about finance and the economy during his presidency.

I extend a special thanks to Leo Melamed, formerly chairman of the Chicago Mercantile Exchange. Leo was generous in sharing his time so that I could get extra insight into the events surrounding the crash of 1987. And Leo doesn't realize it, but he's responsible for my TV career, such as it is.

Thank you as well to Eric Scott Hunsader for his time and for his insight into the Flash Crash of 2010. No one knows more about the market microstructure of today's electronic markets, and he was gracious in sharing his knowledge with me.

Finally, thanks to Wendi for her help and encouragement.

SOURCE NOTES

All five modern stock market crashes have received copious academic and media attention, so any chronicler is fortunate to have contemporaneous newspaper and media accounts that put the events in the context of their time. Several crashes have also been the subject of serious full-length works and scholarly papers that explain them more fully with the advantage of the perspective of time.

Stock market data has come from a variety of sources. All end-of-day prices for the Dow Jones Industrial Average are courtesy of S&P Dow Jones Indexes (www.DJIndexes.com). Other market data comes from additional sources.

Panic—1907

History of Crises Under the National Banking System, by O. M. W. Sprague, 1910.
    Chapter 5, "The Crisis of 1907" (pp. 216–320), is the most helpful, in-depth study of the Panic of 1907.

"The American Crisis," *Economic Journal,* by O. M. W. Sprague, September 1908
    (pp. 353–72), was Sprague's first scholarship on the Panic of 1907.

The Panic of 1907: Lessons Learned from the Market's Perfect Storm, by Robert

Bruner and Sean Carr, 2007, is a wonderful general history of the causes and course of the Panic of 1907.

Details of the assassination of President McKinley are available in the State University of New York at Buffalo archive of the Pan-American Exposition held in Buffalo (http://library.buffalo.edu/pan-am/exposition/law/czolgosz/).

The story of Theodore Roosevelt's return from the Tahawus Club hunting lodge is told in Edmund Morris's *Theodore Rex* (prologue).

There are many books describing Roosevelt's service as a Rough Rider, including Edmund Morris's *The Rise of Theodore Roosevelt* (pp. 618–94) and *Rough Riders: Theodore Roosevelt, His Cowboy Regiment, and the Immortal Charge Up San Juan Hill,* by Mark Lee Gardner.

Details of Boss Thomas Platt's assistance in getting Roosevelt elected governor and nominated for vice president are available in the online history of the United States Senate (https://www.senate.gov/artandhistory/history/common/generic/VP_Theodore_Roosevelt.htm) and in Edmund Morris's *The Rise of Theodore Roosevelt* (pp. 695–746).

The *New York Times* obituary of Senator Thomas Platt appeared on Monday, March 7, 1910.

Mark Hanna's remark about Roosevelt is available in the online history of the United States Senate (https://www.senate.gov/artandhistory/history/minute/Hanna_1896Election.htm).

The progress of McKinley's recovery and ultimate death after being shot is told by many contemporary newspaper accounts, including the *New York Times.* For example, p. 1, September 7, 1901.

Details about Standard Oil can be found in *Titan: The Life of John D. Rockefeller, Sr.,* by Ron Chernow.

Drafts of Roosevelt's speeches as president are available at the Theodore Roosevelt Center and Digital Library at Dickinson State University. Images of the text Roosevelt edited and eventually spoke from are often available showing the progression of his remarks as well as any last-minute changes and ad libs (http://www.theodorerooseveltcenter.org/).

The events surrounding Northern Securities are told in several narratives, including Cornell University Law School's Legal Information Institute (https://www.law.cornell.edu/supremecourt/text/193/197); the Theodore Roosevelt Center, which includes biographies of E. H. Harriman and James J. Hill (http://www.theodorerooseveltcenter.org/Learn-About-TR/TR-Encyclopedia/Capitalism-and-Labor/The-Northern-Securities-Case

.aspx); "The Northern Securities Case," by James Wilford Garner, in *The Annals of the American Academy of Political and Social Science,* 1940; and "A History of the Northern Securities Case," by Balthasar Henry Meyer, Ph.D., *Bulletin of the University of Wisconsin,* 1906.

The stock market reaction to the Northern Securities corner is told in contemporaneous newspapers, including "Northern Pacific Corner Exposed" and "Disaster and Ruin in Falling Market," *New York Times,* May 10, 1901.

The Knight Sugar case is detailed in "The Knight Sugar Decision of 1895 and the Modernization of American Corporation Law," *Business History Review,* Autumn 1979.

Details of the role of J. P. Morgan in the formation of Northern Securities are told in *Morgan: American Financier,* by Jean Strouse (pp. 418–55); *The House of Morgan,* by Ron Chernow (pp. 91–94); and *J. Pierpont Morgan,* by Herbert Satterlee (pp. 309–40). Satterlee was Morgan's son-in-law and offers a particularly intimate point of view.

Jack Morgan's note about the stock market in January 2006 can be found in his letters at the Morgan Library and Museum and in *The Panic of 1907* (p. 16).

Many of the details of the San Francisco earthquake and fire are from "The Story of an Eyewitness," by Jack London, *Collier's,* May 5, 1906.

Details of the geology of the earthquake are from the U.S. Geological Survey (https://earthquake.usgs.gov/regional/nca/1906/18april/).

Details of the financial impact can be found in "Real Shock, Monetary Aftershock: The San Francisco Earthquake and the Panic of 1907," by Kerry Odell and Marc Weidenmier, National Bureau of Economic Research.

The text of Roosevelt's speeches, including his May 4, 1906, address to Congress, can also be found at the Almanac of Theodore Roosevelt, www.Theodore -Roosevelt.com.

The story of the lawsuits against Standard Oil played out in the newspapers, including the *Wall Street Journal* and the *New York Times* (p. 1, August 18, 1906, "Standard Oil Indicted").

David Pietrusza's full-length biography of Kenesaw Mountain Landis is titled *Judge and Jury: The Life and Times of Judge Kenesaw Mountain Landis.*

Rockefeller didn't appear in Landis's courtroom for the verdict; he preferred to play golf. But the details are included in Ron Chernow's *Titan* (pp. 519–60).

Professor Lough's address regarding panics on March 14, 1907, was covered by the *New York Times* in the next day's paper (p. 2), as well as in the *Bulletin of the American Institute of Bank Clerks,* vol. 8 (p. 295).

The events at the Gridiron dinner are detailed by Satterlee on p. 437 (although Satterlee suggests the dinner was held on the evening of Sunday, January 27, 1907, which is unlikely, because the *New York Times* reported on the event in its paper dated the twenty-seventh). The *Times* story was on page 1 of part five.

The text of Roosevelt's Decoration Day speech is available at www.Theodore -Roosevelt.com. The *New York Times* reported on his speech on page 1, Friday, May 31, 1907.

Fascinating detail of the proceedings on August 3, 1907, when Landis imposed his fine on Standard Oil, including descriptions of the courtroom and Landis's wardrobe, can be found in the *Chicago Sunday Tribune,* August 4, 1907 (pp. 1–2) (http://archives.chicagotribune.com/1907/08/04/page/1 /article/forces-new-war-on-standard-oil-after-limit-fine).

An image of the original version of Roosevelt's Provincetown speech given on August 20, 1907, with handwritten edits, confirmed to the author by the staff of the Theodore Roosevelt Digital Library as being in Roosevelt's hand, are available from the Theodore Roosevelt Digital Library. Also available is the image of the letter Roosevelt wrote to his son Kermit, on White House stationery but sent from Oyster Bay, New York, dated August 21, 1908. In this letter Theodore discloses that his "amusing thing" was indeed ad-libbed.

The fascinating story of Fritz Augustus Heinze is told in *Copper King at War,* by Sarah McNelis (University of Montana Press, 1968); "Life Stories of Successful Men," *Technical World,* vol. 2, September 1904 (pp. 60–62), which includes the story of his education, start, and first years in Butte; "The Copper King's Precipitous Fall," *Smithsonian Magazine,* September 2012, includes details of Heinze's successes in Butte and his involvement in the Panic of 1907; "United Copper Booming," *New York Tribune,* October 15, 1907; "The Story of Heinze: A Tale of Copper—and Brass," *Current Literature,* vol. 44, January–June 1908 (pp. 34–36); "The Fight of the Copper Kings," *McClure's Magazine,* vol. 29, May 1907 (pp. 1–16), provides particular detail and insight into Heinze's battles with Amalgamated Copper, including the "Apex Theory"; information regarding Judge William Clancy can be found in "The Revenge of the Trust," *American Heritage,* vol. 41, no. 3, April 1990.

Charles Morse was a captivating personality, undeniably at the heart of the three largest scandals to hit New York City during the first decade of the twentieth century. His involvement with Fritz Heinze is told in the sources mentioned above, but additional information can be found in *Charlie Morse: Ice King & Wall Street Scoundrel,* by Philip H. Woods, 2011; "Whispering Pines: Opening Act: Charles W. Morse—Ice King, Prince of Financiers, and Steamship Magnate," *Bowdoin Daily Sun,* June 11, 2015; and "The Story of Morse," *Current Literature,* vol. 47, January–June 1910.

Stock market prices for United Copper are from the *New York Times.*

The story of the attempted short squeeze in United Copper and the immediate impact on the stock market is best told in *The Panic of 1907* (pp. 43–49), as well as in contemporaneous newspapers, including the *Chicago Tribune* (p. 4), October 15, 1907; *Wall Street Journal* (p. 8), October 15, 1907; *New York Times* (p. 11), October 15, 1907; *New York Times* (p. 13), October 16, 1907; *Wall Street Journal* (p. 4), October 16, 1907; *Chicago Tribune* (p. 2), October 17, 1907; *Wall Street Journal* (p. 3), October 17, 1907; and *New York Times* (pp. 1, 12, and 13), October 17, 1907.

The critical role the trust companies play in the Panic of 1907 is told by "The Bank Panic of 1907: The Role of Trust Companies," by Jon Moen and Ellis Tallman, *Journal of Economic History,* vol. 52, no. 3, September 1992 (pp. 611–30).

The run on the Knickerbocker Trust Company and its failure is told by Sprague (1910: pp. 251–77); and *1907* (pp. 65–70).

The course of the Panic of 1907 after October 17 is told by Satterlee (pp. 454–93), from the point of view of J. P. Morgan; Strouse (pp. 573–93); and Chernow (pp. 121–30).

The story of J. P. Morgan's efforts to save the Trust Company of America is told by Satterlee (pp. 466–73). His now famous quote, "This is the place to stop the trouble," appears on page 469.

Details of J. P. Morgan's efforts to prevent the premature closure of the New York Stock Exchange are told in contemporaneous newspaper accounts but are told most succinctly by Chernow (pp. 124–26).

Crash–1929

The Causes of the 1929 Stock Market Crash, by Harold Bierman Jr., 1998, is a concise history. Bierman is a professor of business administration at Cornell

University. This work is a bit dense in places, but it points to other great resources.

The Great Crash 1929, by John Kenneth Galbraith, originally published in 1954 but updated since, is the best-known history of the crash.

Several excellent histories focusing on the social, business, and political atmosphere of the 1920s have been published, including *1929: The Year of the Great Crash,* by William Klingaman, 1989; *Rainbow's End: The Crash of 1929,* by Maury Klein, 2001; and *Only Yesterday,* by Frederick Lewis Allen, originally published in 1931.

The most accessible early biography of Michael Meehan was published in the *New York Times,* March 18, 1928 (Section 10, p. 3), which includes details of his career before finance. A slightly earlier biography appears in the *New York Times* on March 14, 1928, as part of a story detailing the inquiry into his first RCA pool (pp. 1 and 13).

Meehan's trading in the Bellanca Aircraft Company and the subsequent SEC action are told in "In the Matter of Meehan," 2 SEC 588 (1937).

Meehan's admission to Bloomingdale Asylum is discussed in *Six Days in October: The Stock Market Crash of 1929,* by Karen Blumenthal, 2002 (pp. 142–43).

The story of Liberty Bonds is told by Richard Sutch and the Federal Reserve at www.FederalReserveHistory.org (http://www.federalreservehistory .org/Events/DetailView/100).

The most extensive biography of Benjamin Strong is *Benjamin Strong: Central Banker,* by Lester Chandler, 1958. His life and activities as president of the Federal Reserve Bank of New York are told ably in *Lords of Finance,* by Liaquat Ahamed, 2009 (chapter 4). Another wonderful biography of Benjamin Strong is included in "Benjamin Strong, Jr.: The Common Monetary Thread," by Richard A. Naclerio, History Faculty Publications, Sacred Heart University, 2014.

Data regarding the Federal Reserve's changes in the discount rate can be found in *Money Rates and Security Markets,* no. 115 (pp. 439–41), from the Federal Reserve Bank of St. Louis.

The history of Radio Corporation of America (RCA) and early commercial radio is told in "RCA: An Historical Perspective," a history the company published prior to 1976.

The story of Warren Harding's life and death is told by the American Presidency Project at the Miller Center, University of Virginia; in *The Shadow of Blooming Grove,* by Francis Russell, 1968; and in many contemporary newspapers.

The friendship and collegial alliance between Benjamin Strong and Montagu Norman is described in *1927: High Tide of the Twenties,* by Gerald Leinwand, 2001 (p. 58), and *One Summer: America, 1927,* by Bill Bryson, 2013 (pp. 201–8), which also includes details of the meeting between Strong, Norman, Schacht, and Rist. Potentially the best source is "Central Bank Cooperation 1924–1931," by Stephen V. O. Clarke, published by the Federal Reserve Bank of New York, 1967 (pp. 123–29).

The minutes of the Federal Reserve Open Market Investment Committee following the July meeting of central bankers are available at www.fraser .stlouisfed.org.

Herbert Hoover's efforts to get the Federal Reserve to reverse its low interest rate policy are explained in his memoirs, *The Memoirs of Herbert Hoover: The Great Depression 1929–1941,* published in 1952 (pp. 9–14).

The history of weekly figures for brokers' loans was published in the *Wall Street Journal,* October 15, 1929. This data was also generally published in the media during the relevant week.

The history of the investment trust in Europe and its emergence in the United States is provided by Galbraith (pp. 47–56).

The scale of operations of investment trusts in the United States just prior to the crash is discussed by Klingaman (pp. 60, 235–36) and Bierman (pp. 74–78).

Information regarding investment trusts' use of leverage is found in Galbraith (p. 56) and Bierman (p. 84, and beginning on 138).

The vulnerability of investment trusts that invested primarily in public utilities is discussed in Bierman (p. 2).

The growth in the number of investment trusts and the assets managed is discussed by Bierman (p. 74), Galbraith (p. 50), and Klein (p. 191).

More information regarding the touting of stocks for money by journalists, including by A. Newton Plummer, can be found in the U.S. Senate Committee on Banking and Currency record of its Hearings on Stock Exchange Practices, 1932 (pp. 447–51).

Information about the evolution of margin requirements can be found in "Margin Purchases, Brokers' Loans and the Bull Market of the Twenties," *Business and Economic History,* vol. 17, 1988 (pp. 129–42).

A description of the 1920s call money market is found in "Was There a Bubble in the 1929 Stock Market?" by Peter Rappoport and Eugene White, National Bureau of Economic Research, February 1991.

The intervention of the Massachusetts Department of Public Utilities in the request by the Boston Edison Electric Illuminating Company to split its stock is described in Klingaman (pp. 249–50) and Bierman (pp. 57–58, 86–91, and 135–39) as well as in the *New York Times* of October 12 and 15, 1929.

Herbert Hoover's comment that there are crimes worse than murder can be found in his *Memoirs*.

The story of the Federal Reserve's ill-fated efforts at "direct pressure" can be found in "The Stock Market Boom and Crash of 1929 Revisited," by Eugene White, *Journal of Economic Perspectives*, vol. 4, no. 2, Spring 1990 (pp. 67–83).

Details of New York Stock Exchange data are from the exchange's market data portal, www.nyxdata.com.

Details of Michael Meehan's second RCA pool can be found in *A Financial History of the United States*, vol. 2, by Jerry Markham, 2002 (p. 150).

More insight into Michael Meehan's brokerage office on board the *Berengaria* can be found in *The Day the Bubble Burst*, by Gordon Thomas and Max Morgan-Witts, 1979 (pp. 168–69, 229–31, and 258).

The heartwarming but ultimately sad story of the little girl sending four dollars to the Standard Oil Company, hoping to buy stock, was told in many newspapers nationwide, including the *New York Times*, September 1, 1929 (section 2, p. 7).

The story of Roger Babson and the "Babson Break" is told in Klingaman (p. 232) and Klein (pp. 194–95).

The fraud perpetrated by Clarence Hatry is described in additional detail by Bierman (pp. 19–28), which also provides a biography of the man. Substantial additional information on the man and his fraud is included in *The Day the Bubble Burst*.

A description of the efforts to support the market in October 1929, including Richard Whitney's purchases of stocks, most notably U.S. Steel, can be found in Klein (pp. 213–14).

Black Monday—1987

The greatest sources for the Crash of 1987 are two governmental reports, *The October 1987 Market Break*, compiled by the Securities and Exchange Commission and published February 1988, and the *Report of the Presidential Task Force on Market Mechanisms*, published in January 1988 and commonly known as the Brady Report after the chairman of the task force, Nicholas Brady. Trading statistics, including those for S&P futures traded at the Chicago Mercantile Exchange, are included in both studies, as are intraday prices and details of sales by portfolio insurers.

The story of the creation of portfolio insurance and its intended uses is best told in *Capital Ideas*, by Peter Bernstein, 2005 (pp. 269–94). Additional information is found in "Leland, O'Brien, and Rubinstein: The Guys Who Gave Us Portfolio Insurance," by Andrew Kupfer, *Fortune*, January 4, 1988.

Details of the Wesray acquisition of Gibson Greetings are available in the *New York Times*, August 7, 1983, and January 21, 1990.

T. Boone Pickens's story of growing up in Oklahoma and Texas, as well as his business dealings, is told in his autobiography, *Boone*, 1987.

Carl Icahn's earliest business dealings are recounted in the *Washington Post*, October 11, 1982. Biographies of his upbringing include *King Icahn*, by Mark Stephens, 1993.

The growth of LOR, including assets under management and employees, is provided in "Leland O'Brien Rubinstein Associates Incorporated: Portfolio Insurance," Harvard Business School, September 15, 1995.

The story of Drexel Burnham Lambert is told in *The Predators' Ball*, by Connie Bruck, 1989. The "highly confident" letter is discussed beginning on page 166.

Specifics about LOR's concerns if portfolio insurance became too popular begin on Bernstein (p. 283) and in *An Engine, Not a Camera: How Financial Models Shape Markets*, by Donald MacKenzie, 2006, chapter 7.

The unfortunate story of P. David Herrlinger is told in the *Los Angeles Times*, June 24, 1987; the *New York Times*, June 24, 1987; and *Chicago Tribune*, June 24, 1987.

William Silber's concerns about portfolio insurance, including his fear that a crash would occur because of too much hedging, are detailed in the *New York Times*, December 15, 1987 (p. 1).

Alan Greenspan's commentary from Sunday, October 4, including the notion

that he'd have to destroy the economy in order to save it, is available in the
Wall Street Journal, October 5, 1987 (p. 2).

Robert Prechter was profiled in *People* magazine's May 11, 1987, edition. Additional information is available in the *Los Angeles Times,* October 8, 1987.

More about Chairman Ruder's suggestions for a total market halt can be found in the *Wall Street Journal,* October 7, 1987 (pp. 1, 3, 22, and 65).

The first news of the Ways and Means Committee's plans for new taxes can be found in the *Wall Street Journal,* October 14, 1987.

Richard Phelan's timeline for October 19, 1987, and October 20, 1987, is most accessible in *Black Monday,* by Tim Metz, 1988. Metz also relates the story of news outlets' handling of Ruder's comment about a potential market halt on October 19, Phelan's press conference performance on the afternoon of October 19, and the specifics of the reopening of trading on October 20, as well as the trading activity in the Major Market Index on that day.

Leo Melamed's story is related in his memoir, *Back to the Futures,* published 1996. Details of the events surrounding October 19, 1987, are recounted beginning on page 348. The details were also confirmed in an interview with the author, including his conversations with Continental Illinois bank, Alan Greenspan, and Richard Phelan. The author asked Melamed to name the firm that owed the Chicago Mercantile Exchange $1 billion on the morning of October 20. Melamed declined to answer.

The U.S. military response to the attacks on the *Sea Isle City* are detailed in the *Wall Street Journal,* October 20, 1987 (p. 1), and the *New York Times,* October 20, 1987 (p. 1).

Meltdown—2008

Anyone writing about the crash of 2008 is presented with an avalanche of sources. The most comprehensive are the governmental reports. The most helpful was *The Financial Crisis Inquiry Report,* published by the Financial Crisis Inquiry Commission (FCIC). The report describes itself as the "Final Report of the National Commission of the Causes of the Financial and Economic Crisis in the United States." It was published January 2011 and can be found, along with additional resources, at FCIC.gov. A second governmental report is by the United States Senate Permanent Subcommittee on Investigations and is titled *Wall Street and the Financial Crisis: Anatomy of a Financial Collapse.* It was released on April 13, 2011. The extensive archive of materials related to the bankruptcy of Lehman Brothers Holdings Inc. is maintained by Jenner & Block, the law firm responsible for the report, at https://jenner.com/lehman.

A helpful overview of the subprime mortgage market is offered by Souphala Chomsisengphet and Anthony Pennington-Cross, "The Evolution of the Subprime Mortgage Market," from the *Federal Reserve Bank of St. Louis Review*, January/February 2006 (pp. 31–56).

The history of the Sandlers and Golden West was first told by the *New York Times* on September 9, 1990 (section 3, p. 1, "Inside the Nation's Best-Run S&L"); and the *Wall Street Journal* on December 8, 2000 ("Small Banking Stocks Vault Over Their Bigger Brethren"). Other good sources include *Forbes*, June 4, 2012, and the *New York Times*, June 4, 2012. Another interesting, albeit potentially self-serving, source is the Sandlers' response to *Time* magazine blaming them for the problems in the subprime market. This response is available at http://content.time.com/time/magazine/pdf /SandlerResponse.pdf.

A comprehensive history of mortgage-backed securities, and the GSEs, is available in "The Origins and Evolution of the Market for Mortgage-Backed Securities," by John McConnell and Stephen Buser, professors at Purdue University and Ohio State University, respectively, published in *Annual Reviews*, 2011.

An analysis of the *Exxon Valdez* disaster is contained in *The Exxon Valdez Oil Spill: A Report to the President from Samuel Skinner, Secretary, Department of Transportation and William Reilly, Administrator, Environmental Protection Agency, Prepared by the National Response Team, May 1989.* An interesting look at the string of errors and occurrences that led to the disaster is included in "Software System Safety," by Nancy Leveson (pp. 18–20), prepared for a Software and Safety class at the Massachusetts Institute of Technology, July 2005.

The story of the invention of the credit default swap has been told many times. One source is "The Dream Machine: Invention of Credit Derivatives," by Gillian Tett, *Financial Times*, March 24, 2006. Another is Tett's more extensive history in *Fool's Gold*, 2009. Events in Boca Raton are recounted on pages 3–22. Blythe Masters's involvement and the BISTRO deal are covered on pages 41–56. Credit default swaps are also discussed in *All the Devils Are Here*, by Bethany McLean and Joe Nocera, 2010, beginning on page 60. Another fascinating history is the oral history compiled by the television show *Frontline* and available at http://www.pbs.org/wgbh/pages /frontline/oral-history/financial-crisis/tags/credit-default-swaps/.

Information about the Bill Clinton birthplace is available from the National Park Service website.

Presidential quotes regarding the desirability of homeownership are included in "Homeownership and Its Benefits; Urban Policy Brief Number 2," U.S. Department of Housing and Urban Development, August 1995, which also includes details of President Clinton's National Homeownership Strategy.

Data on homeownership are available from the St. Louis Federal Reserve Economic Data (FRED) database (https://fred.stlouisfed.org/series/RHORU SQ156N). FRED is also the source for data on the Federal Reserve's more recent interest rate history.

The purpose and scope of the Alternative Mortgage Transaction Parity Act, passed in 1982, is described on the website of the U.S. government's Consumer Financial Protection Bureau (http://www.consumerfinance.gov /eregulations/sxs/1004-1/2011-18676?from_version=2011-18676).

The story of Cornelius Vander Starr is told by the Columbia University Libraries (https://exhibitions.cul.columbia.edu/exhibits/show/cvstarr) and in a history by C. V. Starr & Company, published in 1970 (http://www.starrfoun dation.org/cv_starr_book.pdf).

The background on the founding of AIG Financial Products is told in *All The Devils Are Here* (pp. 71–77). The story of AIG FP's entry into the credit default swap market is told on pages 77–81. Michael Lewis also tells a portion of the story focusing on Joseph Cassano in the August 2009 issue of *Vanity Fair* in an article titled "The Man Who Crashed the World."

Data regarding the quantity of mortgage-backed securities outstanding is available from the Securities Industry and Financial Markets Association website (sifma.org) and the FCIC report.

Alan Greenspan's biography is available from many sources, including his own autobiography, *The Age of Turbulence: Adventures in a New World*, 2007 (pp. 19–53). Details about his Ph.D. thesis are reported in *Barron's*, "Looking at Greenspan's Long-Lost Thesis," April 28, 2008.

Historical long-term interest rate data is available from Bloomberg.

Data on foreign ownership of U.S. mortgage-backed securities is available from the U.S. Department of Treasury (https://www.treasury.gov/resource-cen ter/data-chart-center/tic/Pages/fpis.aspx).

A good, nontechnical discussion of the impact of monetary policy (Federal Reserve interest rate policy) on the housing market is presented by John Taylor, a professor at Stanford University and one of the leading advocates for a more rules-based monetary policy, in "Housing and Monetary Policy," National Bureau of Economic Research, Working Paper 13682, December 2007. Additional information is available in the FCIC report (pp. 103–4).

The press release describing President Bush's "zero down payment initiative" is available in the U.S. Department of Housing and Urban Development Archives. The initial release was HUD number 04-006 and is dated January 19, 2004.

The story of Angelo Mozilo and the founding of Countrywide has been told many times. One enjoyable biography is Connie Bruck's from the *New Yorker*, June 29, 2009. Another is related by McLean and Nocera (pp. 21–24).

Details of David Sambol's quote and changes in underwriting standards are included in the FCIC report (p. 105).

Details of the Home Ownership and Equity Protection Act of 1994 are available at the Cornell University School of Law Legal Information Institute (https://www.law.cornell.edu/uscode/text/15/1639).

The warnings that subprime mortgages should be addressed by the Federal Reserve are described in the *New York Times* article "Fed Shrugged as Subprime Crisis Spread," December 18, 2007. Sheila Bair's position is described in her interview with *Frontline* (http://www.pbs.org/wgbh /pages/frontline/meltdown/interviews/bair.html).

The Fed's position that it would not routinely conduct consumer compliance exams was promulgated on January 20, 1998, in release CA 98-1.

The circumstances surrounding Hank Greenberg leaving AIG are discussed beginning with the *Wall Street Journal* article "U.S. Probes AIG Deal, Greenberg Role," on March 4, 2005, then "AIG Probe Focuses on Risk Transfer," on March 8, 2005; and "How Investigations of AIG Led to Retirement of Longtime CEO" on March 15, 2005, discusses his leaving AIG.

David Li's Gaussian copula is discussed in his paper introducing the concept, "On Default Correlation: A Copula Function Approach," *Journal of Fixed Income*, March 2000 (pp. 43–54); "Recipe for Disaster: The Formula That Killed Wall Street," by Felix Salmon, *Wired*, February 23, 2009; and "How a Formula Ignited Market That Burned Some Big Investors," including Li's own reservations, *Wall Street Journal*, September 12, 2005.

Information about the rating agencies, including data about Moody's IPO and rating criteria, can be found in "Did Going Public Impair Moody's Credit Ratings?" by Simi Kedia, Shivaram Rajgopal, and Xing Zhou, October 22, 2013.

The rating agency business model, revenue per engagement, and quotes regarding failures can be found in a series of Bloomberg articles, including "Bringing Down Wall Street as Ratings Let Loose Subprime Scourge," by Elliot Blair Smith, September 24, 2008, and "'Race to Bottom' at Moody's, S&P Secured Subprime Boom, Bust," September 26, 2008. Additional information regarding their failures and the quote that mentions "cows" can be found in "Summary Report of Issues Identified in the Commission Staff's Examinations of Select Credit Rating Agencies," published by the Securities and Exchange Commission, July 2008. The quote regarding "cows" appears on page 12.

Angelo Mozilo's emails lamenting the quality of recent mortgages and describing some products as "toxic" are available on the SEC.gov website (https://www.sec.gov/news/press/2009/2009-129-email.htm) as part of the commission's investigation of Countrywide.

The New Century emails are included in the SEC's criminal complaint against Brad Morrice, Patti Dodge, et al., filed on December 7, 2009. The email discussing the decline in liquidity appears on page 25.

The downgrades by S&P and Moody's on July 10, 2007, and the market reaction are detailed in "Ratings Cuts by S&P, Moody's Rattle Investors," by Serena Ng and Ruth Simon, *Wall Street Journal,* July 11, 2007.

Discussion of the collateral calls received by AIG can be found in McLean and Nocera (pp. 322–26, 330–34, and 339–41).

The discussion of Lehman Brothers' balance sheet is in FCIC (pp. 324–43).

Bernanke's speech regarding recent subprime originations was delivered at the Federal Reserve Bank of Kansas City's Economic Symposium, Jackson Hole, Wyoming, August 31, 2007. The speech is available on the Federal Reserve website (https://www.federalreserve.gov/newsevents/speech/bernanke20070831a.htm).

The transcript of AIG's investor call held on December 5, 2007, is available on the FCIC website (http://fcic-static.law.stanford.edu/cdn_media/fcic-docs/2007-12-05%20AIG%20Conference%20Call%20Transcript.pdf).

PricewaterhouseCoopers' extensive documentation (including internal memos) of their disagreement as to loss recognition for AIG's credit default swap portfolio can be found on the FCIC website.

Many have written the history of the GSEs. One concise version is available from the Federal Housing Finance Agency (https://www.fhfaoig.gov /LearnMore/History).

Alan Greenspan's comment that the difference between the GSE's cost of capital and return on capital was "a big fat gap" was made before the U.S. Senate Banking Committee on February 24, 2004.

The story of the conservatorship of the GSEs is told in Henry Paulson's memoir, *On the Brink*.

The discussions held the weekend of September 13, 2008, are told in Paulson's memoir, *On the Brink*. They are also told in the documentary movie *Hank: Five Years from the Brink* and the book *Too Big to Fail*, by Andrew Ross Sorkin, 2009.

The analysis that Lehman Brothers may not have been insolvent is presented in "The Fed and Lehman Brothers," by Laurence Ball, July 2016, for the July 14, 2016, meeting of the NBER Monetary Economic Program.

The legislative path of TARP was told contemporaneously by many media outlets and by Paulson, beginning on page 265.

Dick Kovacevich's interview on CNBC suggesting that taking TARP funds was not voluntary aired on September 13, 2013. He references *On the Brink* as proof.

Flash Crash—2010

The best resource for information and data regarding the Flash Crash on May 6, 2010, is the joint Commodity Futures Trading Commission (CFTC) and Securities and Exchange Commission (SEC), *Findings Regarding the Market Events of May 6, 2010*. The preliminary report was released on May 18, 2010, and the final report was released September 30, 2010. The preliminary report includes extensive, minute-by-minute trade data for the S&P E-mini futures that trade on the Chicago Mercantile Exchange's Globex electronic trading system, including the number of trades, total volume, opening price (for that one-minute period), high, low, last, and additional data. This is the source of the trade data cited.

Details about the firebombing of the Marfin Bank are available from a number of media outlets, but the story of the frustrations of young Greek nationals is also told by the *Wall Street Journal*, November 27, 2010, by Marcus Walker. The story, including photographs, is also told by CNN in "Sacrificed for a Future That Never Came."

The story of Greece's repeated indebtedness to foreign lenders is told in "The Pitfalls of External Dependence: Greece, 1829–2015," by Carmen Reinhart and Christoph Trebesch. A timeline of Greek defaults is offered on page 12, while narrative details of each default begin on page 13.

The story of the creation of the euro currency, from the pre-euro political landscape in Europe to the rationale for the creation of the common currency, is told in *The Euro Crisis and Its Aftermath*, by Jean Pisani-Ferry, 2011.

Information on the Greek debt crisis is contained in "Greece's Debt Crisis: Overview, Policy Responses, and Implications," by the Congressional Research Service, April 27, 2010.

A fascinating look at Greek tax avoidance and how it became institutionalized is offered in "Tax Evasion Across Industries: Soft Credit Evidence From Greece," by Nikolaos Artavanis, Adair Morse, and Margarita Tsoutsoura, September 2012.

Germany's demand for a no-bailout clause is discussed by Pisani-Ferry beginning on page 54.

The *Independent* newspaper is the source for infuriating information on the overly generous Greek pensions, including those occupations considered arduous or unhealthy and deserving of early retirement. "Greece to Call Time on Cushy Pension Deals for 'Unhealthy' Jobs," by Menelaos Tzafalias, *Independent*, May 20, 2010.

Details of the Greek securitization deals executed to hide their budget gap are available from "Details of Those Other Greek Debt Deals," by Tracy Alloway, *Financial Times*, February 25, 2010. Additional information is from "How 'Magic' Made Greek Debt Disappear Before It Joined the Euro," by Allan Little, BBC, February 3, 2012. Alloway also covers the story for Bloomberg in "It's Another Tough Day for Titlos, the Tarnished Greek Swaps Deal," May 4, 2015. The *New York Times* covered it in "Wall St. Helped to Mask Debt Fueling Europe's Crisis," by Louise Story, Landon Thomas Jr., and Nelson Schwartz, February 14, 2010.

Additional stories of statistical manipulation, tax avoidance, and government waste, including the oddly high number of teachers in Greek schools, are told in "Beware of Greeks Bearing Bonds," by Michael Lewis, *Vanity Fair*, October 2010.

Information regarding the rating agencies work in Greece is chronicled in "Ratings Firms Misread Signs of Greek Woes," by Julie Creswell and Graham Bowley, *New York Times*, November 29, 2011.

The story of Greek perfidy in joining the euro zone is told in "Greece Admits Faking Data to Join Europe," by Anthee Carassava, *New York Times,* September 23, 2004; "Greece 'Cheated' to Join Euro, Former ECB Economist Issing Says," by Christian Weinberg, Bloomberg, May 26, 2011; "Greece Admits Fudging Euro Entry," BBC, November 15, 2004; and "Greece Admits Deficit Figures Were Fudged to Secure Euro Entry," by Daniel Howden and Stephen Castle, *Independent,* November 15, 2004.

Details of the 2008 rioting are from "How Police Shooting of a Teenage Boy Rallied the '€700 Generation,'" by Maria Margaronis, *Guardian,* December 12, 2008.

Details on the progress toward a bailout are related by Pisani-Ferry beginning on page 77.

Waddell & Reed has been identified by many media outlets as the firm that sold 75,000 S&P E-mini futures on May 6, 2010. For example, "Lone $4.1 Billion Sale Led to 'Flash Crash' in May," by Graham Bowley, *New York Times,* October 1, 2010, and "Waddell Named as Mystery Trader in Market Plunge," DealBook blog, *New York Times,* May 14, 2010; "Exclusive: Waddell Is Mystery Trader in Market Plunge," by Herbert Lash and Jonathan Spicer, Reuters, May 14, 2010; and "How a Trading Algorithm Went Awry," by Tom Lauricella, Kara Scannell, and Jenny Strasburg, *Wall Street Journal,* October 2, 2010. On May 14, 2010, Waddell & Reed issued a news release admitting they executed S&P E-mini trades on May 6, 2010, but they did not specify the size of the trades executed.

Barclays has been identified as the executing broker for the trades in question, including by Reuters. See "CFTC, Barclays Discussed Waddell Algorithm-Source," by Herbert Lash, Reuters, October 22, 2010.

On September 2, 2010, Eric Scott Hunsader, founder of Nanex, a market data analytics firm, appeared on CNBC to describe the Waddell & Reed trading as executed by Barclays. The Nanex website (www.Nanex.net) also offers several items naming both Waddell & Reed and Barclays as the sellers of 75,000 contracts on May 6, 2010.

During an interview with the author, Hunsader disclosed that Waddell & Reed had given him their detailed trade data to allow him to do an analysis that he presented to the board of directors of Waddell & Reed. During that interview, Hunsader reiterated that Waddell & Reed was the seller of the 75,000 contracts and that Barclays was the executing broker, and he described the specific parameters of the Barclays algorithms.

In a research note titled "May 6th Flash Crash Analysis Final Conclusion," published October 14, 2010, Nanex discusses the impact of a single price change in the S&P E-mini and the phenomenon of quote saturation. Another note, "Analysis of the 'Flash Crash,'" published June 18, 2010, analyzes the delays in price data transmission, saying they were "stuck in a queue for transmission."

The complete list of stocks and ETFs trading more than 60 percent from their "reference price" on May 6, 2010, was provided by the Securities and Exchange Commission pursuant to a Freedom of Information Act request from the author.

INDEX

Printed in the USA
CPSIA information can be obtained
at www.ICGtesting.com
LVHW031751290124
770227LV00016B/366

9 780062 467287